I0815839

ZODIACTUALLY

THE REAL STORY OF A FAKE SERIAL KILLER

A Feral House Book

ISBN 9781627311724

FERAL HOUSE
1240 W Sims Way #124
Port Townsend WA 98368
www.feralhouse.com
info@feralhouse.com

Designed by Ron Kretsch
Cover model: Clay Parker

ZODIACTUALLY

THE REAL STORY OF A FAKE SERIAL KILLER

BY EDDIE McNAMARA

fh

CHAPTER 1: EVERYTHING YOU KNOW ABOUT THE SIXTIES IS BULLSHIT

"When the legend becomes fact, print the legend."
—Maxwell Scott, *The Man Who Shot Liberty Valance*

THE IMAGE OF AN ANGRY WOMEN'S-LIBBER TOSSING HER bra—once seen as the symbol of a repressive, patriarchal society—into a flaming trash can endures as a cultural stereotype to this day. The term "bra-burning feminist" is still used as derisive shorthand for a certain type of activist: one who is out of touch with mainstream women and unserious in the battles she chooses to fight. It belittles the struggle. It trivializes the movement. And like much of what we remember about the 1960s, it's based on an event that never actually happened. The myth of the bra-burning feminist perfectly represents American history in the late 1960s.

Here's how it really went down. In 1968, activists gathered in Atlantic City, New Jersey, to protest the Miss America pageant. They created a "Freedom Trash Can" where feminists dumped symbols of female oppression like bras, corsets, copies of *Cosmopolitan* magazine, girdles, and high heels.[1] A reporter for the *New York Post* named Lindsay Van Gelder wrote an article about it. No bras were burned at the event. She never claimed any bras were burned.

According to Van Gelder, "I loftily compared this effort to the heroic young men of the era who were burning their draft cards to protest the Vietnam War. But the un-nuanced headline written by the copy desk for my article—'Bra Burners and Miss America'—pretty much gave my editors the laugh they were looking for. And an idiotic trope was born."[2] The image was too powerful. The editors create the headlines, not the reporters. The editors opted to print the legend. In doing so, an enduring myth was created. Years later, Van Gelder said, "I shudder to think that will be my epitaph— 'She invented bra burning.'"[3]

Chroniclers of history often choose myth over fact. Facts can be proven, but myths are the sticky stories we remember. Legends—popular, but unauthenticated, pseudo-historical stories—are easier to digest because they make sense of the world in a neat and clever way. Above all else, legends sell more newspapers and books. Legends get more eyeballs on your documentary or website than dry facts. Facts can be unpleasant. Facts can tear a legend down.

Another legend shapes the story of the "bystander effect," a psychological theory suggesting that individuals are less likely to help a victim when others are around, because responsibility is diffused in a group. It serves as a condemnation of urban apathy and city life, centered around shared spaces and public transport, in favor of the wholesome isolation of suburban car culture. We believe this nonsense because of the story of Kitty Genovese. The problem with the theory, which still lingers today, is that it's entirely based on bullshit.

In the middle of the night on March 13, 1964, Kitty Genovese, a 28-year-old butch lesbian bartender and convicted bookmaker from Queens, New York, was raped and stabbed to death in front of the apartment building she lived in. The *New York Times* published an article lamenting the "fact" that no fewer than thirty-eight of Ms. Genovese's neighbors witnessed the attack, but none of them intervened. It's the classic uncaring New Yorker story jacked up with some times-they-are-a-changin' scares because fear of violence and societal change sells papers. It defined a city and an era and was taught in psychology classes for decades after. According to *American Psychologist* magazine, as recently as 2007, "a survey of ten leading undergraduate psychology textbooks found the Genovese case in all ten of them, with eight textbooks suggesting that witnesses watched from their windows as Genovese was murdered." [4]

Other newspapers didn't print the story because reporters and editors could not verify the salacious details. They knew the story was garbage and made the ethical decision not to print it. They knew the hook about the neighbors doing nothing wasn't true, but they didn't bother to call out the *Times* for reporting dystopian fantasy instead of the news.

In 2016, the *Times* finally admitted that the reporting was "flawed" and "grossly exaggerated the number of witnesses and what they had perceived."[5] Neighbors did shout at the attacker to stop. Multiple neighbors called the police to report the attack. A neighbor named Robert Moser chased the attacker away, and Sophia Ferrar ran to Genovese and told her, "Help is on the way."[6] She held Kitty in her arms until an ambulance finally arrived at 4:15 a.m., a full hour after the first emergency calls were made to the police. Kitty died in the back of the ambulance while being transported to the hospital. Kitty's attack wasn't fatal because of uncaring neighbors who refused to get involved. The real scandal was how long it took emergency services to get to a woman bleeding out on the sidewalk.

In both the bra-burning case and the Genovese murder, what we remember often bears little resemblance to the facts. History is a collection of stories we make up about ourselves and our ancestors to explain how we ended up here. The news media present stories we tell about our communities to explain the now in real time. These stories seldom fully align with reality. And with every passing year the stories are less tethered to the truth.

It's not conspiracy, it's commerce.

In 1969, the Woodstock Music and Art Fair was held August 15-18, on Max Yasgur's dairy farm in Bethel, New York. About 400,000 groovy young Aquarians attended all or part of the three-day music and peace festival. But, once the concert film *Woodstock* was released to enraptured audiences, the significance of the event exploded. Woodstock became the single moment that defined the counterculture in the mainstream. Millions of people who were thousands of miles away claimed they were there. People wanted to be associated with the sense of cool that came with attending Woodstock a lot more than they wanted the reality of the monsoon rain, omnipresent mud, and bad acid. I'm convinced that nearly every baby boomer has told someone about the time they smoked some grass and hitched a ride to Woodstock just in time to catch Hendrix play "The Star Spangled Banner."

Before Woodstock, going to concerts was mostly for teenyboppers. Adults did adult things and children went to rock 'n' roll shows. But Woodstock shifted the dynamic. The media relentlessly covered the naked girls, the drugs, and the debauchery at the Woodstock festival, which changed society's relationship with live music. No one wanted to miss out. Suddenly, grown men became concertgoers in search of the thrills available at Woodstock.

Consider this: in 1968, the year before Woodstock, the iconic rock band the Doors performed at New York City's coolest rock venue, the Fillmore East. This was at the absolute height of their fame and popularity. They drew 2,600 fans, almost entirely teenage girls—over two nights.

In January of 1970, a washed-up, no-longer-relevant version of the Doors returned to New York. This time, they played concerts in two nights at Madison Square Garden's Felt Forum theater. They drew twice as many fans as the Fillmore East shows, and those fans were dressed to the Woodstock nines. The expectations were different—these fans did not come to scream, "I love you," at Jim Morrison. They came for an adventure of their own.

Much of what we believe about the 1960s today is simply not accurate. We are taught that hippies changed the world, ushering in an era of racial equality and parity between the sexes. Former hippies claim that they helped to end the Vietnam War and fostered peace, love, and understanding. None of this is true. The United States did not get out of Vietnam until the 1973 Paris Peace Accords went into effect. The cost of that war was 50,000 dead Americans, two million dead Vietnamese civilians, and over one million dead Viet Cong fighters. In the United States, radical left-wing activists set off thousands of bombs a year in the sixties and seventies. Violent crime rates soared, quadrupling between 1960 and 1991. The hippies did not make things peaceful; they made a mess. If the hippies did anything besides drugs, they made such an unappealing show of themselves at the 1968 Democratic National Convention that it led directly to the election of conservative arch-villains like Richard Nixon as president and Ronald Reagan as governor of California. The rebellious kids succeeded in pissing off their parents, and Mom and Dad taught those kids a lesson by voting Republican.

Lore is a powerful thing. Take Vincent Bugliosi, the Los Angeles prosecutor, who sold a trial jury on the far-fetched tale of the brainwashed Manson Family. He then repackaged the story and sold it to the world in his true-crime book, *Helter Skelter*. He was the inventor and chief public-relations officer for the Helter Skelter theory. He turned a two-bit pimp with a guitar named Charles Manson—a man who thought it was a good idea to sell ass in San Francisco during the Summer of (free) Love—into America's boogeyman.

When that didn't work, Manson took his show on the road to Los Angeles. He brought San Francisco's spirit of free love to the uptight city of angels. Like the pimp he was, Charlie recruited some young, troubled girls and plied them with drugs. But this time, Charlie didn't charge. He became a novelty in L.A.'s celebrity circles, the guy from the Haight who offered free drugs and free love, courtesy of his drugged-out teenage stable, who were willing to do anything with anyone.

Dennis Wilson of the Beach Boys took Charlie and his merry band into his home. Doris Day's kid, a record producer named Terry Melcher who gave the world "Turn, Turn, Turn" and "Mr. Tambourine Man," wanted to make a documentary about Manson and record his music—until he lost interest in the music part and just wanted to televise the freak show. Charlie held a grudge. When Melcher was palling around with Charlie, he lived at 10050 Cielo Drive—the same home where Sharon Tate was murdered.

Bugliosi sold "the Manson Family" as a cult with Manson at the helm and his rabid followers at his beck and call. In reality, it was just a new-age pimp's stable. Charlie was Daddy to the girls, and he kept rough characters around as muscle. Charlie supplied the girls with drugs and coerced them to have sex with random strangers. Pimp shit.

In the tale Bugliosi told, Manson tried to mastermind a race war by ordering his followers to commit the August 1969 Tate–LaBianca murders. The "Family" scrawled messages like "Pig" and "Death to Pigs" on the crime scene walls in the victims' blood. Somehow, according to Bugliosi, this was supposed to set off a chain reaction—a crime wave fueled by angry Black men deprived of sexually available white women—that would lead to slaughter and a full-scale race war.

Jurors actually believed this nonsense. The public not only believed it, they ate it up and bought the book. It defined the era. It created the True-Crime Industrial Complex. Sales eclipsed Truman Capote's *In Cold Blood*. *Helter Skelter* is still the best-selling true-crime book of all time. As soon as the camera light came on, Manson played his part like a trained seal, pretending he was the evil master manipulator Bugliosi made him out to be. Manson loved being famous, and Bugliosi's crackpot theory was his ticket to fame. He may have wanted to be a rock star, but *Helter Skelter* allowed Manson far greater cultural significance.

Charles Manson continued to play his given role in his statement after being convicted of the Tate–LaBianca murders: "Mr. and Mrs. America—you are wrong. I am not the King of the Jews nor am I a hippie cult leader. I am what you have made me and the mad dog devil killer fiend leper is a reflection of your society . . . Whatever the outcome of this madness that you call a fair trial or Christian justice, you can know this: in my mind's eye my thoughts light fires in your cities."[7]

The Helter Skelter theory is bonkers. What really went down is a far less fantastical chain of events. The Tate–LaBianca murders center on the mundane criminal trifecta of drugs, money, and gangs: Bobby Beausoleil, a Manson Family associate and an actor in Kenneth Anger's *Lucifer Rising,* found himself in a pickle. Beausoleil brokered a drug deal for one thousand hits of mescaline between the supplier, the L.A. hippie renaissance man Gary Hinman, and the buyer, the Straight Satans motorcycle gang. Shortly after receiving the drugs, the bikers realized they were scammed—they had bought strychnine instead of mescaline. They demanded their money back. Bobby went to confront Hinman about the rip-off and get his $1,000 back. (That's approximately $8,600 in today's money.) He needed that cash to get the Straight Satans off his ass. Bobby brought Manson girlfriends Susan "Sadie" Atkins and Mary Brunner along with him on the trip to Hinman's house in Topanga Canyon.

Gary Hinman was murdered—stabbed twice in the heart. His cars were stolen, and somebody wrote "Political Piggy" in Hinman's blood on the wall. Beausoleil said they did it to get the heat off of them by making it look like the killing had something to do with Hinman's radical political activism instead of his drug dealing. Six days later, the California Highway Patrol found Beausoleil sleeping in Hinman's stolen car with the murder knife. The cops arrested him on the spot.

According to the journalist A. L. Bardach, who interviewed Beausoleil for the November 1981 issue of *Oui* magazine, "Three days after Bobby's arrest, all the occupants of the Sharon Tate and La Bianca homes were brutally slaughtered. Though epithets written in blood on the walls were a common factor at all three murder sites ('Pig' on the Tate wall and 'Death to Pigs' on the LaBianca refrigerator), investigators initially failed to make the link. According to Beausoleil, this came as something of a shock to the Manson Family, who had hoped the authorities would assume the same killer was responsible for all three homicidal sprees, then release Beausoleil. Their logic was that if Beausoleil was in jail during the Tate–LaBianca killings, he couldn't be the Hinman killer."[8]

Around the same time, in the Bay Area, there was a lesser-known figure who, unlike Manson, lacked main character energy and messianic rock star ambitions. This guy wanted to be seen as a criminal mastermind. He sent letters, secret codes, and ciphers to newspapers, taking credit for murders and threatening the good citizens of the Bay Area with violence. His letters were goofy. They sounded like comic-book nonsense intended for Batman's Gotham City or Superman's Metropolis instead of real-life Northern California. He was an attention whore who threatened to go on kill sprees, shoot children on school buses, and set off bombs. He did none of those things. But he told lots of lies. He called himself the Zodiac.

He was a troll in the pre-internet era whose letters to newspapers got his message out. He took credit for a slew of real crimes that had nothing else in common besides his letters. The cops investigated the murders, but the newspapers printed the legend. It was interactive: buy a paper and try to solve the "My name is" cipher at home. That's a brilliant marketing strategy.

The Zodiac Killer claimed responsibility for at least thirty seven murders in his letters. His identity has stumped professional and amateur investigators for over half a century. In an era when nearly 80% of homicides were closed by the police, the Zodiac's five "confirmed" murders and the more than thirty "unconfirmed" murders he boasted about are still unsolved. What if the reason his identity remains a mystery until today is that the Zodiac was a hippie-era media boogeyman and not a real person?

The Zodiac existed in the imagination of the troll who wrote letters and cryptograms to the newspapers. The Zodiac existed on the pages of the newspapers that reported on his comic-book supervillain antics. The Zodiac existed in the imagination of a frightened public. The Zodiac Killer never existed in real life.

The Zodiac became a bona fide star when Robert Graysmith's best-selling book *Zodiac* was published in 1986. In 2007, David Fincher made a film starring Robert Downey, Jr., Jake Gyllenhaal, and Mark Ruffalo, based on the *Zodiac* book. It made $84.7 million at the box office. Graysmith and Fincher turned the Zodiac Killer into a star for people who weren't around for his initial run in the '60s and '70s. Print the legend. Create the myth. Make it larger than life, then make a big-budget Hollywood film about it. Think of the profits.

But who benefits from a serial killer who can't be caught? So, so many people. There have been hundreds of books about the notorious Zodiac Killer. Dozens of documentaries, and thousands of podcast episodes and YouTube videos have been devoted to monetizing the mystery of the Zodiac Killer. What's missing from these books and documentaries? Well, not one of them will come right out and tell you this inconvenient fact: in the more than seven hundred pages of publicly available FBI reports about the Zodiac case, only one suspect is named concerning the authorship of the Zodiac letters. That name? Inspector David Toschi—the lead investigator on the Zodiac case from 1969 to 1978. They don't want you to know that the lead investigator (Mark Ruffalo's character in the movie) was investigated by the San Francisco Police Department (SFPD) for writing the Zodiac letters. The people tasked with solving the crime were the ones creating the legend, then tipping off their friends in the press to print the legend.

The true-crime grifters also overlook the fact that there isn't a single piece of hard evidence linking the murders. Each attack involved a different weapon. There are no fingerprint matches between crime scenes or from letter to letter. There are no confirmed DNA matches between crime scenes or between any of the letters (with one supposed match between two letters, which was later believed to have been fabricated by Toschi). The physical descriptions of the perp don't match either, unless you believe someone can gain and lose fifty-five pounds and almost twenty years of age between crimes.

None of this deters the fans in the online Zodiac community (which is almost entirely male—never a good sign). They love to pick the safest pet suspects—generally dead, harmless Bay Area eccentrics. They never seem to look for convicted murderers, especially those still living, when championing a suspect. Why bother looking at someone who committed similar murders when you can just blame it on a dead guy who wrote an underground newspaper, a guy who wrote a *Lord of the Rings* fanzine, the Unabomber, the Black Dahlia Avenger, someone involved with the military psy-ops program at the Presidio, or a member of San Francisco's Church of Satan? (These are all real examples.) That's not even considering the dozens of ridiculous "My daddy/grandpa/stepdaddy was the Zodiac" books that have flooded the market. For any of this to make sense, you really must want to believe—or be a soulless grifter.

So, was the Zodiac Killer bullshit? The answer is yes, and you're about to find out why.

CHAPTER 2: WHAT WE'RE TALKING ABOUT WHEN WE TALK ABOUT THE ZODIAC

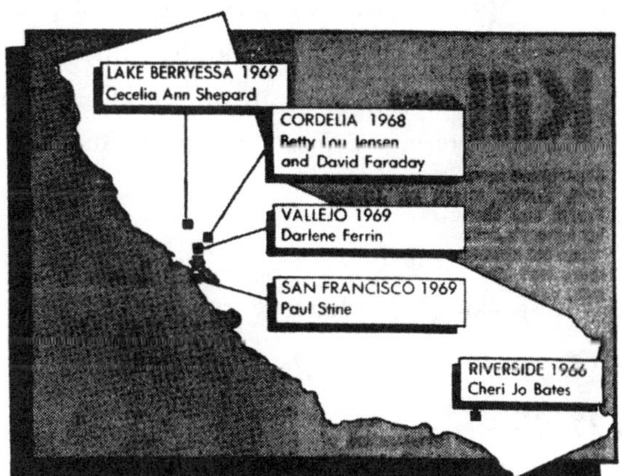

ZODIAC MURDER MAP. *SAN FRANCISCO CHRONICLE*, MAY 4, 1981.

THIS ISN'T ONE OF THOSE BORING TRUE-CRIME BOOKS about the Zodiac that's 90% rehash of his crimes and 10% baseless opinion and speculation. There are dozens of those and they're all terrible. But, for the sake of clarity, and to make sure we're on the same page, here's a timeline of the canonical Zodiac murders and correspondences.

DECEMBER 20, 1968

Seventeen-year-old David Faraday and sixteen-year-old Betty Lou Jensen were shot to death with a .22-caliber semi-automatic pistol at a lover's-lane parking area on Lake Herman Road in an unincorporated no-man's-land between Vallejo and Benicia, California.

JULY 4, 1969

While parked at a lover's-lane area at Blue Rock Springs Park in Vallejo, twenty-two-year-old Darlene Ferrin and nineteen-year-old Mike Mageau were both shot multiple times with a 9mm semi-automatic pistol. Darlene was killed, but

Mike survived. At 12:40 p.m. a man called the Vallejo Police Department from a gas-station payphone and claimed responsibility for the murder as well as the murders at Lake Herman Road.

JULY 31, 1969

The *Vallejo Times-Herald, San Francisco Chronicle,* and *San Francisco Examiner* each received a letter claiming responsibility for the murders at Lake Herman Road and Blue Rock Springs. The letter-writer included details about the shootings, the victims, and the weapons used in the crimes. He also sent one-third of a cipher to each newspaper, threatening to kill again if his ciphers weren't published. The letters were signed with a crossed-circle symbol.

AUGUST 4, 1969

A letter arrived at the *San Francisco Examiner,* beginning with the salutation, "This is the Zodiac speaking." The letter-writer provided more information about the murders.

AUGUST 8, 1969

The Zodiac's cipher was decoded by Donald and Bettye Harden, two civilian puzzle enthusiasts. It said, "I like killing people because it is so much fun. It is more fun than killing wild game in the forest because man is the most dangerous animal of all."

SEPTEMBER 27, 1969

At Lake Berryessa in Napa County, California, twenty-two-year-old Cecelia Shepard and twenty-year-old Bryan Hartnell were attacked by a man in a hooded costume with the Zodiac's crossed-circle symbol on it. They were tied up at gunpoint and stabbed multiple times by the masked man. Cecilia died and Bryan survived. The Zodiac symbol and the following message were written in marker on Hartnell's car door: "Vallejo 12-20-68, 7-4-69, Sept 27-69-6:30 by knife". At 7:40 p.m., a man called the Napa Police Department from a payphone to report a double murder, saying, "I'm the one who did it."

OCTOBER 11, 1969

Paul Stine, a taxi driver, was shot to death in his cab in the Presidio Heights neighborhood of San Francisco, California. Stine was the last confirmed Zodiac victim.

OCTOBER 13, 1969

A letter was mailed to the *San Francisco Chronicle*. It began with the salutation, "This is the Zodiac speaking." The letter-writer claimed, "I am the murderer of the taxi driver," and threatened to kill schoolchildren on a bus. The letter was accompanied by a piece of Paul Stine's bloody shirt.

NOVEMBER 8, 1969

An envelope containing a greeting card was mailed to the *San Francisco Chronicle* along with another piece of Paul Stine's bloody shirt, and a 340-character cipher.

NOVEMBER 9, 1969

A seven-page letter was mailed to the *San Francisco Chronicle*. The Zodiac claimed responsibility for the murders of seven victims. He also stated that two police officers had stopped him on the night of the Paul Stine murder but "pulled a goof" by letting him walk free. The letter included a bomb-making recipe and a diagram of a bomb.

DECEMBER 20, 1969

A letter containing another piece of Paul Stine's bloody shirt was sent to the prominent San Francisco defense attorney Melvin Belli at his home. This letter did not look or read like any of the previous Zodiac letters.

APRIL 20, 1970

A letter was mailed to the *San Francisco Chronicle*. The Zodiac claimed responsibility for the murders of ten victims. He included a new bomb diagram along with a cipher, which he said contained his name.

APRIL 28, 1970

A humorous greeting card was mailed to the *San Francisco Chronicle*. On the back, the Zodiac wrote, "If you don't want me to have this blast you must do two things. 1 Tell everyone about the bus bomb with all the details. 2 I would like to see some nice Zodiac butons [*sic*] wandering about town."

JUNE 26, 1970

A letter was mailed to the *San Francisco Chronicle*. The Zodiac claimed responsibility for twelve victims and included another cipher. If decoded, the cipher was said to reveal the location of his "bus bomb." The Zodiac was angry that people weren't wearing his buttons. He also claimed to have shot a man in a parked car with a .38.

JULY 24, 1970

A letter was mailed to the *San Francisco Chronicle.* The Zodiac again complained about people not wearing his buttons. He also took credit for the attempted abduction of Kathleen Johns and her baby after the story was reported in the newspaper.

JULY 26, 1970

A letter was mailed to the *San Francisco Chronicle.* The Zodiac complained about the buttons yet again. The Zodiac claimed responsibility for thirteen victims and quoted from the Gilbert and Sullivan opera *The Mikado.*

OCTOBER 5, 1970

A card with thirteen holes punched in it was sent to the *San Francisco Chronicle.* This letter, which contained the phrase "city pig cops," was initially believed to be a hoax.

OCTOBER 27, 1970

A Halloween card signed by the Zodiac was mailed to *San Francisco Chronicle* reporter, Paul Avery. It claimed fourteen kills.

MARCH 13, 1971

A letter was mailed to the *Los Angeles Times* from the Zodiac claiming responsibility for seventeen victims. Unlike previous Zodiac letters, which were postmarked in San Francisco, this one was sent from Pleasanton, California. In the letter, he praised the police for uncovering his involvement in the 1966 murder of Cheri Jo Bates in Riverside, California.

JANUARY 29, 1974

A letter was mailed to the *San Francisco Chronicle.* The Zodiac claimed responsibility for thirty-seven victims, quoted from *The Mikado,* and gave his opinion of the film *The Exorcist.*

APRIL 24, 1978

After four years of silence, a new letter from the Zodiac arrived at the *San Francisco Chronicle.* The letter was believed to be a hoax. ⌖

CHAPTER 3: A TRAGEDY AT LAKE HERMAN ROAD

DAVID FARADAY. *VALLEJO TIMES-HERALD,* MARCH 30, 1969.

BETTY LOU JENSEN. *TENNESSEAN,* OCTOBER 19, 1969.

LET'S TALK ABOUT THE MURDERS OF DAVID FARADAY and Betty Lou Jensen without the specter of the Zodiac Killer clouding things up. Let's talk about what was going on near Lake Herman Road that night and look at this case without linking it to the others and that jackass who wrote letters to the papers.

Between 9:30 and 10:00 p.m., William Crow and his girlfriend tested out her new sports car on Lake Herman Road. If that sounds like a euphemism, it's not. Like many young couples in the area, they pulled over near the pump station. The location was a lover's lane—a place where young people who still live with their parents go for some alone time with their dates. It was also known as a party spot where people went to buy and use drugs.

According to Crow, he wasn't there for heavy petting, smoking grass, or drinking beer. He was adjusting her car's motor. If *that* sounds like a euphemism, it's because it probably is. A blue car, possibly a Valiant, drove past Crow and his girlfriend on Lake Herman Road. Crow was not a car guy. In the police report, he called his girlfriend's new car a "sports car" instead of identifying it by make and model. Maybe he saw a Valiant. Maybe he didn't. He wasn't color-blind, though—the car was blue.

He spotted two white guys in the blue car, which came to a dead stop in the middle of the street. Crow saw the car's white reverse lights engage in the dark as the car backed up toward him and his girlfriend. Terrified, they jumped into her sports car. He floored the gas, and they sped away. The blue car gave chase. It was speeding towards them, trying to force them off the road. Crow turned off towards Benicia. The blue car and the two men inside continued on Lake Herman Road towards Vallejo.

Sometime after 10:00 p.m., about 2,000 feet away from the pump station, two Benicia Police Department detectives, Pierre Bidou and Steve Armenta, served a search warrant at the Cottage on Lake Herman.[9] The cops got the warrant based on an anonymous tip from a concerned citizen. The Cottage, a lakefront property owned by the city, was known to locals as the Pink House.

According to the tip, a major drug deal was about to go down at the Pink House. And if a major drug deal is about to go down in Northern California in 1968, the Hells Angels know about it. The Hells Angels are a motorcycle club. In '68, the Hells Angels were the Mafia on two wheels. Two Solano County deputies, Russell Butterbach and Wayne Waterman, were dispatched by their sergeant to the Hells Angels clubhouse on Warren Street in Vallejo at about the same time the warrant was being served on the Cottage at Lake Herman. They spent about forty-five minutes at the Hells Angels crash pad.

Bidou and Armenta's bust was the big one. According to the *Benicia Herald,* it was the biggest-ever drug bust in Benicia at the time.[10] They reported that cops seized one kilo (2.2 pounds) of marijuana, with a street value of $150 (the equivalent of about $1,400 today) from the house. Charles Anthony Borcich, the twenty-two-year-old grandson of the caretaker, and a resident of the Cottage at Lake Herman, was arrested at the scene.[11]

In the 2007 documentary *This Is the Zodiac Speaking*, Bidou said, "We confiscated about a pound and a half of marijuana, which in the 1960s was a big drug bust. Today it wouldn't get very high on the Richter scale. We had left and were heading back to the police department to put the marijuana into evidence and, as we drove by, we didn't see or observe anybody in that area. There's a turn there [the crime-scene turnout] and your headlights shine right in there as you go by. As I was pulling into the lot at the police department, we heard the Benicia Police Department dispatcher put out a call about a possible shooting and victims on Lake Herman Road and described the location. My partner and I turned around at that time and responded to the call." [12]

The problem with this chain of events: how is it possible that Bidou and Armenta, en route to Benicia police headquarters, presumably with Charles Borcich in custody in the back seat of their vehicle, get the call about the shooting at Lake Herman Road, then spin right around and respond to the job? What did they do with Borcich? They're certainly not going to the scene of a shooting with a civilian in the back seat of their car. Bidou never accounted for their prisoner in his retelling of the events.

That's not the only inconsistency with this story.

It sounds like a great bust for the cops and a disaster for the criminals involved in the drug deal. (Actually, it wasn't as big of a drug bust for the cops as Bidou or the *Benicia Herald* claimed, either. The numbers don't add up. Bidou was mentioned in a 1967 article that referenced a Benicia marijuana bust in the $5000-$7000 range—worth up to $65,000 in today's money.)[13] Another 1967 article tells of Bidou and his partner shutting down a dealer with a $40,000 (about $370,000 in today's money) bank roll trying to set up shop in Benicia.[14] Not sure why a seasoned narcotics enforcement officer and future chief of police called this particular bust out as a "big" one in his quote. It was clear that somebody snitched. Somebody nearby was missing a kilo of marijuana. Somebody owed somebody money for the kilo of marijuana that was now sitting in Benicia police evidence. Somebody's fucked.

At 10:30 p.m., fourteen-year-old Stan (his last name has been redacted in the copies of police reports made available to the public since he was a minor at the time) was in a car with a friend on Columbus Parkway, headed towards Blue Rock Springs. He saw a blue two-door hardtop Oldsmobile and a blue 1963 Chevy Impala with two people in it at the intersection of Columbus

Parkway and Lake Herman Road. The Impala with the two guys in it turned onto Lake Herman Road, heading towards Blue Rock Springs.[15]

Now for the victims. Seventeen-year-old David Faraday was the post-war American ideal in the form of a high school student. He was beyond a good kid—not just a Boy Scout, he was an Eagle Scout. He even won something called the God and Country Award. He was a member of the high school wrestling team. He was the kind of kid who confronted a drug dealer at the Pancake House and threatened to turn him in to police for pushing grass at school.[16]

At 7:10 p.m., David drove his sister Debbie to a meeting of the Rainbow Girls at the Pythian Castle on Sonoma Boulevard. David told Debbie he was going to Lake Herman Road later that night with some other kids.[17]

At 8:00 p.m., David arrived at the home of sixteen-year-old Betty Lou Jensen, whom he had met a few weeks earlier at the Pythian Castle. He was picking her up for their first date. It might have been her first-ever date. He met her Christian Scientist parents and got their permission to take her to a Christmas concert at her high school, followed by a party at her friend's house.

Even Eagle Scouts are capable of lying—there was no Christmas concert at Hogan High School on December 20, 1968. There had been one the previous week, but not that night. It was a wholesome story to reassure her parents, but David and Betty Lou had other plans. He promised Betty Lou's parents he'd have her home by 11:00 p.m. [18]

At 11:20 p.m., Stella Medeiros, a seventy-year-old local resident on the way to pick up her grandson at the movie theater, drove by the turnout at Lake Herman Road. The headlights of her car illuminated David's Rambler station wagon. Medeiros reported seeing "a boy and he had looked like he had fallen out of the open door. The girl was lying on her side facing the road."[19] It seemed that Medeiros found the unfortunate couple shortly after their shooter did. She sped off toward Benicia, slamming her car horn until she got the attention of a police officer. Capt. Daniel Pitta was the first cop on scene, at 11:28 p.m. David was still breathing. Betty Lou was dead on scene in a pool of her own blood. Emergency services transported David to Vallejo Hospital where he was pronounced dead on arrival at 12:05 a.m. by a Dr. Siebert.

The murders took place in an unincorporated area on Lake Herman Road. The murder investigation didn't go to the Vallejo Police Department, who were used to dealing with serious crime, drug offenses, murder, and mayhem,

DET. SGT. LES LUNDBLAD. *VALLEJO TIMES-HERALD*, DECEMBER 22, 1968.

or the Benicia Police Department, who were less experienced with such serious crimes. The job went to the Solano County Sheriff's Office.

Detective Sergeant Les Lundblad, who had worked on murders before, caught the case. He looked the part of a hard-charging detective—a stern-faced, gray-haired old-timer who wore severe horn-rimmed glasses, a fedora, and an overcoat.

At 12:05 a.m., Lundblad arrived on scene at Lake Herman Road and took charge. He sent his deputies, Butterbach and Waterman—the same pair that had been off at the Hells Angels caper earlier in the night—to the hospital to gather information.

David had been shot once in the head, at the left ear. The wound had powder burns, which only occur when the individual was in close proximity to a gun going off. An experienced investigator like Lundblad would immediately know that the presence of powder burns means the gun had been pressed to David's head or close enough.

David wasn't robbed—he had his class ring, wallet, money, and a watch on his person when he died. A single small-caliber shot to the head from behind the ear sounds a hell of a lot like an execution-style murder.

But why would someone want to execute David, an Eagle Scout on a harmless date?

Lundblad brought in neighboring police departments from Vallejo, Martinez, Fairfield, Benicia, and others for mutual aid. He even called in the California Department of Justice for assistance with the investigation. And he was a perfectionist with the witnesses—he checked how fast or slow their clocks were and nailed down their travel times to get a firmer grasp of the timeline.

The California Department of Justice identified the weapon—a .22-caliber, semi-automatic long-barreled pistol. Either a J. C. Higgins Model 80 or a High Standard Model 101. (Those are both the same gun with different brand names. The J. C. Higgins brand was a High Standard M-101 sold under a different name exclusively at Sears, Roebuck, and Company stores.) This gun had a distinctive appearance. It was known as the "space gun" because it looked kitschy, like something spacemen in a 1950s B-grade science-fiction movie would use to fight aliens. It looked like a ray gun. If somebody pulled this gun on you, you'd remember it. It was a decent target pistol for the price, also known as a "plinker" gun because of the "plinking" sound that a fired round made when it hit a metal target, like a beer can or road sign.

Betty Lou was shot five times in the back. Maybe the girl tried to escape and the killer shot her in the back. Maybe the killer convinced her his issue was with David, not her, and he'd allow her to leave. Then, as she was leaving, he shot her in the back when she wasn't expecting it.

Lundblad and his deputies aggressively questioned those closest to David and Betty Lou. Betty Lou's sister Melody told him that, on the evening of the murder, Betty Lou had told her she was afraid of a boy named Ricky Burton. According to Betty Lou's friend Sharon and Ricky himself, Ricky and Betty Lou "went with" each other at school for two weeks (from December 1st to14th) and talked on the phone often but never went on a date. Once Betty Lou met David, she dropped Ricky. Ricky had threatened to tell the Jensens that their daughter smoked cigarettes and went on dates. Betty Lou told her sister that Ricky said he was going to beat up David Faraday with brass knuckles.[20]

Melody also told Lundblad that David, a student at Vallejo High, came to Betty Lou's school, Hogan High, and confronted Ricky. She said that Betty Lou had even asked her to close the blinds because she suspected Ricky was prowling around the outside of the house and spying on her.

The cops searched Betty Lou's school locker and found an interesting note about Ricky Burton signed by her:

> **DO YOU KNOW A KID NAMED RICHARD BURTON? I WAS GOING WITH HIM, UNTIL TWO DAYS BEFORE THE INSTALATION. HE STILL PHONES ME AND IS THREATENING ME TO KEEP AWAY FROM DAVE. HE SAID IF HE'S EVER CLOSE ENOUGH TO DAVE, HE WOULD PUNCH HIM ONE IN THE TEETH, I TOLD HIM TO LEAVE ME ALONE, IF HE KNOWS WHAT GOOD HIM.** [21]

Cops also talked to David's friend Joe, who told them that David had no enemies. Ricky, according to Joe, was just a big talker with no friends. Other friends of David and Betty Lou reiterated that Ricky was a harmless blowhard.

The cops followed up and interviewed Burton and his family. According to them, at the time of David and Betty Lou's murder, Ricky was at home with a roomful of people, including family members and a police sergeant from Mare Island. They were having coffee and cake, and watching the movie *A Global Affair*, starring Bob Hope and Yvonne De Carlo. Cops kept looking into Burton. They showed him a copy of Betty Lou's note about him; he agreed that it was her handwriting and acted unfazed about it. Ricky agreed to take a polygraph test, and his parents consented to it too. The next morning, Ricky's father informed police that Ricky would not be taking the polygraph because he was too nervous. After the refusal, the cops moved on from Ricky Burton.

You know who didn't move on? Ricky Burton.

On February 13, 1969, an article appeared in the *Vallejo Times-Herald* about students at Vallejo and Hogan High raising money for the Jensen-Faraday Reward Fund to help catch their friends' killers. The student leading the efforts to help find the real killer at Betty Lou's school? Ricky Burton.[22] This kid was either a really good friend to Betty Lou and was legitimately trying to help, or he was pulling an O. J. Simpson.

Cops talked to the mother of Betty Lou's friend Sharon, who told a story about David confronting a drug dealer at the Pancake House and threatening to turn him in to the police. The police report concluded with, "The above information will be checked out."[23]

Based on publicly available police records, the information was not followed up on. Links between the major drug bust at the Cottage and David's reputed snitching on a drug dealer were not investigated by the Solano Sheriff's Office. This is unfathomably negligent police work. Once investigators determined that neither David nor Betty Lou used drugs, they completely dropped the drug angle despite information that David informed the police about a local drug dealer who pushed grass at Vallejo High School. Only three days after the murders, the media were running with another narrative, supplied by investigators: the murders could be the work of a "murderous maniac who was not acquainted with either victim."[24]

Local witnesses came forward. Apparently, Lake Herman Road after dark, in the late December cold, had been a hub of activity. Two guys hunting raccoons, Robert Connelly and Frank Gasser, said they saw a light-colored '59 or '60 Chevy Impala at 9:00 p.m. parked at the turnout. A local shepherd, Bingo Wesner, also saw a white Impala by the pumping station at 10:00 p.m.[25] Helen Axe claimed to have seen David's Rambler at the lover's-lane turnout at 10:15 p.m.

At 11:00 p.m., a married couple, Peggy and Homer Your, were driving home from Sacramento when they saw David's Rambler with a white male and female in the front seat. They also saw Connelly and Gasser holding a long-barreled gun and got the hell out of there. They passed the turnout again around 11:15 p.m. and saw the Rambler with the white man and the white woman still in the front seat. (The hunters also saw David's Rambler sometime between 11:00 and 11:15 p.m., but they said there was no one in it.) A police range master, George Parks, ran ballistics tests on the hunters' guns, which were not a match for the gun that shot David and Betty Lou.

James Owen, who was driving to work the graveyard shift at the oil company, thought he passed the scene around 11:20 p.m. and saw David's unoccupied Rambler and another mystery car parked ten feet away. Police determined his clock was six minutes fast. Owen was the last person to pass the pumping station, at 11:14 p.m., before Medeiros found David and Betty Lou at 11:20 p.m.

On January 3, 1969, just three weeks after the murders at Lake Herman Road, another person was murdered in a parked car in Solano County. The victim was forty-six-year-old Matthew Burrell. He was celebrating his birthday with friends at the Kentwig Lodge, a motel bar where he was a regular.

According to guests and employees, everyone was drinking and laughing and having a grand old time.

Burrell was shot through his car's rear window by a .30-caliber M-1 carbine at about 1:30 a.m. Then, proving it was no accident, the shooter ran up to Burrell and shot him a second time. He died and his car rolled into the Kentwig Lodge's motel sign at Interstate 80 and Magazine Street.

Burrell, a Black man, weighed 260 pounds. The few newspaper accounts that bothered to cover the story never fail to mention that. That's a massive man in 1969. The average American adult male in the 1960s weighs 166 pounds. "Fats" Burrell (clever nickname) had a hundred pounds on the average guy. He was a bricklayer with an ex-wife and no enemies. The newspaper article describes him as "jovial." Of course they did.

Meanwhile, Lundblad had another motiveless murder of an innocent person shot in a parked car on his hands. The third in three weeks.[26]

The media started asking questions about the connection between the murders of two teenagers parked in a car at Lake Herman Road and the murder of Matthew Burrell parked in his car near the Kentwig Lodge. Det. Sgt. H. P. Kramer told the *Napa Valley Register* that, although similarities between the two crimes existed, the murder weapons were different. "Of course, it's possible we've got a real goofball around here," he said.[27]

Or maybe they had two goofballs. A witness told police that on the night Burrell was murdered they saw two young men milling around the parking lot acting erratically, as if they were under the influence of drugs. Later that night, police found a car stolen out of Berkeley abandoned on Columbus Parkway with shotgun shells in the front seat.

Like the murders of David and Betty Lou, Burrell's murder was never solved. As a middle-aged Black man, the papers didn't follow his story the way they did that of two white teenagers at a lover's lane. His death made the papers first because of the possible connection to the Lake Herman Road murders and six months later because the gun that killed him was also used to kill a white man called Steven Tompkins during a crime spree. The Solano Sheriff Office's investigation went nowhere.

CHAPTER 4: WHO KILLED DAVID AND BETTY LOU?

WHILE DIGGING INTO THE FIRST TWO MURDERS attributed to the Zodiac Killer, I found myself wondering why the original police investigators on the case, the detectives who worked the Zodiac as a cold case in 1991 and '92, and David Fincher, who directed the movie *Zodiac,* all believed that the Zodiac Killer had nothing to do with the murders of David Faraday and Betty Lou Jensen at Lake Herman Road. Turns out, in 1970, David Magris, a death-row inmate, confessed to his involvement in the Lake Herman Road murders—murders that the Zodiac took credit for. Fincher didn't even include a Lake Herman Road depiction in his film.

See, here's the thing: in real life, most crime is boring. It's just dumb people doing awful things for ridiculous reasons. Victims often aren't carefully chosen. They're just people who happened to be in the wrong place at the wrong time.

The concept of a master criminal is soothing. The narrative of a mad genius committing murders and evading police detection for very specific, very mysterious reasons is an attempt to make sense of senseless slaughter. Manifestos and secret codes show a level of thought and care absent from the brutality and poor impulse control present in real crimes as opposed to "true crime."

"True crime" is a fairy tale. Real crime, like the brutal murders of David Faraday, Betty Lou Jensen, Matthew Burrell, and Steven Tompkins, isn't always well-thought-out. Real crime just happens, without an elaborate backstory to explain the motivation. Two teenagers making out in a car two thousand feet away from the location where police made a major drug bust were likely shot and killed because the guys who were supposed to pick up the drugs the cops intercepted got pissed off. "True crime" is the television program *Crimes of the Century* not airing their interview with Terry Cunningham, who is identified in the producer's notes as: "Detective who doesn't believe there *is* a Zodiac. Knows who murdered the first 2 kids and rest are random killings for which a nut took credit." In order to preserve the bankable narrative, "true crime" has to cherry-pick its sources. What purpose could the police officer who took the confession for the first two Zodiac murders possibly serve in a Zodiac documentary?

Back to David Magris. What was he up to in Vallejo around the time of the murders of David Faraday and Betty Lou Jensen? Before we get to that, let's set the scene properly.

In 1968, two years before Magris confessed to Sgt. Terry Cunningham of the Solano County Sheriff's Office, San Francisco was the coolest place in the world. Thousands of young Americans flocked there to smoke grass, drop acid, fuck strangers, and be seen at Vietnam War protests by strangers they hadn't fucked yet. Hippies turned parts of the city into an amusement park for rich kids from Anytown, U.S.A. The privileged progeny of the generation who lived through the Depression and killed the Nazis thumbed their noses at the post-war prosperity and the suburban stability they grew up with. They stuck a flower in their hair, ditched their shoes in a trash can, and lived ten to a room with other LARPers making the scene.

Watch a television news report from the era—the correspondents treated the Haight as a human zoo. *Behold, their wild attire and poor hygiene. Their drug-fueled baby boomer radical politics. These could be your little darlings if you're not careful!*

The news media are in the fear business. Fear is the product the media sells to an addicted audience jonesing for the next story that will give them a rush. Long-haired, anti-establishment hippies scared the shit out of America. The cultural shift, framed by sensational coverage of assassinations and unrest across the country, turned daily newspapers into penny dreadfuls. The TV nightly news was stuffed with gruesome war footage from Vietnam and urban riot scenes, becoming an anthology of cinema verité horror films detailing the rapid decay of a once-wholesome society.

Vallejo, California, is about thirty-three miles from the intersection of Haight and Ashbury in San Francisco, but it might as well be a million miles away. You could make the drive in under an hour, but it would feel like traveling back a decade in a time machine. Vallejo ain't San Francisco. In 1968, it was still 1958 in the scrappy, blue-collar city. It was a company town for the U.S. Navy.

The Mare Island Naval Shipyard was the only game in town. It was by far the biggest employer. The Cold War was raging. Vietnam was already a clusterfuck. The war business was booming, and ships needed to be built and repaired. A civilian army of machinists were paid a good wage by Uncle Sam to help crush the Viet Cong. In 1950, the city's population was 26,038; by 1968, it had more than doubled, to over 66,000 people. And, like the boomtowns of the Old West, Vallejo, a boomtown of the New West, was besieged by an increase in violence, vice, and mayhem to go along with its newfound prosperity and population explosion.

In San Francisco, they burned draft cards. In Vallejo, young men like David Luis Magris enlisted in the United States Marine Corps during wartime. The hippies in Berkeley had free love and the birth-control pill, and Vallejoans like Magris had a wife and a baby before their twentieth birthday. Magris even looked a decade out of style in the late '60s. Magris's aesthetic suggested an affinity for the 1950s teen idol Ritchie Valens. His jet-black hair was slicked back in a greasy pompadour with a spit curl dangling across his forehead. He wore cuffed Levi's jeans and bomber jackets.

His partner in crime, Jon Holmberg (this name has been changed for legal reasons), had a mop of red hair and was tall and jacked with boot-camp muscle —six-foot-three according to his Solano County Jail booking sheet. He looked like a devilishly handsome jailhouse biker version of Shaggy from *Scooby-Doo* with his beatnik goatee and floppy red hair.

MEET DAVID MAGRIS

Magris started out as a good kid, a gifted and talented kid before that phrase became meaningless. According to his mother, he began formally studying with the famed dancer Lodena Edgecumbe at the age of eight. He wasn't just one of those kids whose parents paid through the nose for dance lessons and bought a ridiculous costume—say, bow tie, a bowler hat, and a vest covered in sequins—just for the displeasure of sitting through one recital with their bored kid shuffling in the background. Magris was the real deal, a prodigy. By age sixteen, he had performed with the world-famous Leningrad Kirov Ballet in San Francisco.[28] The *Solano-Napa News Chronicle* even printed glowing articles about their local celebrity. His Clayton Valley High School yearbook

DAVID MAGRIS YEARBOOK PHOTO. CENTRAL VALLEY HIGH SCHOOL, 1966.

picture looks like a show kid's headshot—he could have been one of the background guys in a doo-wop group. Not Dion or Frankie Lymon, but definitely one of the Belmonts or the Teenagers.

According to an August 1993 article in the *Sun* magazine, Dancing Dave lived a double life. "I was leading an exemplary life in the daytime as a dancer," Magris said. "I was determined to be a star. But at night I was doing burglaries, drinking, taking, and selling drugs."[29]

As a fifteen-year-old, he stole his dance teacher's car and crossed state lines into Nevada with a fourteen-year-old girl. This landed him in juvie. After juvie, he bounced around foster care until he ended up at a cousin's house. Through all this upheaval, Dave kept dancing. He danced his way on stage with the big-time Soviet ballet. Then, just a few months later, while still in high school, he gave up on dancing and joined the Marines.

Magris served his country and was discharged in January of 1968. He returned to Vallejo born-again hard. No more dance recitals. If any well-meaning family member or judge thought that a couple of years in the Corps would give him the discipline needed to straighten his life out, they couldn't have been more wrong.

Magris was a half-a-gangster who dove headfirst into the North Bay criminal world. In '68, when the local paper wrote about Dave, it was for setting up a shooting gallery and selling drugs out of an illegal squat at 322 Capitol Street. The cops raided the joint, arrested eight people, and discovered a cache of codeine, morphine, Demerol, and syringes, plus other gear. They also found several underage teenage girls, mostly runaways from out of state.[30]

One of the girls, a local, had a two-year-old baby. Det. George Bawart made the bust—in *Zodiac Unmasked,* he told Robert Graysmith, "They were wired on reds and screwy as bedbugs."

"Reds" was the street name for the drug Seconal, a powerful barbiturate used for anesthesia, sedation, and treating insomnia. They're knockout pills if you take one or two. They're blackout-for-days pills if you grind them up and shoot them in your vein. They were the drug of choice for the zoned-

DAVID MAGRIS, UNDER ARREST. *SOLANO-NAPA NEWS CHRONICLE*, JUNE 3, 1969.

out characters in *Valley of the Dolls*. They were the same pills that killed Judy Garland and Tennessee Williams. David and his friends had a never-ending supply—bags and bags containing hundreds of reds from their biker associate called Darrell "Pus Gut" Cussins.

Magris got lucky. A kid from Cleveland named John Ferrette was investigated for a violation of the Mann Act. To cops and prosecutors, drugs are bad, but transporting underage girls across state lines for the purposes of prostitution is straight-up diabolical. Magris was allowed to plead guilty on the narcotics beef and only got sixty days in jail.

After getting out, Magris fell in love. He was over the moon for a sixteen-year-old named Dian Stevens. They met on Wilson Avenue, the notorious street where Vallejo's "freaks" hung out. Stevens had just gotten back from hitchhiking across the country with Mike Lebovitz, one of the guys who got arrested with Magris at the Capitol Street squat, and another guy called Happy Jack who took fifty hits of acid and disappeared.

Stevens was pretty and petite and more badass than all the tough guys in Vallejo put together. For her sixteenth birthday, her father gave her a .32 automatic pistol for self-defense. He worked double shifts as a machinist at Mare Island—if he couldn't physically be there to protect his daughter due to work obligations, she'd have to do it herself.

When Stevens protested the war in Vietnam, it wasn't to virtue-signal. It was because she was sick of seeing young men return to Vallejo in pieces—literally or figuratively. In an era when nearly every young person had at least a casual fling with drugs, Stevens didn't use drugs. She hated drugs. Her older sister was an addict who had overdosed.

One day, Stevens, with Magris in tow and a .32 in her purse, drove to confront the dealers who sold her sister the dope—they were teenagers outside a high school. She pulled the gun to get some answers. Somebody called the cops. The cops hit the siren. Magris decided it was time to split, so he grabbed the gun from Stevens and stuck it in his waistband. As they ran, the gun went off and he shot himself in the leg.

Stevens remained calm. She knew that he needed to get to the hospital, but if he went to the ER with a bullet lodged in his leg the hospital would call the police and they'd put two and two together. She took Magris home and removed the bullet with household utensils, then she brought him to the hospital. The ER nurse winked and said, "Whoever took that bullet out did a good job."

Meanwhile, Magris was again living a Jekyll-and-Hyde double life. He was a sweetheart boyfriend to Stevens. He paid her compliments and took her out dancing. He didn't get high when she was around. And if he had to conduct business at a drug spot, Stevens waited in the car. He didn't do this to shelter her from Vallejo's underworld; she was well acquainted with the characters and didn't need his protection. She just didn't want to be around drugs and had put her foot down. Dian had had enough of that drama while hanging out with her wild-child sister and her sister's boyfriend, a guy named Jim Flowers. In 1967, Dian had tagged along with the couple for a trip up to the Haight. Jim drove, Dian's sister went to score drugs, and Dian sat with some hippie girls and glued pennies to the sidewalk. Dian was arrested for malicious mischief. Her picture ended up on the front page of the underground newspaper the *Berkeley Barb* with the headline "Malice in Blunderland."

Dian had also been a passenger in Jim Flowers's car the time he stopped at a gas station in San Jose and decided to rob the place. Jim asked Dian to tie up the attendant while he stole the cash and Blue Chip Stamps. She flatly refused. The quick-thinking attendant pretended to be tied up, and nobody got hurt. The next time Jim Flowers drove to a gas station in San Jose with Dian in the passenger seat, she stayed in the car.

At sixteen years old, Stevens understood the concept of plausible deniability. Magris met some of Stevens's less drug-averse friends and put a crew together. He enlisted the Donohue brothers, Robert (an ex-boyfriend of Stevens) and Matthew. They were movie-star handsome knock-around guys who came up the hard way. Like many people who get caught up in criminal activity, they came with a tragic origin story. Their sad tale made the *San Francisco Examiner* for the first time on June 19, 1956. Their father was working out of town. Their mother took his absence as an opportunity to leave her six children, ranging in age from one to eight, at home in their Mission District apartment for "twenty minutes" while she went shopping. Twenty minutes turned into nine hours while Mommy Dearest went on a bender. Neighbors called the cops at 1:00 a.m. The kids were crying. They were starving—the only food in the house was a loaf of bread and a box of pancake mix. Three days later, Mrs. Donohue telephoned the Juvenile Bureau to inquire about the whereabouts of her kids, but "gave no indication she planned to get them."[31]

JONATHAN HOLMBERG JOINS THE CREW

Stevens's best friend was a seventeen-year-old called Cindy (this name has been changed) who had married a twenty-three-year-old veteran named Jonathan Holmberg. Magris and Holmberg, a couple of guys fresh out of the military, become instant friends and partners in crime.

Holmberg was medically discharged after two years due to a service-related injury. With an IQ of 130, he was the smartest person in the room—any room. Most importantly, he had a solid connection to the Hells Angels through his sister Joyce. She was an "old lady," the girlfriend of a club member, who made the papers on several occasions, in a number of locations, for getting arrested with the motorcycle club.[32] She was also arrested in Vallejo for possession of Benzedrine.[33]

Benzedrine was a form of speed. An upper. The drug Jack Kerouac took while writing spontaneous prose in marathon sessions that eventually became the classic American novel *On the Road*. Even the drugs in Vallejo were straight out of 1958.

That's how Magris's gang had a rock-solid hookup with the biggest drug suppliers on the West Coast, the Hells Angels. Holmberg introduced Magris to Darrell "Pus Gut" Cussins and his right-hand man Darryl Walters. Pus Gut was the kind of upstanding citizen who got arrested for painting swastikas and writing "Hitler's Youth" on a guy named William Black's house.[34] The bikers quickly became part of the crew—the gang's drug suppliers.

If you were a high-school kid in Vallejo looking to get high in 1969, David Magris was the guy to know. If you didn't look old enough to get into the Kat Pad strip club on Sacramento Street, you could track him down at the apartment he shared with the Donohue brothers and a slew of teenage girls.

Magris often sat in the middle of the Capitol Street apartment, spaced out, on a bare mattress, wearing an oversized pair of Ray-Ban sunglasses to hide his scrambled pupils and dark undereye bags.

Cornell Johnson, a six-foot-three twenty-year-old high-school senior, was literally a man among boys at Benicia High School and one of Magris's best customers. He looked old enough to get into the Kat Pad, but in 1969 it probably wasn't a great idea for a Black man and his girlfriend to score drugs at a biker and peckerwood hangout. Late-'60s Vallejo wasn't exactly integrated. You could call Dave and Jon a lot of things, but it would be inaccurate to call them racists. Magris's drug spots were practically inclusive safe spaces where all were welcome. Local newspapers regularly featured stories of Cornell's dominance on the court in high-school basketball games. When basketball wasn't in season, Cornell would casually walk onto the team in other sports, as some kind of side quest, and dominate. He smashed home runs for the baseball team. He messed around with track and field a little and wound up setting a school record for the high jump. The most remarkable thing about these athletic achievements? He managed to accomplish all of this while ensnared in the grips of hard drug addiction. Cornell might have liked sports and girls, but his one true love was drugs.

Cornell bought his dope at the illicit drug mini-marts Magris ran out of Vallejo apartments. These places were filled with drugs, weapons, and teenage girls. They were places to hang out, places to buy drugs, places to use the drugs you just bought, and maybe even places to hook up with a girl. They were drug spots, shooting galleries, social clubs, and cathouses all rolled into one.

Cornell Johnson brought a girlfriend named Mollie to the apartment. Dave, Jon, and a half dozen high-school-aged girls, half of them named Debbie, were as screwy as bedbugs on handfuls of reds and handfuls of uppers. Cornell was annoyed at the impaired state of everyone. He just wanted to get his gear and get the hell out of there as fast as possible. He was nervous. A warrant had recently gone out for his arrest. He had gotten caught up in a burglary caper. He boosted $850 (about $8,000 in today's money) worth of stereo equipment.

There was a knock at the door. Someone outside shouted, "Vallejo Police." Cornell freaked out and thought the cops were there to arrest him.

Mollie and one of the Debbies answered the door. It really was the police. The cops wanted to speak to Jon Holmberg about a stolen '57 Chevy. The girls knew not to let the cops in. Jon played it smart by walking outside and surrendering to the cops, who took him in for questioning about the stolen car. He slammed the front door shut so the cops couldn't see what was happening inside the house or enter the house.

In the grips of a full-blown panic attack, Cornell ran into a bedroom at the back of the apartment. He pulled a .30 caliber M-1 carbine from under his jacket and slid it under the bed. If he got caught in this place, with that gun, with a warrant on his head, he could get a long stretch in prison. Cornell wasn't about that life. He was a ballplayer, not a gangster. He didn't want the gun anymore; it made him too nervous. He gifted David Magris a powerful gun, a weapon that would get him much more respect (and trouble) than the dinky .22 pistol he was tooling around with.[35]

Another regular at the Capitol Street apartment was the gang's associate Johnny Doyel. He was a subsistence drug-dealer, an eighteen-year-old who dealt Methedrine supplied by Magris to fund his own habit. Methamphetamine was marketed under the trade name Methedrine by Burroughs Wellcome. In the 1960s, it was prescribed by medical doctors for everything from weight loss to depression to fatigue. It became a popular cure-all, used and abused by American housewives, students, truck drivers, bikers, and mods. A 1965 study indicated that "pep pills" (meth) were the most-used illicit substance among students at San Francisco State College.[36] America became speed-crazy, with millions of daily users.

Doyel was such a fixture at the gang's dope spot that he considered Holmberg a "good friend." He even began a serious relationship with Holmberg's sister, Sarah, and intended to marry her. Sometimes he brought his teenage brother Paul around to hang out at the apartment. They got high and drunk, sitting on a mattress and talking shit with the other kids milling around.

As much as Doyel enjoyed getting high on free drugs and sharing laughs with his new friends, they scared the shit out of him. He later testified that he had been at the apartment on January 3, 1969, when the boys came home in the middle of the night and Magris, dazed and exhilarated, bragged, "I shot someone. A Negro."[37] Killers almost always tell someone. They can't help themselves.

Doyel also swore under oath that he had been on the back porch at Holmberg's rental on Fifth Street when Magris, out of his mind on speed and LSD, fired shots at a random stranger walking down the street. He watched Holmberg calmly wrestle the gun away and take control of a dangerous situation without hesitation.

He dealt his drugs, supplied by Magris, to students at Vallejo High and Hogan High. The Doyel brothers knew David Faraday before his death—and Johnny Doyel was likely the high-school drug pusher Faraday argued with at the Pancake House and threatened to report to the police. Paul Doyel was Betty Lou's classmate at Hogan High. Johnny Doyel was not subtle about the fact that he could get high-school kids whatever drugs they needed, and David Faraday, being the God and Country Award–winning member of the Knights of Dunamis, varsity wrestler, and Eagle Scout, wasn't exactly subtle about his feelings concerning a drug dealer setting up shop at his high school. Like a lot of other people in the Vallejo drug scene, Doyel probably heard the rumor on the street that Magris and a partner murdered Faraday and the girl he was with at Lake Herman Road because Faraday snitched about a big-time drug deal.

As much as those two incidents disturbed him, what bothered him most was what happened to the dog.[38]

THE THING WITH THE DOG

One day when he was at the apartment, Johnny Doyel got involved in a stoner conversation about the ferocious watchdog at a grocery store called the Dairy Farm.

"Dairy Farm?" Magris asked.

"Yeah," Johnny Doyel said. "They got a real mean German shepherd that watches the place after hours. He's the best guard dog around. They're the only store in Vallejo that's never been robbed. That dog chewed a bunch of burglars up. They never got nothing from there. I figure if anybody ever gets past that dog and robs the Dairy Farm, somebody big, like the Mafia, would notice and hire them." [39]

"That dog'll get its lumps one day," Paul Doyel said.

"What the hell do you know about the Mafia?" Magris said.

"Just stories," Johnny Doyel said.

"Stories from who?"

"The boys who run the coin-ops. They're connected."

"The hell they are," Magris said. "If they were connected, I'd know about it. My father's a Mafia hitman. He's on death row back east because of it." Magris believed in his family's private lore. He believed he was cursed with bad blood, criminal blood. He told people he was half-Italian and bragged about his family's criminal underworld connections, boasting about being a descendent of Mafia royalty. His biological father, he explained, was a Cosa Nostra button man. Magris really believed this because his grandfather told him an outlandish story explaining his father's absenteeism.[40] None of this was true, of course.

David's mother's surname was Ramos when his parents split. Magris was raised by his maternal grandparents, and they were Puerto Rican. He was as Italian as mofongo, but that didn't stop him from holding on to the orphan's outlaw fantasy. His death notice in 2023 even listed a man named Frank Zona as his father.[41] Frank Zona was an insurance agent and the head of the men's club at St. Catherine's Catholic Church in San Mateo, California.[42] He was not a Mafia hitman. The guy was a good citizen, a never-got-a-parking-ticket type, not a gangster.

The Doyel brothers, sensing the mood had turned dark, took their supply of meth and hit the road. They knew some truly frightening bikers were behind the speed—everybody knew that. Magris and Holmberg got their speed from the outlaw biker Pus Gut, who supplied drugs to local dealers. The club was not officially involved in the drug game, but some individual members like Pus Gut were. Pus Gut was a heavy hitter. The only guy above him in the local drug game was the president of the Hells Angels Nomad chapter, James Dewey Witt, Jr., who was at the top of the drug-dealing pyramid. Doyel was at the bottom of the pyramid. Magris, whom he considered to be a dangerous, murderous psychopath, was a rung above Doyel but well below Pus Gut and his boss Witt.

Vallejo cops raided Witt's home and seized $80,000 worth of drugs (over a million dollars today), $12,500 in cash (about $150,000 today), and an arsenal that included bazookas, rockets, and machine guns.[43] Despite being found guilty of nine heavy charges, Witt was only sentenced to a year in jail by a Solano County judge.[44]

The drugs were fronted by Magris, meaning they were given to Doyel on credit. After Doyel sold the speed and weed, he paid him. Magris would then pay Pus Gut, who bought wholesale quantities from Witt. As soon as the Doyel brothers left the house, the clock started ticking for everyone. Everyone understood the consequences if they failed to uphold their end of the bargain.

In the middle of the night, after closing time, Magris drove Dian Stevens's dad's white Chevrolet Impala to the Dairy Farm. He smashed a window on the back door. The fearsome attack dog ran towards the disturbance. Magris remained behind the closed door as the dog charged at him. Anticipating the dog's aggression, he kept himself out of harm's way and fired two shots into the German shepherd. The dog didn't drop. He made another charge at the door. Magris aimed and got off a headshot. The dog went down.

Magris reached through the broken glass and turned the door handle open. The dog whimpered and gave a last growl. Magris fired two more shots, killing the dog. He robbed the store of cash and cigarettes. He grabbed a bottle of milk for the road and left a note—"Thank you. The Cat."

Magris's street name was the Cat because he was a slick burglar who moved with the suddenness and silence of a cat. It was a better nickname than the Ballerino, which would more accurately describe his graceful movement. Magris drove to the Doyel house and met Johnny Doyel outside. He laughed and handed the confused Doyel the bottle of milk. "I just pulled a job and shot the dog."

As far as I'm concerned, this is a chilling glimpse into the unhinged mind of David Magris. The idea of intentionally shooting a dog is so disturbing to the average person that the cinematic *John Wick* franchise has managed to make four movies based on it. But the true horror is what that mindset might lead to when applied to a human life. Take the case of a man murdered in his car on his birthday. Is it so difficult to infer that two hopped-up junkies looking for an excuse to try out their new gun did the crime? Or that a drunk psychopath's idea of the best way to end a night of partying was to rob a gas station, kidnap the attendant, pretend that you're letting him go, then use that carbine that was so fun to shoot to kill him in cold blood? It's random and it's fucking frightening, but there's a very real possibility that David Faraday, Betty Lou

Jensen, Matthew Burrell, and Steven Tompkins were shot to death because two twisted guys simply thought it would be fun to shoot them. That's at least as terrifying as the idea of a Zodiac Killer who's motivated to collect the souls of people he's killed as slaves in the afterlife. The Zodiac, with his cryptic letters and dark lore, is the stuff of a horror B-movie. Real crime is spontaneous and messy. It's splatterpunk. But if the public requires a cute nickname to attach to the violent criminals responsible for these deaths, let's call them exactly what they are—the Vallejo Thrill Killers.

INTRODUCING THE VALLEJO THRILL KILLERS

On January 3, 1969, just two weeks after the murders of David Faraday and Betty Lou Jensen, Matthew Burrell was murdered in a motel parking lot in Vallejo. He was killed by a .30-caliber M-1 carbine—Magris's .30-caliber M-1 carbine.[45] The abandoned car police believed to be associated with Burrell's murder had been stolen out of Berkeley, just a couple of blocks from the drycleaning plant where Holmberg worked.

Magris turned twenty-one on June 2, 1969. Honoring tradition, the boys had a few drinks at a topless and bottomless go-go bar called the Kat Pad to celebrate. The Kat Pad was a class joint that sometimes offered a "spaghetti feed" at 7:00 p.m. That's not a euphemism for something illegal—they fed customers free spaghetti to keep them on premises, spending money on booze and girls, instead of going home for dinner. The featured attraction in 1969 was Little Annie Fanny and Her Special Act. The Department of Alcoholic Beverage Control eventually suspended their beer license for thirty days when they found evidence the establishment "permitted lewd conduct by female employees," whatever the hell that meant in 1969. Maybe it was a shakedown by the state, and maybe happy endings were being doled out on premises. Whatever the case, after a thirty-day BYOB interruption, everything went back to business as usual.

By 1:00 a.m. closing time, Magris's gang sought out another way to raise some hell—they went on a crime spree. First, they hit Vallejo's Standard Oil Service Station at the intersection of Florida Street and Interstate 80. The

THE VALLEJO THRILL KILLERS UNDER ARREST. *VALLEJO TIMES-HERALD*, JUNE 6, 1969.

KAT PAD ADVERTISEMENT. *VALLEJO TIMES-HERALD*, FEBRUARY 27, 1969.

station was open twenty-four hours, but only one person worked the graveyard shift from midnight to 8:00 a.m. His name was Steven Tompkins.

At 1:30 a.m., the manager of the Standard Oil station, Bryce Clyma, was awoken by the cops. His employee, Tompkins, was missing. Clyma rushed to the station. Two cops were already there. Tompkins really was missing, and so was the cash box. There was a yellow rubber glove lying on the gas pump. $54.38 was unaccounted for.

What happened that night after twenty-year-old Tompkins pumped gas into the Magris gang's car? According to Magris and the Donohue brothers, Holmberg brandished the .30-caliber carbine "enforcer" and told the gas-station employee to fill a bag with money. Tompkins took the money from the cash box and handed it over. Holmberg told the gang, "Get ready, I'm going to pop this guy."[46] But he didn't pop the guy. The Donohue Brothers protested—they didn't want to kill the attendant. Holmberg agreed and forced Tompkins into their car. They drove him to the outskirts of town, to Blue Rock Springs, where he was let out of the car and told he was free to walk away. Tompkins thought he had escaped the nightmare as he ran from the car, but Jon Holmberg blasted him in the back five times with an M-1 carbine. He died instantly. They left him in a ditch on the side of the road.

This is the same way Betty Lou Jensen was murdered at Lake Herman Road—shot five times in the back as she walked or ran away from David Faraday's car.

The Magris gang wasn't finished yet. They then drove to the Texaco station on Sears Point Road in Vallejo. Like the Standard station, it was open all night with just one man working. Dennis Tapp was that man. The gang's car pulled into an isolated area of the service station where they stored U-Haul trailers. Sometime after 2:00 a.m., Tapp walked over to the car—which he later described as a blue 1959 Oldsmobile or Pontiac—and asked if the men needed help.

They asked Tapp to use the bathroom. He said, "Go ahead," and walked back to the station. Matthew Donohue and Magris followed him in. Magris pulled the .30-caliber carbine. Tapp lifted his shirt to show he was unarmed. He told the robbers, "Take everything in the house." He handed them the money in the cash box. Magris asked, "Do you have any Blue Chip Stamps?" Tapp went to the safe and got the stamps. Magris demanded his wallet and Tapp slid it on the floor to Donohue. Magris told Tapp to sit down on the floor and turn away from the men as he left. Magris shot Tapp two times and left.

Tapp survived. He was rushed to Kaiser Hospital in critical condition. Doctors weren't sure he was going to make it. He would be partially paralyzed for life. He later gave cops a description of the assailant, whom he described as "a Latin type" in his twenties, about five-foot-nine, 150 pounds, in the blue car the boys were in.

The Magris gang got away with just $20 in cash and some Blue Chip Stamps. They returned to the house on Nebraska Street and partied. Holmberg had an intense argument with his wife and they left the house.

That's when Dian Stevens noticed something was off with Magris. He looked shell-shocked. As soon as they were alone, he burst into tears and hysterically told her what happened. She acted quickly. The couple burned Tapp's wallet and any other incriminating evidence Magris was holding in a wash basin in the backyard of the rental home. She wiped the fingerprints off the M-1 carbine with a blue baby blanket, wrapped it up, and put it in the furthest corner of the crawlspace under the house.

Vallejo police arrested Magris and the Donohue brothers at the home they shared with three high-school girls based on the information Tapp gave them. Stevens was caught hiding under a pile of clothes in the closet and arrested. Tapp was given twenty-four-hour police protection at the hospital. The Vallejo police knew who they were dealing with and understood how dangerous they were.

Holmberg and his wife were arrested outside another twenty-four-hour market along with the Meyi brothers. The cops believed they were all casing the joint. The Meyi brothers, two light-skinned Black men with beards, could have almost matched the description of the two bearded "Mexican" guys who had just pulled a gunpoint robbery at the Texaco station on Tennessee Street. Apparently, it was open season at twenty-four-hour Vallejo service stations on the night of David Magris's twenty-first birthday. Jon Holmberg absolutely did not match the description of a short, dark-skinned "Mexican" man with a beard, and it's absurd that cops claimed they stopped and questioned him based on his resemblance to that description. The stop was lousy, but cops found a yellow rubberized glove that matched the one from the Standard Oil crime scene in Holmberg's blue 1959 Oldsmobile.

That same night, Pus Gut and Darryl Walters were arrested on armed-robbery charges after a home invasion at the apartment of twenty-year-old Dorman Bell, a sailor they mistook for Jon Holmberg.[47] The bikers were higher than a seagull's bollocks and grabbed the wrong guy. They pointed a different .30-caliber M-1 carbine at the sailor, stole his stereo, and smashed his apartment up. The bikers were arrested, and their gun was seized and later destroyed.

Pus Gut told the cops that Holmberg had failed to pay him for the blue 1959 Oldsmobile he had recently bought from him. During questioning, the bikers passed out cold in the police station from all the Seconal in their system before cops could thoroughly investigate. Cops never asked Pus Gut, a well-known drug-supplier, if it was his blue Oldsmobile that had been in the area around the time David Faraday and Betty Lou Jensen were murdered and a kilo of weed were seized when a drug deal went belly-up at the Cottage on Lake Herman on December 20, 1968.

THE PEOPLE V. MAGRIS AND HOLMBERG

Zodiac researchers are forever searching for a harmless Bay Area eccentric to pin suspicion on while avoiding actual murderers who were busy killing people in the same area at the time. What came out at the 1969 trial, *The People v. Magris and Holmberg,* shows that not only were they capable of committing such crimes, but they already had.

A criminal trial is, many times, a storytelling contest between a government lawyer whose only job is to cherry-pick the most winnable contest and the best attorney a poor person charged with a crime can afford. It's not exactly rigged, but the deck is heavily stacked against the defense unless the defendant is rich. It's the state, the cops, civil servants, and an army of paid experts against an overworked, bottom-of-the-class Legal Aid lawyer and their broke client.

The People v. Magris and Holmberg was the wildest criminal trial in the fall of 1969. It got more coverage in the *Vallejo Times-Herald* and other local news outlets than the July 4th murder of Darlene Ferrin and the attempted murder of Michael Mageau at Blue Rock Springs. It got as much, if not more, coverage than the spooky letters the Zodiac Killer sent after taking credit for both the Lake Herman Road murders and the Blue Rock Springs killing.

It wasn't just a murder trial, it was theater—a melodramatic blockbuster. Before the proceedings even got underway, Magris and Holmberg tried to break out of jail with hacksaws allegedly sneaked in by seventeen-year-old girls. We're talking about Billy the Kid dime-novel stuff. Teenage thugs who attended the trial as spectators were arrested in the courtroom.[48] The pretrial hearing was the longest in Solano County history. Half the Vallejo underworld testified on behalf of or against the duo. Defense lawyers bickered with each other to the point that the trial was stopped multiple times and the courtroom cleared because the whole thing turned into a melee.

If you read the court transcript and reports, you can almost feel Holmberg's attorney L. Byron Coan's exasperation whenever the surviving shooting victim Dennis Tapp repeatedly identified Jon Holmberg, a six-foot-three-inch-tall redhead of Nordic heritage, as the shooter he had previously and repeatedly described as short or average-height and Latino. Tapp insisted that his shooter was around five foot nine and a "Latin type" because he'd "be hard-pressed to tell the difference between a Mexican a Cuban or a Puerto Rican," yet every time he was asked to identify his shooter, he picked the whitest man in the history of white men instead of the guy who was actually five-foot-eight and Latino (that would be Magris). This farce began at the pretrial hearing and continued until the final verdict.

It was even suggested by a cop, testifying under oath, that Holmberg's Viking-blond-and-red beard gave him the impression that he was Latino and that was the justification for the stop that led to his arrest. That's called testi-lying. There's a zero-percent chance that the cop initiated contact with Holmberg because he thought he was the small "Mexican" man cops were looking for. There was no probable cause for that stop. The glove evidence discovered in Holmberg's car following the stop should have been thrown out as fruit of the poisonous tree. Coan repeatedly had his long-legged, ginger-haired client stand up when he asked whoever was testifying if Holmberg appeared to be Latino or five-foot-nine.

Everyone, including Det. Sgt. Les Lundblad, said no. Holmberg was *still* convicted for shooting Tapp. Years later, Magris would admit to shooting Tapp and Tapp would admit to being shot by Magris.[49] Tapp even managed to forgive Magris and spent time with him when he was released from prison. Holmberg was absolutely railroaded for the Tapp shooting.

On September 21, 1969, shortly before the trial began, a seventeen-year-old recent graduate of Hogan High, Chuck Doyel, was shot in the neck and the stomach while working nights at a service station located on Georgia Street in Vallejo. It was clear to police that robbery wasn't the motive because the shooter didn't take anything from the cash box, and there was plenty of money in there. A guy walked in and asked for change. Doyel turned his back to get the change for him. The guy shot him in the neck, then the stomach, with a .22 pistol, then split. Doyel didn't get a good look at the shooter. Best he could come up with was a skinny white guy in his twenties with long blonde hair.[50]

The cops investigating couldn't find a single person who had a grudge against Doyel. He wasn't involved with gangs or drugs. Doyel was into cars—he liked working on them and racing them. Cops were baffled by the shooting. Doyel was clearly targeted, but they couldn't figure out why. Even though the whole thing was fishy, they ultimately shrugged their shoulders, declared it an "attempted robbery," and never looked further.

A couple of weeks later, Chuck Doyel's first cousin, Johnny Doyel—yes, Magris and Holmberg's drug-dealing pal—was sworn in to testify as an alibi witness for Holmberg. Holmberg's only alibi witnesses were his mother and his mother-in-law, who made it clear she didn't like him. Johnny Doyel took the stand and claimed he had been with Holmberg the night Dennis Tapp and Steven Tompkins were shot, so he couldn't have been involved in the murder, kidnapping, or robbery. Holmberg was adamant that he had had an argument with his wife because she didn't want him to go drinking and carousing at the Kat Pad with Magris and the Donohues. Holmberg said that argument was so heated that he spent the night packing up his belongings in boxes and putting them in the garage so he could move out the next day.[51] His mother, mother-in-law, and Johnny Doyel all testified that they saw him packing boxes with his stuff in the garage between midnight and 1:30 a.m. when Tapp and Tompkins were being robbed and shot. Holmberg's story never wavered while being questioned by three attorneys for five hours: he hadn't been with Magris and the Donohues at all that night—he had just let them borrow his car, the same car he hadn't paid Pus Gut for.

Maybe it was pure coincidence that Johnny Doyel's cousin got shot up at a service station. Maybe it had nothing to do with someone intimidating Doyel to appear as an alibi witness. Or maybe these guys or their outlaw associates on the outside were green-lighting kids to compel their family members to testify on their behalf or to silence a witness who could prove that Holmberg couldn't have been involved in the murder and couldn't be their patsy.

As crazy as that may sound, it wasn't unprecedented for this case. The Vallejo City Council approved $4,180 (over $40,000 today) to pay reserve police officers to guard both Dennis Tapp and the "Zodiac" victim Mike

Mageau 24/7 while they recovered in the hospital. Vallejo's police chief, Jack Stiltz, said, "There is a good possibility of both Tapp and Mageau, as well as doctors, nurses, and others attending them, being killed by the suspect at large, or associates of the accused."[52] The Chief explained that threats had been made to police against Tapp's life by people connected to Holmberg and Magris, indicating that they would "take care" of Dennis Tapp because of his lies. Stiltz felt that both Tapp and Mageau were in imminent danger of being "rubbed out" before being able to testify.

Sgt. Terry Cunningham of the Solano County Sheriff's Office discovered during his investigation that criminal associates acting on behalf of the Magris gang attempted to engage in witness intimidation against Tapp by approaching his father and making threats on his life. This was made obvious when Tapp insisted that the man who had shot him was Holmberg, despite the whole world knowing Magris had shot him and the fact that Magris had told Dian Stevens that he had shot Tapp.

The trial became truly shocking when the extent of Magris and Holmberg's crime spree was revealed. Doyel returned to the stand a month later and testified that Magris was the shooter of Matthew Burrell and the guard dog at the Dairy Farm. A mental-health counselor from Horizon House named Katherine Greenblat testified that Holmberg had admitted to her that he had killed Burrell.[53] An incarcerated criminal associate of Magris who went unnamed due to fear of reprisal testified that Magris had bragged about shooting a Black man, later determined to be Burrell. Magris provided the detail that he had narrowly missed shooting a woman—she bent over and the shot went through the window of Burrell's car. In a surprising twist during cross-examination, this unnamed witness admitted under oath that he had confessed to Magris that he had committed the Blue Rock Springs "Zodiac" murder while high on LSD.[54]

A criminologist, Jerry Chisim, testified that the slug in Burrell's neck matched the slugs from the Tapp and Tompkins shootings. The gun that killed Tompkins and Burrell belonged to David Magris.[55]

The abandoned car found on Columbus Parkway and tied to the Burrell murder was stolen out of Berkeley, California. Jonathan Holmberg worked at a drycleaning plant a short walk from where the car had been stolen in Berkeley. The evidence indicated that Magris and Holmberg had committed the Burrell murder.

With all this information and evidence coming out in court, it seems as though Det. Sgt. Les Lundblad would be able to close that open murder, right? Nope. Lundblad was the one and only defense witness in the pre-trial hearing, called to testify by Holmberg's attorney. Lundblad testified that Holmberg did not match the description of the man who shot Tapp. The Burrell murder remains unsolved by the Solano County Sheriff's Office. They know who did it and what weapon they used, but they didn't pursue justice in the Matthew Burrell murder case.

Magris and Holmberg had a pact—they wouldn't testify against each other. But that didn't last long. In the end, Magris and the Donohue brothers took the stand and pinned the whole thing on Holmberg while minimizing their own involvement. Holmberg never budged, sticking to his story that he wasn't with Magris and the Donohues but had let them borrow his car that night. Jon's wife, Cindy Holmberg, testified that he had allowed Magris and the boys to use his car to go to the Kat Pad. Matt Donohue's seventeen-year-old girlfriend, Debbie Watkins, who rented the apartment they were all staying at, testified that Holmberg hadn't left the apartment with Magris and the Donohues and that he had returned to the apartment much later than the other three.[56]

Dian Stevens and Cindy Holmberg had an airtight alibi. While the boys were shooting and kidnapping gas-station attendants, they were locked in a cell at the police station. Earlier in the night, Cindy was arrested for shoplifting bobby pins from a store called Mayfair Market in a strip mall.

After six weeks of twists, turns, testimony, and theatrics, the jury finally got to deliberate. They came back quickly with a guilty verdict.

When all was said and done, Judge Ellis R. Randall said, "Having found absolutely no redeeming qualities about you, I hereby sentence you to death in the gas chamber."[57] Bad news for two very bad men—Magris and Holmberg were toast. The Donohues were tried and found guilty of lesser charges in a separate trial.

THE ZODIAC CONNECTION

The evidence that surfaced during the trial—evidence that seemed to link Magris and Holmberg to the notorious Zodiac killings at Lake Herman Road—was far from incidental and should not have been overlooked.

Magris was convicted of robbing the Short Stop Market in Vallejo on May 29, 1969. The store clerk, David Drew, said Magris used a .22 to rob him. A long-barreled .22 pistol was used to kill Betty Lou Jensen and David Faraday in the supposed "Zodiac" Lake Herman Road murders.

Magris was also convicted of robbing a different Short Stop Market in Benicia on June 1, 1969. The store clerk, Burl Van Gieson, said Magris robbed *him* with a long-barreled pistol.

And Al Ross, owner of a store that sells ammunition in Vallejo, when called to testify, produced a receipt from May 24, 1969. He had sold three boxes of Remington .22-caliber ammo and one box containing Remington .30-caliber carbine soft-point bullets to Holmberg.

The coincidences were starting to pile up, one after another. Were any of the cops attending the trial capable of connecting the dots? Apparently not, because the "coincidences" kept on coming. The car that the gang used for the gas-station spree was a blue 1959 Oldsmobile sedan. Two Lake Herman Road witnesses, William Crow and "Stan" (last name redacted), contacted police, and each described a blue sedan as the suspicious vehicle they had encountered shortly before the supposed "Zodiac" Lake Herman Road murders. "Stan" even specified that he saw a blue hard-top Oldsmobile. On the night of the Lake Herman Road murders, this hard-top 1959 blue Oldsmobile belonged to the big-time Vallejo drug-supplier and Magris criminal associate Darrell "Pus Gut" Cussins.

The other vehicle of interest on the night of the Lake Herman Road murders was a white Chevrolet Impala. Dian Stevens, Magris's teenage girlfriend, owned a 1962 Volkswagen Beetle, but often drove her parents' white Chevrolet Impala—and Magris had access to it. The Lake Herman Road witness "Stan" saw a Chevy Impala driving with the suspicious blue Oldsmobile on Lake Herman Road. Robert Connelly and Frank Gasser saw an empty Impala parked at the pumping-station turnout where David Faraday and Betty Lou Jensen were murdered by the "Zodiac" shortly before the killings. And a statement by a shepherd named Bingo Wesner in the police report confirms the Impala: he was checking his sheep at approximately 10:00 p.m. (east of the Benicia pumping station) and he observed a white Chevrolet Impala sedan parked by the south fence of the entrance to the pumping station. Finally, decades after the fact, the non-car-guy Crow amended his original statement when he told Tom Voigt of zodiackiller.com that the car he had seen was a light-colored, four-door Chevrolet.

According to a newspaper account, after Magris and Holmberg's conviction, the prosecutor introduced a forty-eight-page police report into evidence during the penalty phase linking Magris and Holmberg to yet another area murder.[58] Unfortunately, when I spoke with a clerk at Solano Superior Court, he told me that the records of the trial had been destroyed. Transcripts of death-penalty cases are not supposed to be destroyed. Luckily, I was able to obtain 1,500 pages of pretrial transcripts. Could that police report have detailed the killings at Lake Herman Road? Of all the open murder cases in Solano and Napa County during the time Magris and Holmberg were acquainted and not in jail, Lake Herman Road is the only one that fits.

How could local police officials have missed the connections between the Vallejo Thrill Killers and the murders of David Faraday and Betty Lou Jensen at Lake Herman Road? They were in the courtroom when this information came out: the Vallejo Thrill Killers had access to the same cars seen by witnesses at Lake Herman Road shortly before the murders—a blue 1959 Oldsmobile and a white Chevy Impala. Magris was convicted of robbing stores with the same model .22 long-barreled pistol that killed David Faraday and Betty Lou Jensen. The Vallejo Thrill Killers allowed Steven Tompkins to run away from a car and shot him five times in the back. Betty Lou Jensen's murderer also allowed her to run away from the car and shot her five times in the back. David Faraday and Dennis Tapp were both shot in the head at close range. Magris and Holmberg were drug-dealing associates of Pus Gut, the outlaw biker who supplied drugs in large quantities to street dealers. The Lake Herman Road murders occurred minutes after the biggest-ever drug bust to date in Benicia, California, foiled a drug deal at the same time the Hells Angels clubhouse was raided. It came out in the police investigation that David Faraday confronted a drug-dealer and demanded he stop pushing grass at school. Johnny Doyel, a "good friend" of Holmberg, dealt drugs for Magris at Vallejo High School. Sgt. John Lynch of the Vallejo Police Department had information that David Faraday ran his mouth about a big-time drug deal and was "eliminated" because of it.

So why did the cops in charge of investigating the Lake Herman Road murders believe they were the work of the mysterious Zodiac and not simply two more murders in the Vallejo Thrill Killers spree?

They didn't.

On the other side of town, in Vallejo, Det. George Bawart had his ear to the street. He had heard things about the death-row inmate who had done the murders at Lake Herman Road. He told Robert Graysmith in *Zodiac Unmasked,* "'Magris and his partner' is the snitch information I got [about] who killed the kids on Lake Herman Road," after arresting a woman on an unrelated charge. She told Bawart, "Magris and his buddy did the Lake Herman Road thing, I swear," Bawart said. "I was semi-convinced Zodiac didn't do it but took credit for it."

According to Sergeant Cunningham, a motorcycle gang member who had a side hustle as a confidential informant gave up Magris and another guy as the shooters at Lake Herman Road, too. A Vallejo waitress told cops that Magris and his redheaded friend had bragged to her about being the Lake Herman Road killers.

A December 23, 1970, article in the *Benicia Herald* called "New Suspects Are Linked in Lake Herman Slayings" backs this up:

> **Local authorities have obtained statements from two persons implicating another man and his accomplice as the slayers. But officers lack sufficient evidence to charge the men, later imprisoned with the murders. For example, the death gun, a 22-caliber automatic pistol, reportedly was hurled into the Bay. The primary witness against the pair is a member of a motorcycle gang. His story is substantiated by a young woman. But neither their identities nor those of the accused killers, for obvious reasons can be disclosed. Officers hope to make the case in the future.**

The top Zodiac researcher Tom Voigt obtained notes from a producer of the 1988 television program *Crimes of the Century*. In an unaired segment, Sergeant Cunningham challenged Zodiac lore by claiming the Zodiac wasn't responsible for the murders at Lake Herman Road... and that he knew who committed them.

The *Crimes of the Century* producer's notes indicated that Cunningham "never believed in that Zodiac thing." Cunningham told the producer David and Betty Lou "weren't Zodiacked."[59] Furthermore, Cunningham interviewed Magris, Holmberg, and the Donohue Brothers in prison, and "he [knew] the red-headed kid killed the two teens." Holmberg had red hair. The confession Cunningham got wasn't for a targeted drug murder, it was a pure thrill killing. Cunningham told the producer, "[The] kids were just cruising, looking for excitement, the red headed one especially, who coerced the others into going along."[60]

The notes said, according to Cunningham, "one of them told him the whole story about Jensen and Faraday—how they were dressed, etc. where shot—not mentioned anywhere. He verified it and passed it on to Lundblad . . . Lundblad was too narrow in his thinking, obsessed. Lundblad was too immersed in Zodiac."

This is the same Detective Sergeant Lundblad who was called as the one and only defense witness at the pretrial hearing on behalf of Holmberg in a death-penalty murder case. The same Lundblad who didn't follow up after three sworn witnesses testified in that trial that Magris and Holmberg were responsible for the January 3, 1969, murder of Matthew Burrell. The same Lundblad who ignored the ballistics match between the gun Magris and Holmberg used to murder Steven Tompkins and the gun used to kill Matthew Burrell. The same Lundblad who ignored intel from the Vallejo Police Department that indicated Magris was involved in the Lake Herman Road murders. Good old Les Lundblad, who didn't bother investigating if the major drug bust and the Hells Angels clubhouse raid that happened minutes before the murders of David Faraday and Betty Lou Jensen at Lake Herman Road had anything to do with the murders. Instead, he focused on scaring teenage girls with interrogations, then throwing his arms up in the air three days after the murders and suggesting the killings might be the work of a maniac.

Occam's razor states that the simplest explanation is usually the best one. Lundblad's razor states that no explanation at all is the best explanation.

None of this makes sense. By all accounts, Lundblad was a dedicated and experienced police officer. How could he botch three unsolved murder cases served up on a silver platter to him with a confession, informants, ballistics, and sworn testimony? And why would he show up as a defense witness for one of the guys implicated in those three murders in a separate murder case in another jurisdiction? What was up with this guy? Was he lazy, incompetent, or crooked? Possibly all three? Or was it something else?

A retired California Highway Patrol officer and Zodiac researcher named Lyndon Lafferty wrote a book called *The Zodiac Killer Cover-Up: The Silenced Badge*. In the book, the badge that was silenced was his good friend Les Lundblad's. According to Lafferty, Lundblad was ordered by his superior officers to destroy his suspect files for the murders at Lake Herman Road and Lundblad complied with the order. Lafferty also alleged that Lundblad was put on ice by a judge who ordered him to stop investigating the Lake

Herman Road case because that judge was having an affair with the wife of his suspect. Lafferty's suspect wasn't Magris or Holmberg, it was a guy named William Joseph Grant, an old queen who cruised Solano County lover's lanes in search of gay sex.

George Bawart, a Vallejo detective during the Zodiac era who worked the case when it was reopened in 1991, questioned the Zodiac's involvement in the deaths of David Faraday and Betty Lou Jensen. Bawart was also interviewed for *Crimes of the Century,* and notes stated he said he was "not sure Zodiac did Lake Herman Road. Two other individuals on a crime spree may have done Lake Herman whacked out on drugs." Sounds a lot like Magris and Holmberg.

Capt. Roy Conway, another Zodiac era cop and the Vallejo Police Department's lead investigator when the case was revived in 1991, said, "The other killing, on Lake Herman Road, happened [seven months] before the Zodiac killing. We had some very good suspects in that case, and Detective Bawart and I are satisfied that the Zodiac didn't really do that case, although we don't have unequivocal proof on that."

The investigators with the most experience on the case did not believe that Lake Herman Road was part of the Zodiac murders.

In a 1986 *Vallejo Times-Herald* article, Sgt. John Lynch of Vallejo P.D. also said, referring to the murders of Betty Lou Jensen and David Faraday, "I never did believe those two were connected to the other [Zodiac] murders."[61]

A few years later, on Geraldo Rivera's tabloid television program *Now It Can Be Told,* Sergeant Lynch spoke about the Lake Herman Road murders as a hit because David Faraday opened his mouth about a drug deal: "This kid had found out one way or another about some narcotics transaction that had taken place, and he was telling other kids about it, and they just eliminated him."

Considering the large-scale drug bust that happened the night of the murders, just 2,000 feet away on Lake Herman Road, this doesn't seem like such a massive leap in logic.

On July 20, 2002, Tom Voigt posted on his zodiackiller.com forum, "I'm not saying I believe Magris (or anyone else in the gang) was the Zodiac; rather, I think it's possible they might have been responsible for the Lake Herman Road killings. Or maybe not. What's so troubling is how many violent criminals were living in that small town."

The Zodiac taking credit for somebody else's murders as his first kills was the worst-kept secret in law enforcement and true crime.

Even David Fincher, director of the film *Zodiac,* considered Magris's involvement. "Magris and his partner are just sociopaths, thrill killers," Fincher told Robert Graysmith in *Zodiac Unmasked.* "The thing I'm interested in is the sociopath who shoots at close range—two guys who rob a filling station and tell the guy 'here's your chance to run' and shoot him in the back . . . The notion that Lake Herman Road is something Leigh Allen [the Zodiac suspect in Graysmith's book and Fincher's film] hears about and goes out and does Blue Rock Springs suddenly makes more sense." Fincher, who hired a team to reinvestigate the Zodiac case before making his big Hollywood film, believed that Magris and a partner likely murdered David Faraday and Betty Lou Jensen at Lake Herman Road. Fincher's statement implies that, rather than believing the Lake Herman Road murders were the work of the Zodiac, he thought they inspired Zodiac to commit the murder at Blue Rock Springs. The true-crime community that keeps the Zodiac case alive are silent about this. If the first two Zodiac murders aren't even the work of the Zodiac, their true-crime cottage industry begins to fall apart. Believing that Dave Magris and not the Zodiac was responsible for the murders of Betty Lou Jensen and David Faraday didn't stop David Fincher from putting out a Zodiac movie generating nearly $85 million in ticket sales. He simply didn't show the Lake Herman Road murders in his film. He avoids covering the first two Zodiac murders. Fincher's movie focused on the people obsessed with solving the case rather than the facts of the case. It wasn't a fact-based true-crime film that had to deal with uncomfortable truths about the investigation. It was intellectual serial-killer-adjacent entertainment starring Jake Gyllenhaal, Robert Downey, Jr., and Mark Ruffalo.

As for Holmberg being the unnamed partner? In the summer of 2019, Sgt. Ed Rust of the Vallejo Police Department was interviewed by *Shadow of the Zodiac*:

> **My recollection of the LHR [Lake Herman Road] killing is that Cunningham and other SO [Sheriff's Office] detectives "firmly believed" that the killer was a local thug named Frank Schwerzzfetter. Not sure now of the actual spelling, but they told me that this guy had used a .22 rifle in a local robbery, and they believed this was the murder gun, but they never could find it. They said it involved drugs and maybe a love triangle. He was convicted of the robbery and went to prison, but without the murder weapon, they could not charge him with the LHR murder.**

Furthermore, in 2022, Rust posted on the "History of the Solano County Sheriff's Office" Facebook page, writing, "I knew and worked with Les [Lundblad] on some cases back in the 70s. Re: The Zodiac case and Lake Herman killing claimed by Z, Les was certain the killer was a local young thug, Frank Fetz------ [he gave an alias because the person is still alive] who knew both victims and used a .22 cal rifle [same as the murder weapon] in a robbery, but he could not find the rifle and had no case." Frank Fetz . . . now, that sounds a lot like Frank Schwerzzfetter, which sounds a lot like the real name of the guy we're calling Jonathan Holmberg in this book. Make of that what you will.

A case could be made for Pus Gut being Magris's partner—or at least in the area at the time of the murders at Lake Herman Road. Jon Holmberg's blue 1959 Oldsmobile belonged to Pus Gut when the Lake Herman Road murders happened on December 20, 1968. Two cars were spotted near the scene of the crime and the intercepted drug deal: a white Impala that Magris (the drug-dealer) drove and the blue Olds that Pus Gut (the drug-supplier) owned. But no one came forward and named Pus Gut as the accomplice. The description given was consistently a red-headed man. Pus Gut doesn't fit that description. He was a grizzly bear of a man with long brown hair and an unruly beard. Those were likely his drugs that the cops found in the Cottage, but Magris and his buddy were the buyers, and the ones linked to the murders. However, when a born-again Dave Magris gave a confession about the Lake Herman Road murders from death row, he claimed the motive was nothing more than a couple of guys looking for some excitement.

Listen. Les Lundblad knew that two of the Vallejo Thrill Killers committed the murders at Lake Herman Road. But, in police work, knowing isn't enough. The standard is higher than just getting a conviction for "knowing" someone did something—you have to have the will, budget, and backing of the district attorney to put them on trial. And you need evidence to prove they did it in a court of law. In 1970, Magris found Jesus and became a born-again Christian. He wanted to unburden his guilty conscience. He wrote a sworn affidavit confessing that it was him, and not Holmberg, who had shot Dennis Tapp in the head. He implicated one of the Donohue brothers in the murder of Steven Tompkins. He admitted to perjuring himself at trial. He even claimed that Holmberg hadn't been with him and the Donohues on their gas-station spree. Holmberg's attorney filed a habeas corpus petition "based on the claim he was convicted because of perjured testimony."[62] Amazingly, instead of releasing him from prison, the appeals court rejected the petition and upheld Holmberg's conviction. This dude not only got railroaded at his trial, but when the guy who railroaded him finally took the blame and admitted to lying on the witness stand to save his own ass by pinning the murders on Holmberg, the court didn't want to hear it and kept him in prison. Somebody powerful really must have had it out for Jon Holmberg.

Magris kept talking. He verbally confessed to the Solano County Sheriff's Office's desk sergeant Terry Cunningham about his involvement as an accomplice in the Lake Herman Road murders but claimed he wasn't the trigger man. Magris told Cunningham that he had used the same .22 in a series of robberies in Vallejo and Benicia. When this gun information came out at his murder trial, an associate on the outside disposed of the gun in the bay.

Remember, producers of the documentary *Crimes of the Century* identified Cunningham as "Detective who doesn't believe there is a Zodiac—knows who murdered the first two kids and thinks the rest are random killings for which a nut took credit."[63]

Les Lundblad was handed a case file on Magris and a partner as the Lake Herman Road killers. It wasn't just a case of Zodiac fever that prevented Lundblad from doing his job—the Solano County District Attorney was actively uninterested in prosecuting the murders at Lake Herman Road. Lundblad was forced to make a very practical decision. Magris and Holmberg were on San Quentin's death row awaiting the gas chamber. He couldn't have known that the death penalty would be done away with in California just two years later.

In 1970, Lundblad had to live with the fact that getting convictions for killing Betty Lou Jensen, David Faraday, and Matthew Burrell wasn't going to kill Magris and Holmberg any more than the gas chamber they were already getting for Tompkins and Tapp. Two additional murder trials and the subsequent appeals that follow would have cost Solano County a ton of money. The death penalty is final justice, and Lundblad had fresh cases. Crime was exploding. Solano and Napa counties had twenty-three murders from October of 1968 to October of 1969.[64] Drugs and crime only got worse as the '60s turned into the '70s. The Zodiac case spanned four jurisdictions, with SFPD taking the helm.

It wasn't a conspiracy. It was a compromise.

Lundblad wasn't authorized to send a team of divers into the bay to look for the murder weapon. His boss didn't want to hear about alternative suspects for the Lake Herman Road murders. The whole world already believed it was a

FOR SHERIFF
*THE QUIET CANDIDATE
(*with the best qualifications)

Sgt. TERRY
CUNNINGHAM

- FBI TRAINED
- 22 YEARS IN LAW WORK
- COMMUNITY RELATIONS ORIENTED
- LITTLE LEAGUE TEAM SPONSOR

Solano County
Deputy Sheriff

SGT. TERRY CUNNINGHAM, CAMPAIGN AD. *VALLEJO TIMES-HERALD*, MAY 25, 1970.

Zodiac case. Telling the public that Lake Herman Road wasn't a Zodiac crime would be like telling a child that Santa Claus wasn't real. Once newspapers printed the narrative, the authorities were tasked with preserving the narrative.

Cunningham was so disgruntled by the way justice wasn't served in the Lake Herman Road case that he declared himself a candidate for Solano County Sheriff in 1970. He ran as a reformer. His campaign slogan was, "Vote for the quiet candidate with the best qualifications."[65] He lost.

WHERE ARE THEY NOW?

The Donohue brothers, Darrell "Pus Gut" Cussins, and Darrell Walters are all deceased.

David Magris was a model inmate during his years in prison. In the 1980s he became a celebrity inmate and vocal anti-death-penalty activist with multiple media appearances on television and in print. He embodied the possibility of redemption in prison. He got a college degree in prison, underwent psychological counselling, and became a born-again Christian. He was paroled in 1985 and became a board member, then president, of Centerforce, a California nonprofit organization that provides re-entry services for incarcerated adults and helps the children of parents in prison. David became

DAVID MAGRIS, A FREE MAN. *SACRAMENTO BEE,* NOVEMBER 13, 1995.

a member of the prison ministry at Calvary Chapel and counseled death-row inmates. "Dancing Dave" even gave senior citizens dance lessons in Boca Raton, Florida. He lived a life of service until he died on August 17, 2023. Everyone I interviewed for this book who knew Dave, even the people who knew him during his years of crime, had enthusiastically pleasant things to say about him. Almost everyone agreed that sober Dave Magris was a sweetheart. Dave on drugs was a completely different story. It's worth noting not only that Dennis Tapp, the man he shot in the head and confined to a wheelchair, forgave Magris, but the two shared a friendship when Dave was released from prison.

Jon Holmberg took a different path. He was paroled in 1989 and quietly opened an auto-repair business. Less than a decade later, he was sentenced to twenty-eight years to life in prison for cooking methamphetamine. While in prison, Holmberg completed gender transition from male to female. She is now Johanna Holmberg, a transgender woman, and one of the first inmates in the history of California to transfer from a men's to a women's prison, where she served the final years of her sentence. I have messaged with her a few times, and she doesn't want to talk about the bad old days when she was on death row and in prison for twenty years, convicted of shooting a man she claims she didn't shoot. She prefers to focus on the present and her freedom. Whatever Johanna may or may not be guilty of, she spent almost her entire adult life behind bars. She's nearly eighty years old.

CHAPTER 5: MURDER AT BLUE ROCK SPRINGS

THE TIMELINE OF EVENTS SURROUNDING THE BRUTAL shootings of Michael Mageau and Darlene Ferrin on July 4, 1969, is a mess of half-truths and contradictions that left even seasoned detectives scratching their heads. That's because what we know about that night—and what the police learned at the time of the investigation—was partially fiction. The truth of this case was obscured by the persons of interest who were questioned. It's human nature to lie to the police. People do it for various reasons, ranging from trying to conceal their involvement in a crime to protecting the reputation of a victim to just feeling nervous around cops. The timeline you're about to explore comes from the police reports. It's confusing and even contradictory at times. If you find your head spinning, you're not alone.

Michael was excited about his movie date with Darlene on the 4th of July. Around 4 p.m., she called the nineteen-year-old on the phone and asked him to see a film that night in San Francisco. She even offered to pick him up at his father's house at 7:30 that evening. Like seemingly every other dude in Vallejo, he had a crush on Darlene, the wild blonde with the soft round features. Deep down he knew that a girl like her was completely out of his league.

Darlene was three years older and a proper adult compared to teenage dirtbag Mike. She owned a house free and clear. She had spent the Summer of Love in San Francisco and traveled to exotic locations in the Caribbean. She drove a Corvair. Michael, though, still lived at his dad's house and worked for his dad's pest-control company. He didn't drive a car, he had a criminal record, and he wasn't even the coolest of the two Mageau twins. (He had a brother, Steven.)

DARLENE FERRIN. *TENNESSEAN*, OCTOBER 19, 1969.

Furthermore, she was married. Twice! She and her second husband, a guy named Dean Ferrin, had a baby daughter together. Maybe Dean was being honest when he later told detectives that he thought that a goofy kid like Michael was just a friend to Darlene. Maybe the Ferrins had an open relationship, or he wanted to preserve his wife's reputation and not come out as a cuckold to all of Vallejo. Too late for that. The rumors that Darlene dated other men—lots of men—weren't whispered, they were practically screamed.

Darlene's father picked up the babysitters, Pamela Key and Janet Lynn, at 7:00 p.m. and drove them to Darlene's house so they could watch her daughter while she went out. Darlene told the babysitters that she and her fifteen-year-old sister Christina were going to the Miss Firecracker contest downtown and she'd be home by 10:00 p.m. She didn't mention anything about the movies or Michael. Perhaps her plans had already changed. Plans always changed with Darlene. She spent the next forty-five minutes getting ready. Then, as she left the house, she told the babysitters that she was going to head out to San Francisco later in the night.

Around 9:00 p.m., the babysitters took a phone message. A woman called and asked Darlene to come to Terry's Waffle Shop, her place of employment.

Around 10:30 p.m., Darlene and Christina went to visit Dean at Caesar's Italian restaurant, where he was a cook. He was scheduled to work until closing time. Darlene told her husband she was going to drop Christina off and then drive the babysitters home.

Darlene got home around 11:30 p.m. She told the babysitters she had changed her mind about going to San Francisco. Instead, she was going to have a small party at home with some friends when Dean got off work. According to the police report, five minutes later, Darlene's boss at Terry's Waffle Shop, Bill Lee, "called Darlene to ask her if she would try to find a fireworks booth open and purchase some as they were going to have a party at 1300 Virginia Street." Darlene lived at 1300 Virginia Street—it was her party. There were no fireworks booths open after 11:30 p.m. on the 4th of July. It was a ridiculous thing to tell the cops. It's an obvious lie. The "fireworks" Lee was looking for were drugs. It was supposed to be that kind of party. Darlene went out again, telling the babysitters she was going to buy fireworks and other party favors and she'd be home by 12:30 a.m.

Around 11:45 p.m., Darlene drove her brown Corvair to Michael's house and finally picked him up. For some reason, on a hot summer night, Michael wore three pairs of trousers, one t-shirt, and three long-sleeved sweaters. This is more absurd than the fireworks story. Something is up with this guy—he's wearing three layers of red flags. He was dressed like Nanook of the North in California in July. Michael had a criminal record for petty theft. Perhaps Michael was dressed for a burglary, ready to shed layers after committing a crime on a night when many people were out of their homes to celebrate the holiday. This is a common criminal tactic used to thwart witness descriptions. Later, he explained his strange attire by claiming he was insecure about being skinny so he wore all those clothes to appear bigger. That's a potentially valid explanation. Kurt Cobain was reportedly insecure about his frail physique and wore layers to look bulkier. However, the police report also indicated that Michael weighed 170 pounds. In 1969, the average American man weighed 166 pounds, so Michael was average size—slightly bigger, even.

Darlene and the very overdressed Michael were both hungry and decided to go to Mr. Ed's Drive In restaurant. At least that's what Michael told the cops. On the way, Darlene told Michael that she wanted to talk to him about something and he suggested they go to Blue Rock Springs Park. The park was a popular lover's lane where a kid who lived with his parents and a woman who lived with her husband could find some alone time. It was also a popular spot to buy and use illegal drugs. Darlene drove to Blue Rock Springs. They didn't go there to buy fireworks. They didn't go to have a deep conversation. And based on Michael's outfit, they didn't go there to hook up either. They stopped there to get "party favors." Strangely, investigators took Michael's statement at face value and didn't pick at the holes in his Swiss-cheese story. Det. Ed Rust and Sgt. John Lynch were sharp and experienced, and they must have known his story didn't add up, but they didn't press him to get to something closer to the truth than the rubbish statement he gave them. Maybe they treated him with kid gloves because he was a traumatized victim of a shooting and they were showing him kindness in the direct aftermath. It's possible that Michael knew a lot more about the context of what was going on that night, but detectives didn't care to get that information from him then or in follow-up conversations.

Around 11:55 p.m., Darlene pulled into the parking lot at Blue Rock Springs. She turned off the motor and the lights and cranked the radio. Three cars full of teenagers entered the parking lot and lit off fireworks, laughing and carrying on. After a few minutes, they left Mike and Darlene alone again.

Five minutes later, another car pulled into the lot and cramped their style. The driver turned off his lights and pulled up to the left side of Darlene's car. He sat there for a minute in silence and darkness. Michael, unnerved by this, asked Darlene if she knew who it was and she said, "Oh, never mind." The car pulled out of the lot and left.

Minutes later, a car, possibly the same car that had just been there, returned, stopping ten feet to the rear of Darlene's car. The driver exited the vehicle with a "high powered flashlight, the type you carry with a handle." Michael thought it was a cop because the guy was acting as a cop conducting a car stop would. Michael, still dressed like a burglar, nervously went through his pockets looking for his identification to present to the cop. He thought he was fucked.

Michael had no idea how fucked he really was.

The man raised a 9mm handgun and fired into the car. Michael was shot in the face. He jumped into the backseat to try and save himself. The shooter fired into the car five times, leaving Michael and Darlene curled up and bleeding. Michael's screams alerted the shooter that he was still alive. The man Michael thought was a cop returned to finish the job. He shot Michael and Darlene twice more, then casually walked back to his car, driving off into the night.

Shortly after the shooting, three "hippie types" called Jerry, Roger, and Debbie drove by Blue Rock Springs. They found Michael and Darlene. Assuring Michael they'd get help, they called the police and spoke with the dispatcher, Nancy Slover. Slover was able to calmly get the relevant information from three hysterical teens.

Around 12:10 a.m., Officer Richard Hoffman of the Vallejo Police Department answered a radio call about two teenagers shot at Blue Rock Springs. He was the first officer to arrive on scene. Just fifteen minutes earlier, Hoffman, who was working a plainclothes detail making sure there wasn't any trouble at Blue Rock Springs or other similar hotspots of drug activity, had stated over the radio that the lover's lane area was "clear of people or motor vehicles." Officer Douglas Clark arrived on scene to assist. Clark and Hoffman attempted to render aid to Darlene and Michael and called for an ambulance. Hoffman rode in the ambulance with Darlene.

At 12:38 a.m. Darlene was declared dead on arrival at Kaiser Hospital by a Dr. Borden. Michael was alive in the intensive care unit. Hoffman noticed his suspicious outfit and placed Michael's clothes into evidence.

Just two minutes after Darlene was pronounced dead, at 12:40 a.m., a phone call was placed to Vallejo police dispatch. Nancy Slover answered again. A man said, "I want to report a double murder. If you will go one mile east on Columbus Parkway to the public park, you will find the kids in a brown car. They were shot with a 9mm Luger. I also killed those kids last year. . . Good-bye." Cops traced the call to a gas-station payphone near Darlene's home.

Dean Ferrin returned home from work at 1:30 a.m. He had no idea what happened with Darlene. He hung out with his brother, Bill Lee, and some other friends looking to party. The babysitters informed them that Darlene wasn't home yet. Ferrin drove the babysitters home. He didn't seem too worried because Darlene was always late.

At 2:35 a.m., Ferrin and Lee were met by police officers who escorted them to the police station to speak with Vallejo Police Department detectives. The detectives informed them that Darlene had been shot. When Ferrin was told that Darlene was killed, he became "very distraught."

Before 7:00 a.m. the next morning, the lead investigator, Detective Rust, returned to the crime scene to look for evidence in the daylight. He didn't find any, but Darlene's sister Linda showed up at the crime scene, telling Rust about a creepy guy who had made unwanted romantic advances towards Darlene. According to her, a bartender named George may have stalked or harassed Darlene. He made her uncomfortable. He got very upset when Darlene didn't pay attention to him. George used to work at the Kentwig Lodge—the same Kentwig Lodge where Matthew Burrell had been shot and killed with David Magris's gun seven months earlier.

Police had a suspect.

Cops contacted Robert Mageau, Michael's father, and informed him that his son had been shot and was being treated at the hospital. He told the cops that Darlene had called the house often, including several times the day before. Mageau didn't know that Michael and Darlene met up that night because he'd stayed at a motel—the Kentwig Lodge.

At the hospital, Michael gave Rust a description of the shooter: white male, adult, "5'8" tall, beefy build, but not blubbery fat, possibly 195-200 pounds, or maybe even larger, short curly hair, light brown almost blond." Michael estimated the man's age as between twenty-six and thirty years old. He didn't get a great look at the shooter—he was shot in the face and had a flashlight blaring in his eyes. Plus, he was loopy from painkillers given to him at the hospital. He thought the guy might have driven a car that looked like Darlene's brown Corvair.

Rust met with Darlene's parents at their home. They told him she had no known enemies but that Darlene was sometimes afraid of Michael. See, Michael pretended to be a dangerous criminal to get Darlene's attention—he told her that he was wanted by the FBI back in New York City. She believed him. He eventually confessed to her that the wanted-criminal thing was a ruse to get to know her. It worked—Darlene spent time with Michael when she believed he was a dangerous man, despite being afraid of him.

Rust then interviewed Mike's mother and twin brother Steven. Steven Mageau confirmed that George harassed Darlene. He told Rust, "George had broken into her apartment and told her that he was going to rape her. Darlene stated that she had talked him out of it. Steven states that neither he nor his brother had taken her seriously and didn't think any more about it." Steven said that Darlene was "deathly afraid" of George but "was friendly towards him in an effort to keep him at a distance." Steven also told Rust that "Darlene often took her boyfriends to Blue Rock Springs Park."

Detectives determined that George was a promising suspect. They enlisted the help of the nearby Napa Police Department because his last known address was in their jurisdiction.

Without being asked, Michael's father turned up at the police station to reiterate that Darlene used to call Michael on the phone every day.

When detectives paid Dean Ferrin a visit, he said he had met George once. He described him as a five-foot-eight dark-complexioned Mexican man to whom he had once sold a 1951 Ford pickup truck. Darlene had set up the truck deal. Ferrin really stuck to the clueless-husband story: though he knew that George used to give Darlene rides home and hang around her job, he told the cops he had had no reason to believe the two were involved.

Vallejo detectives determined that George's full name was George William Waters. They spoke to his previous employers at Kaiser Steel, the Elks Club, and the Kentwig Lodge. He had a spotty work history, leaving the steel company after completing his training, only working special functions as a bartender at the Elks, and getting fired from the Kentwig Lodge after one night behind the bar.

MUGSHOT OF GEORGE WATERS. SOLANO COUNTY SHERIFF'S OFFICE, DECEMBER 3, 1964.

The owner of the notorious Kat Pad strip club, a man named William Pollard, came forward with information about the murder at Blue Rock Springs. He told cops that a regular customer named Walter had told a Kat Pad waitress that another regular named George had bragged about killing the two people at Blue Rock Springs. The cops went to the Kat Pad to find out more at the club. They waited for Walter, who stopped in for drinks and dances every night before and after his night shift at Mare Island.

Pollard's business partner, a man named William Lose, owned the equally notorious topless and bottomless club called the Krazy Kat on 663 San Pablo Avenue in Albany. George Waters owned a rental property in San Pablo, less than a ten-minute drive from the club. George had been a regular at the Krazy Kat a year earlier. George and Lose had been drinking buddies for a while, hitting up the bars in Alameda County. Lose claimed that George told "goofball stories about being rich" but drove a crappy car: a white-over-blue '55 or '56 Chevy.

Cops quickly confirmed, based on physical descriptions and information obtained at the Kat Pad strip club, that George Waters was the same George Waters that Darlene's family and friends had told them about. The man who had stalked Darlene, broken into her apartment, and threatened to rape her was the same man who had apparently bragged about killing her at Blue Rock Springs. Six days after the murder of Darlene Ferrin, Vallejo police had a solid suspect who knew Darlene, threatened Darlene, and bragged about killing Darlene.

Cops learned that George had also harassed Linda, the Kat Pad's manager, often grabbing her legs and pulling her hair. One night, George got especially rough and threw her against the hood of his car. Linda had had enough. She punched George in the face, pulled his hair, and fought him off. Somehow, George was not banned from the club for getting physical with the manager.

Being manager of the Kat Pad was a dangerous gig. Another manager, twenty-two-year-old Lillian Morgan, was later shot to death with one bullet from a .25 automatic in the back of the head. Richard Hoffman (the same officer who had been first on scene of Darlene's murder) told newspaper reporters that Morgan had threatened and attempted suicide in the past.[66] Why would he say that about someone who clearly didn't die by suicide? It was determined forensically that Morgan couldn't have possibly shot herself in the back of the head. Hoffman also failed to mention to reporters that Lillian's boyfriend, an outlaw biker and drug-dealer with a history of violence and attempted murder named Robert Gilday, had been recently released from a one-year prison term for shooting a youth in the head.[67]

LILLIAN MORGAN. *VALLEJO TIMES-HERALD,* NOVEMBER 10, 1972.

Unsurprisingly, the drug-dealing, head-shooting boyfriend was later jailed for Morgan's murder. But we should probably not be shocked that the Solano County district attorney never brought Gilday to trial for murder. Just another case of a young woman murdered in Vallejo and prosecutors failing to even attempt to get justice. Five months later, Gilday was back in jail and back in the newspapers. Another attempted-murder case—this time, he slashed and stabbed a twenty-two-year-old man in a house full of meth. Morgan was an organ donor, and her heart was transplanted into a fifty-one-year-old man at Stanford University Hospital. At least someone involved in this tragedy was capable of decency.

Walter showed up at the Kat Pad after his shift. When the cops spoke to him, his story had completely changed. He told the cops he didn't know George (even though they hung out at the same bar every night). Walter also told police that he was a friend of Darlene's family and that he got his information from them.

Seven days after Darlene's murder, Rust and Lynch finally tracked George Waters down from a post office box in Yountville, California, about twenty-five miles away from Vallejo in Napa Valley's wine country. George found work as a bookkeeper and office manager in nearby St. Helena. Waters was not Mexican. Born in the Philippines, his heritage was a mix of Spanish, Irish, and Filipino, and he was not an American citizen. He claimed he didn't own a gun. He was described in the police report as a slightly overweight, olive-complected, twenty-nine-year-old married man with black hair who weighed

150 pounds. That description does not do George Waters justice. He looked like Elvis Presley from the '68 Comeback Special. George was a strikingly handsome man who'd put on a bit of weight by 1969. He certainly didn't weigh 150 pounds in July of 1969. That number was likely copied from an arrest report from five years earlier. His wife Judith said that he had gained a significant amount of weight and no longer looked like the young, skinny kid in the mug shot the police had from his earlier arrest. In the summer of '69, George was closer to 200 pounds than 150.

George Waters was arrested in 1964 for assaulting his first wife and later for violating a restraining order. During the 1960s, restraining orders or orders of protection were not as common or as comprehensive as they are today. Domestic violence was not treated with the seriousness it receives now. This arrest provides insight into George Waters's character. Given that cops in the 1960s often overlooked such matters, George must have exhibited significantly dangerous behavior to get locked up for violating a restraining order.

George readily admitted to knowing Darlene. He told the cops he used to work for Kaiser Steel and tended bar at a handful of establishments in Vallejo. He ate at Terry's Waffle Shop every night after the bars closed at 2:00 a.m. and regularly gave Darlene rides home after her shift ended. In fact, he said Darlene often called him at home and asked for rides to work. He told the cops that her husband Dean knew all about it. George said that Darlene sometimes got angry with him when he teased her. But he claimed he hadn't seen her in about a month and a half since he brought his wife to Terry's Waffle Shop for a meal and Darlene was their waitress.

George gave the cops an alibi for July 4th: he played in a Napa-P.D.-sponsored softball game that morning and then watched the fireworks display at the Veteran's Home with his wife that night. He claimed he was in bed by 11:00 p.m. It should be noted that Yountville is just a thirty-minute drive from Blue Rock Springs. Even if he was in bed at 11:00 p.m., he could have sneaked out, left Yountville, and made it to Blue Rock Springs with more than thirty minutes to spare before Darlene and Mike were shot. George's alibi is far from rock solid, and the only person to confirm it was his new wife, who'd later claim he was "controlling" and "abusive" and that he "terrorized" her.

At this point in the investigation, George Waters should have been considered an excellent suspect for Darlene's murder. He had a history of stalking and harassing women, including Darlene. He had a history of violence against women. He showed up drunk at Darlene's job often. He chauffeured her to and from work. Her friends and family identified him as a stalker who broke into her house and threatened to rape her. They told cops she was "deathly afraid" of George. And his alibi wasn't exactly airtight. He also reportedly bragged about killing Darlene.

This had to be the guy.

For some inexplicable reason, Sergeant Lynch signed off on the report concerning the interview with George, and that was the end of George Waters as a suspect. If you follow the paper trail, the Vallejo police investigation into George ended with that interview. This was a massive fumble by Sergeant Lynch, but it wouldn't be his last massive fumble in the Zodiac investigation.

Then there was another hurdle for the case. Two weeks after the Zodiac struck in Vallejo—just a week after detectives spoke to George Waters—the police went on strike. On July 17, 1969, the Vallejo Police Department and the Vallejo Fire Department went on strike together for five days.[68] It was the first joint police and fire strike in a single municipality ever. All but twenty of the city's 173 uniformed members of the fire and police services walked off the job, leaving a skeleton crew to deal with fire and police emergencies for a busy city of 66,000.

To make matters worse, during the strike, the makeshift fire crew had to respond to around thirty-five false fire alarms per night compared to the less-than-one average before the cops and firefighters made themselves scarce.[69] This made for an incredibly dangerous situation in the city. Vallejo fire hydrants were turned on by saboteurs and ran all day and night. While a fire crew was occupied by a false alarm, a garage was torched with Molotov cocktails. The buildings where false alarms were often had taunting notes directed towards the fill-in firefighters saying "ha ha ha" or something similarly half-witted. This was clearly a labor action by striking firefighters. We don't know how many fake police emergencies the striking officers called in just to mock the scab cops. The local newspapers didn't want to touch *that* story. Why would they? Newspaper reporters depended on a good relationship with the police for information and quotes for their stories. No reason to burn the sources of their information. The strike would eventually end, and the reporters would still need the cops.

The investigation into George Waters was entirely derailed by the strike. After the initial interview, no supplemental reports were filed to verify his alibi or clear him. The cops went on strike in the middle of investigating George

Waters and completely lost momentum in the Darlene Ferrin murder case. No record of a follow-up exists in the publicly available Vallejo police files. George doesn't show up in police reports again until almost two months later, on September 9, 1969, when investigators asked Darlene's friend and fellow Terry's waitress Bobbie Ramos about him. She knew George but hadn't seen him in almost a year.

During the Vallejo Police strike, other law-enforcement agencies did their best to hold down the fort and keep the investigation into Darlene Ferrin's murder alive. On July 21, 1969, ten days after Vallejo investigators filed their last report about the Blue Rock Springs murder, Dep. Ben Villareal of the Solano County Sheriff's Office phoned to inform Vallejo police that he had arrested two guys who might be of interest to them in the Ferrin case. Villareal worked narcotics. He had noticed two men hanging around near a known drug spot. When he approached to question them, he saw a gun-shaped bulge in one man's waistband. When Villareal frisked the man, he discovered a concealed 9mm automatic handgun. Darlene Ferrin and Mike Mageau had been shot with a 9mm handgun. The men were arrested for loitering and taken to the sheriff's office headquarters for booking and questioning.

The man with the 9mm was identified as twenty-four-year-old Donald Warren Blank (this name has been changed for this book). The other man was identified as nineteen-year-old James Phillip Flowers. Dian Stevens's friend Jim Flowers was now a person of interest in the murder of Darlene Ferrin. That's quite the coincidence—that her ex-boyfriend confessed to the first two Zodiac murders and her sister's ex-boyfriend was a suspect in the third Zodiac murder. Both men were questioned by police. Blank claimed he had the gun because he was supposed to have a fight with "some guy" and that that guy had a shotgun. Blank refused to name the person who gave him the gun, telling cops it was an ex-con from San Francisco. Flowers told a different story, about how they were looking for a friend named Willie. Flowers claimed he didn't know anything about Darlene's murder and told cops he had gone to San Jose (his favorite place to rob gas stations) on July 4th and didn't return to Vallejo until the 5th. After questioning, Flowers was searched more thoroughly before being brought to the holding cell, and cops found a .32 revolver hidden in his underwear.

One of the men—the name is redacted in the publicly available Vallejo police report—blurted out, "I'm going to be booked for murder," when officers discovered the gun.

Whoever said it was correct. Blank and Flowers were booked for the murder of Darlene Ferrin. The 9mm handgun and the loaded clip were sent out for ballistic analysis the following morning when the Vallejo police returned to work from their strike. Nothing ever came of the murder charge. Blank was back in the newspaper on October 1, 1969, for getting arrested after stealing a car in Fairfield, California. The concealed weapon and prowling charges stuck, but the murder rap went away within a week. Normally, you'd assume that this was because the ballistics weren't a match, but there's nothing normal about this case, so I won't make that assumption—and neither should you.

The police and firefighter strike worked. They got their raises, plus improved working conditions and the changes to labor rules they had sought. The city of Vallejo also agreed to revise its policy by using the general city budget to call in and pay reserve officers for special protection details, rather than assigning an on-duty officer at straight time from the police budget. This became a sweet side hustle for reserve cops looking to make extra money by standing around and doing nothing. Reserve officers were put on a twenty-four-hour protection detail for Michael Mageau and the surviving Magris–Holmberg victim Dennis Tapp during their hospital stays. Instead of assigning one on-duty cop to the hospital as they would have under the old standard operating procedures, the Vallejo Police Department were now required to call up one reserve officer assigned to Tapp and another reserve officer assigned to Mageau. Six reserve cops were getting paid overtime every day for the hospital protection detail. An August 20, 1969, report in the *Vallejo Times-Herald* showed that the city had coughed up $4,180 (about $40,000 today) for two months of watching Dennis in the hospital and one month of watching Michael. That's an outsized amount of money for babysitting. When the police received an anonymous letter on August 7, 1969 (the day after Michael was released from the hospital), threatening to "rub out" surviving witness Tapp, the 24/7 protection detail was restored and extended for Michael for his life outside the hospital. Think about this for a second: just one day after the Michael Mageau overtime protection detail came to a natural conclusion, cops got a letter threatening a different shooting victim and used that letter to justify spending money on a new Michael Mageau 24/7 protection detail. That looks like a blatant cash grab.

Why would a threat to Dennis Tapp in the hospital put Michael's life outside of the hospital in danger? Dennis had been shot by a vicious drug gang with dangerous connections, while Michael had been reportedly shot by the Zodiac Killer. Did the cops believe that Michael might have run afoul of a drug gang? Did Darlene meet with Michael to score drugs on the 4th of July? Were the cops unwilling to shut the overtime protection detail tap off? Or maybe a bit of all three?

Michael wanted nothing to do with cops hanging around. He didn't stick around to answer any of these questions or get hassled with a police protection detail. Michael skipped town soon after leaving the hospital.

The cops weren't exactly beating his door down trying to get more information about the shooting at Blue Rock Springs. On September 29, 1969, police learned from his father that he had been living in San Pedro for a month and a half. That means detectives never felt the need to follow up with Mageau, a guy they claimed required around-the-clock protection, for the entire ninety days he was out of town. If he knew more about the circumstances surrounding the murder of Darlene Ferrin, as some investigators and Darlene's sister suggested, the Vallejo police didn't care to know or hear about it.

On July 25, 1969, Vallejo police received an anonymous letter possibly connecting the murder of Darlene Ferrin to the murders of David Faraday and Betty Lou Jensen as well as drug activity at Lake Herman Road. The letter reads:

> **To whom it may concern**
>
> **There is a young man who used to live in the pink house bordering Lake Herman. His name is Charles Borcich. He is around 22 and is short and heavy set. I do not know if this boy still lives at this residence or if he is guilty. I do know that he is off balanced by things he has done in the past and is very capable of committing the murders that were committed in that area and at Blue Rock. If he is innocent I will not have hurt him, but if he is guilty and another person died, I would never forgive myself. Please check this man out!**

This is the same guy who was arrested when the Benicia police made the major drug bust at the Cottage at Lake Herman on the night David and Betty Lou were murdered. This is Charles Anthony Borcich, the caretaker's grandson. The letter to police connected the shootings of David Faraday and Betty Lou Jensen with those of Darlene Ferrin and Mike Mageau a week before the first three letters from the Zodiac made that link. Whoever wrote this letter scooped the Zodiac's big reveal and offered up a suspect. Borcich was not a known criminal. He worked at Mare Island Naval Shipyard and was a student at Mt. Diablo Community College. He was a former honor student, football player, and track and field star from Benicia High School. He had served his country in the Army.

Lynch and Rust took a copy of Borcich's mug shot from the drug bust to Michael at the hospital. Mageau didn't recognize Borcich. He claimed that to the best of his knowledge Borcich was not his shooter.

Nothing came of Borcich's arrest at the Cottage, either. His lawyer filed multiple motions to suppress evidence obtained by Detective Bidou's warrant, arguing that "the warrant was insufficient on its face" and that "evidence obtained wasn't described in the warrant." A third motion was filed to "reveal the identity of the informant who allegedly led to his arrest."[70] That's the last time the story was reported on in local newspapers, leading some with knowledge of the case to suspect that the unnamed informant may have been David Faraday. Borcich was accepted into the Army Corps of Engineers and was the building inspector for the city of Lewiston, Idaho. None of that would have been possible if he had had a criminal record for Bidou's drug bust. Borcich's drug case appeared to have magically disappeared.

The letters kept coming. One, a threatening note linked to an associate of Magris and Holmberg and directed at Vallejo police, claimed that "Dennis Tapp is a liar." This caused concern and further justified the need for a protection detail. Another letter, allegedly from Holmberg himself, was sent to the *Vallejo Times-Herald*. In it, he declared his innocence and expressed his contempt for Dennis Tapp. Holmberg, then in jail and on trial for the Tompkins murder and Tapp shooting, claimed to have no knowledge of the letter. His lawyer, while claiming that he knew who had written it, refused to reveal the identity of the author, insisting that it wasn't his client. There was a prolific letter-writer in Vallejo with a strong interest in the Vallejo Thrill Killer crime spree.

Further linking the cases, Magris's girlfriend, Dian Stevens, and her friend, Marybeth Newsome, were arrested by Vallejo police on the night of July 4, 1969, while driving on the backroads near Blue Rock Springs in the direct aftermath of Darlene Ferrin's murder. Doesn't this feel like too many coincidences to be just a coincidence? According to Stevens, Newsome's mother was listening to the drama unfolding on the police frequency of a ham radio and heard cops arresting her daughter and Dian. Mrs. Newsome arrived at the police station before the cops got there with Marybeth and Dian in the back of the patrol car. If someone wanted to listen in on what the local cops were up to, they could. If someone wanted specific details about the crime scene at Blue Rock Springs, all they had to do was listen to the police frequency.

CHAPTER 6: THIS IS THE ZODIAC LYING

ON JULY 31, 1969, THE ZODIAC KILLER WROTE THREE virtually identical letters and sent a three-part cryptogram to three different Bay Area newspapers taking credit for the murders of Betty Lou Jensen, David Faraday, and Darlene Ferrin, plus the attempted murder of Michael Mageau. This was the communication sent to the *Vallejo Times-Herald*:

Dear Editor

This is the murderer of the 2 teenagers last Christmass at Lake Herman and the girl on the 4th of July near the golf course in Vallejo

To prove I killed them I shall state some facts which only I + the police know.

Christmass

1. Brand name of ammo
   Super X
2. 10 shots were fired
3. the boy was on his back with his feet to the car
4. the girl was on her right side feet to the west

4th July

1. girl was wearing paterned slacks
2. The boy was also shot in the knee.
3. Brand name of ammo was western

Over

Here is part of a cipher the other 2 parts of this cipher are being mailed to the editors of the Vallejo Times + SF Examiner.

I want you to print this cipher on the front page of your paper. In this cipher is my idenity.

If you do not print this cipher by the afternoon of Fry. 1st of Aug 69, I will go on a kill rampage Fry. night. I will cruse around all weekend killing lone people in the night then move on to kill again, untill I end up with a dozen people over the weekend.

Was this legit, or was it bullshit meant to cause a panic like the false alarms and taunting notes left by the fire department during the strike? Were these letters real or were they like the cynical letters that kept funds flowing for the Tapp and Mageau protection details? The first three Zodiac letters could have been nothing more than a post-strike police labor action meant to frighten the public into feeling that the spoils of the strike were justified because they needed cops to protect them from a mysterious code killer.

Are the Zodiac letters taking credit for the Lake Herman Road and Blue Rock Springs murders bullshit?

Vallejo's police chief, Jack Stiltz, didn't go on strike with the rank and file. He worked twenty-hour shifts when they were on the picket line playing pranks. And he thought the letters were bullshit. Stiltz told the FBI that all the information provided by the letter-writer was reported in the newspaper. Stiltz goaded the letter-writer into giving more details. He publicly asked the writer to write back and send better information to prove he was telling the truth. On August 4, 1969, the writer obliged:

Dear Editor
This is the Zodiac speaking.

In answer to your asking for more details about the good times I have had in Vallejo, I shall be very happy to supply even more material. By the way, are the police haveing a good time with the code? If not, tell them to cheer up; when they do crack it they will have me.

On the 4th of July:
I did not open the car door, The window was rolled down all ready.

The boy was origionaly sitting in the front seat when I began fireing. When I fired the first shot at his head, he leaped backwards at the same time thus spoiling my aim. He ended up on the back seat then the floor in back thashing out very violently with his legs; thats how I shot him in the knee. I did not leave the cene of the killing with squealling tires + raceing engine as described in the Vallejo paper,. I drove away quite slowly so as not to draw attention to my car.

The man who told the police that my car was brown was a negro about 40–45 rather shabbly dressed. I was at this phone booth haveing some fun with the Vallejo cops when he was walking by. When I hung the phone up the dam X@ thing began to ring + that drew his attention to me + my car.

Last Christmass

In that epasode the police were wondering as to how I could shoot + hit my victoms in the dark. They did not openly state this, but implied this by saying it was a well lit night + I could see the silowets on the horizon. Bull Shit that area is srounded by high hills + trees. What I did was tape a small pencel flash light to the barrel of my gun. If you notice, in the center of the beam of light if you aim it at a wall or celling you will see a black or darck spot in the center of the circle of light about 3 to 6 inches across. When taped to a gun barrel, the bullet will strike exactly in the center of the black dot in the light. All I had to do was spray them as if it was a water hose; there was no need to use the gun sights. I was not happy to see that I did not get front page coverage.

—No Address

The writer, now calling himself the Zodiac, filled in the story but provided nothing new. The Zodiac's letters repeated many details that police already knew, using the same wording found in their own crime reports. For instance, the Zodiac noted that Michael Mageau had jumped into the back seat of the car after being shot. This was a curious detail because it hadn't been mentioned in local newspapers, but it was information that local police—or anyone with access to the reports—could have known. One thing is certain: the Zodiac letter-writer had access to the police files.

The call was coming from inside the house. The letter-writer wasn't subtle enough to hide the fact that they were quoting directly from Benicia, Solano, California Department of Justice, and Vallejo police reports. When describing the crimes, the language used in the Zodiac letters closely mirrors the phrasing in those police reports—dry, detached, and very "cop-like."

Everything in the letters comes directly from the police reports. The Benicia police report for the Lake Herman Road murders, written by the first officer on scene, Capt. Daniel Pitta, describes David Faraday's positioning: "Victim #2 was lying face up." The Zodiac Killer wrote, "the boy was on his back." Captain Pitta's report says that Faraday was discovered "with his feet to the right rear wheel." The Zodiac Killer copied that and wrote that Faraday had been left "with his feet to the car." Like a child who cheats on a test and changes one little thing in an attempt to fool the teacher, the Zodiac rephrases Pitta's "his feet to the right rear wheel" to "his feet to the car," and Pitta's "face up" to "on his back" in the Zodiac letter.

Pitta's police report said that Betty Lou had been found with her "head to the east." The Zodiac not-so-cleverly switched that up and described Betty Lou's positioning as having her "feet to the west."

Officer Hoffman's report about Darlene Ferrin quoted Stella Medeiros: "The girl was lying on her side facing the road." The Zodiac added a word and a spelling error to Stella's quote and stuck it in his letters: "the girl was on lyeing her right side."

The Zodiac even copied mistakes. When he plagiarized a Vallejo police report, he wrote that the "girl was wearing patterned slacks."

However, Darlene was actually wearing a floral pantsuit. Hoffman, who wrote the report, wasn't a fashion expert and mistakenly described her floral pantsuit as a "patterned slack dress." Anyone familiar with fashion knows there's no such thing as a "slack dress," not in 1969 and not today. Hoffman made an error, and the Zodiac simply copied it.

The Zodiac was a hack.

The Zodiac was caught in another lie when he tried to impress the chief by expanding on the dry police-report details provided in the first batch of letters. In the letter, the Zodiac showed himself to be a fantasist with a pulp-fiction imagination when he bragged about his ingenious flashlight contraption taped to the barrel of his gun, as if 1960s pencil flashlights had enough power to illuminate a pitch-black area. And who the hell tapes a flashlight to the thin barrel of a .22 squirrel pistol? He was proven to be a liar when he claimed that he sprayed the kids at Lake Herman Road with bullets as though he were using a water hose. This is complete nonsense that doesn't match the facts of the case. David Faraday was shot once, execution-style, in the head. There was no spraying. If the letter-writer was the killer, he would have known that David had been shot at point-blank range. Stiltz's suspicions were right: the Zodiac letter-writer was lying when it came to the first two Zodiac murders. The letter-writer was talking out of his ass about the murders of Betty Lou Jensen and David Faraday.

The Zodiac was a proven fraud.

CHAPTER 7: EVERYBODY LOVES DARLENE

THE TRAGEDY OF DARLENE FERRIN'S MURDER WAS made worse when she was cast as the scandalous female lead in the bizarre narrative spun around the Zodiac Killer. During her short life, she lived on her own terms. She was a liberated young woman in a time and place that wasn't ready for someone who fully embraced her freedom.

At just twenty-two, Darlene had already spent much of her life surrounded by abusive, dangerous men. She had close ties to real-life bad actors—she didn't need to become a supporting character in the twisted saga of a fake serial killer. The Zodiac didn't murder Darlene. The Zodiac never existed beyond the pages of the newspaper. He was a distraction, a figment of a mid-wit imagination. Tragically, this manufactured boogeyman kept Darlene's true killer, along with the killers of other "Zodiac" victims, from ever being brought to justice.

The first bad man in her life was her father, Leo Suennen, Jr. He fathered three boys and five girls, one of whom was Darlene Suennen. To offer insight into his character, it's important to note that on March 22, 1991, he was arraigned on four counts of sexual assault involving a child under the age of fourteen. Ten years later, he was once again arrested and charged with lewdness towards a child under fourteen years of age. Suennen copped a plea. Child sexual abuse isn't something people pick up in their retirement years. If old man Suennen preyed on children, you can bet that he was an even more prolific abuser in his testosterone-fueled youth. Perhaps even while raising Darlene and her three brothers and four sisters.

If Darlene grew up under a child predator's roof, it's no great leap to imagine how her upbringing influenced her relationships with men. It might help explain her self-destructive behavior, her distorted relationship with intimacy, and her attraction to toxic men and abusive relationships. According to the National Institutes of Health, "half of child sexual abuse survivors are sexually victimized in the future."[71]

Teenage Darlene ran away from her parents' house of horrors due to a massive "family dispute" and into a marriage with James Douglas Phillips, who had an IQ of 138 and a dishonorable discharge from the army. He worked in the newspaper business and wrote editorials. Jim told Darlene he was a "secret agent" and some kind of undercover military badass, and she believed him. Maybe that's what made him attractive to her. They lived a "gypsy existence" in the Haight, Reno, Pennsylvania, upstate New York, and the Virgin Islands.

Jim was brilliant and volatile. The longtime Zodiac researcher and Suennen family friend Sandy Betts remarked in an October 15, 2018, post on zodiackiller.com, "According to Darlene, Jim beat her often, so badly that she had to go to the hospital three different times."[72] The Zodiac researcher Mike Morford spoke to Phillips decades after Darlene's murder. "It sounded as if he hated her with a passion, still up to the moment I spoke with him," Morford wrote on the zodiackiller.com forum, "as if whatever wrong he felt she did to him was fresh in his heart & mind. I could feel it through the phone, it was that strong in my opinion. He used a few strong choice words as I recall, and I am going by memory; bitch, cunt, slut, whore come to mind. I remember hanging up the phone and saying to myself—WOW, and then thinking, I really hope he was ruled out properly."[73]

Darlene eventually grew tired of her nomadic, bohemian lifestyle with Phillips. She longed for stability. She thought she found it with Dean Ferrin, the short-order cook at the diner where she worked. Darlene's father, in an attempt to repair their relationship, gave Dean and Darlene a large sum of money to help them buy a house near her family in Vallejo. She divorced Phillips in June of 1967 and married Ferrin just two months later, changing her name from Darlene Phillips to Darlene Ferrin. In January 1968 she gave birth to a daughter, which suggests Darlene was still married to her first husband when she began her affair with her second, and Darlene's daughter was conceived while she was still married to James Phillips.

There are some intriguing details about Phillips. In 1969, he changed his name to James Crabtree. He was raised by a California Highway Patrol officer. While

DARLENE FERRIN WITH UNIDENTIFIED MAN.

in the army, Crabtree (né Phillips) married a woman in Germany, got her pregnant, and never bothered to divorce her before marrying Darlene. Early police reports regarding Darlene's murder didn't mention James Phillips or Crabtree—her ex-husband and an eventual suspect in a murder they believed was driven by "jealousy"—until January 1970. A psychic grifter who contacted Darlene's family appears in the police reports before her violent, angry ex does.

It's not that he wasn't suspicious. He was a newspaperman with a strong need to express his ideas in the print media, who understood how newspapers were run and what made it onto the page. He had a military background, intimate knowledge of police procedure through a cop father figure, and delusions of grandeur. Plus, he was a self-proclaimed "secret agent" who boasted about being a military cryptographer with top-secret clearance. He had spent time in a mental institution after deserting the army and living on the streets of New York, then served six months in the army brig at the Presidio. Yet it was the psychic, using information from Darlene's mother, who initially brought the suspect James Crabtree to the police's attention.

There were a lot of head-scratching decisions made in the Ferrin murder investigation. Why did it take so long to investigate James Crabtree—a guy who couldn't have had more Zodiac red flags if he tried? Criminal profiling didn't exist in the 1960s, but commonsense did, and commonsense would suggest that the ex-husband James Crabtree should have been near the top of the suspect list from July 4, 1969. It's hard to understand why detectives neglected to follow up with the surviving witness, Michael Mageau, and get to the bottom of what was really going on the night Darlene was murdered. It's impossible to wrap your head around why investigators stopped investigating George Waters after they went on strike. It's almost as if the cops weren't looking too hard into Darlene Ferrin's murder.

In the summer of 1969, the Zodiac wasn't that big of a cultural phenomenon. There were no true-crime podcasts and goofy serial-killer fan websites selling

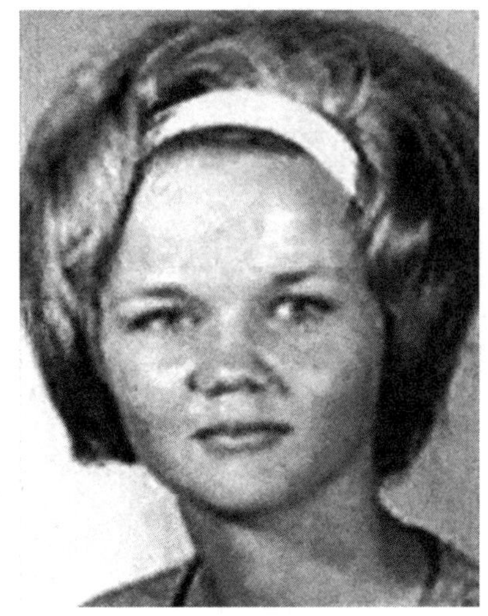

DARLENE ELIZABETH FERRIN (NÉE SUENNEN), AGE 18, 1966.

Zodiac Killer merch. Graysmith didn't publish his best-selling *Zodiac* book until 1986. David Fincher didn't put his big-budget Hollywood film out until 2007. The Zodiac didn't strike in San Francisco until October of 1969. Zodiac was a local story, a Vallejo, Benicia, North Bay story. The local papers wrote about the Zodiac, but the cops weren't looking for fake supervillains.

By late 1969, several Vallejo detectives working the Ferrin homicide, a police captain, and the chief of the department had soured on the notion that a Zodiac Killer even existed. Informants flooded Vallejo cops with information that David Magris and a partner did the Lake Herman Road murders because David Faraday snitched about a big-time drug deal. Solano deputies knew this too. Magris even corroborated that intel with a confession to Sergeant Cunningham about his involvement in the Lake Herman Road murders.

Even if the Zodiac Killer was a complete fraud, surely Vallejo cops would doggedly pursue the killer of Darlene Ferrin, a twenty-two-year-old mother and Vallejo local. As details of Darlene's dating life surfaced, things became a bit more complicated for the police and the investigation landed too close to home. Darlene liked cops. She really, really liked cops. A thorough investigation into Darlene Ferrin would entail an awkward investigation into several happily married members of the Vallejo Police Department and Solano Sheriff's Office. When you couple that with the obvious overlap between the Zodiac letters and the police reports, it doesn't take a genius to see why the investigation never went anywhere. If investigators really wanted an answer about this murder, they were going to have to take a hard look into fellow police officers. There's a taboo in police culture against that sort of thing. Investigate your fellow cop and you're a rat. The cops investigating Darlene's murder were no rats.

Darlene's trysts with Vallejo-area cops were addressed by officers who worked the Zodiac case in Robert Graysmith's *Zodiac Unmasked.* Detective

Bawart said, "If you're working the swing shift, the graveyard shift, and a new waitress came on, it would be a contest to see who could get in her shorts first. That's the way cops were back then. There were a lot of cops pursuing her. She was a pretty loose gal, Darlene was." Sgt. Jack Mulanax added, "Darlene had a rep as being pretty fast and loose. She was dating a lot of different guys. Certainly during the time she was working as a waitress out at Terry's . . . Before her death, she saw three Vallejo cops, one 'a drive-in Romeo' and another a deputy in the sheriff's office."

One cop Darlene dated was a Solano County Sheriff's Office deputy named Howard "Buzz" Gordon. Gordon claimed in an interview with Brooke Sulski that his relationship with Darlene started as a "'sex thing' but became significantly more intimate. They spent a lot of time together—hours upon hours"—and "Buzz said he knew Dee better than anybody, and that includes her husband and her girlfriends who only scratched the surface."[74]

Gordon also said that before and after their relationship "Dee was into drugs, pot, speed, hash, LSD, Reds." If Darlene was using reds, a.k.a. Seconal, that puts her one degree of separation away from Darrell "Pus Gut" Cussins. If you were popping reds in Vallejo in 1969, chances are you were doing Pus Gut's drugs. On December 31, 2016, Sandy Betts, a Zodiac researcher who also had a relationship with Buzz Gordon, posted on a Zodiac Killer internet forum, "I know for a fact that Darlene was involved in selling drugs."[75] Darlene's home at 1300 Virginia Street was only three minutes away from Pus Gut's pad at 943 Capitol Street. That's a dangerous orbit for a woman involved in selling drugs and dating cops to be in.

During the Vallejo police strike (two weeks after Darlene's murder), Buzz Gordon got into a public fistfight with Officer Richard Hoffman on the picket line. Hoffman vowed revenge. This is the same Richard Hoffman who first responded to the shooting of Darlene and Michael, who rode in the ambulance to the hospital with Darlene and filed the police report. The same guy who coined the term "slack dress." Later, Gordon got fired from the force when he was charged, arrested, and found not guilty of two counts of statutory rape.

The cop rumor mill said that Hoffman was having an affair with Darlene around the time of her murder. Darlene's sister Linda claimed that Darlene knew Hoffman—that he was a guest at Darlene's house.

Before he was attacked, Mike Mageau reached for his ID because he believed that his attacker was a cop. Darlene was cheating on her husband with at least three cops, including the first officer who responded to her murder, a guy who was confirmed to be at the location of the crime at Blue Rock Springs fifteen minutes before the attack. The other cops she had affairs with were even sketchier than Hoffman.

In February of 1970, a full seven months after the murder of Darlene Ferrin, Vallejo detectives finally made contact with the angry ex, Jim Crabtree, at Santa Cruz Municipal Court where Crabtree was dealing with a traffic ticket. He was advised that he was a suspect in the murder of Darlene Ferrin. He told cops he didn't even know that Darlene had been killed, or that she had changed her name to Ferrin. He was living as a semi-off-the-grid hippie with a new common-law wife in a rural area about twenty minutes from Santa Cruz. He cooperated with the police and let them search his place. He also gave a handwriting sample. Cops took his prints.

Crabtree told cops that the marriage had ended with Darlene because she had been running around with other men. He had an alibi for July 4, 1969: he was with his new wife at a hippie encampment in Boulder Creek. There was a concert that night. Phillips's truck broke down, so he couldn't leave the campsite. The cops liked Crabtree—not as a suspect, but as a person. They believed him. Sergeant Mulanax even opined in the official report, "It is the opinion of RO [reporting officer] that Phillips is in no way connected with the murder of Darlene Ferrin."[76]

What stands out about the February 1970 interview of Crabtree is that Vallejo detectives were investigating Darlene's murder independent of the Zodiac murders. By the time they finally spoke to Crabtree, the Zodiac had claimed to be responsible for two other murders following Darlene's: one in Napa County and one in San Francisco. The Vallejo detectives weren't trying to tie Crabtree to either of those other crimes; they were looking for the murderer of Darlene Ferrin. Zodiac lore played no part in their investigation into Darlene's ex. That indicates that Vallejo detectives didn't fully buy into the whole Zodiac thing.

Another one of Darlene's lovers, a twenty-one-year-old Navy man named Gordon Arthur Spence, contacted the police. Spence had met Darlene at Terry's. After her shift, he'd drive her to Blue Rock Springs for a tryst, then drive her home. For some reason, Darlene insisted that Spence meet her husband. Eventually, Spence met Ferrin—he later said that Dean was friendly and aware that the two were spending time together.

When the Navy transferred Spence to Idaho Falls, Darlene begged him to take her with him. She wanted to leave Ferrin. Spence didn't go for it. Darlene had a baby daughter and a husband at home—she belonged with them. He took Darlene out one last time in the Bay Area and left for Idaho. Darlene wrote to him while he was away, asking him to call her on the phone. When he did, she said she was pregnant. The implication was that the baby was his. The next letter she sent him was from the hospital. Spence assumed she had an abortion. He got angry and wanted nothing more to do with her. That is, until he showed up at Terry's looking for her months after her murder. That's when he found out the cops wanted to talk to him.

Another awful man attached to Darlene was Charles Wayne Lindsey. Lindsey was a deputy with the Solano County Sheriff's Office, where he worked as an identification technician, specializing in handling evidence and obtaining identification. Lindsey appears in Robert Graysmith's book *Zodiac* under the pseudonym "Jack." According to Graysmith's sources, Lindsey dated Darlene.

According to Lindsey's roommate, he had photos and evidence from the Blue Rock Springs crime scene at their home. Lindsey also had photos of Darlene and the other Zodiac victims displayed at their home. In the late '70s, Graysmith spoke to Sgt. Ralph Wilson of the Solano County Sheriff's Office, who said that Lindsey was considered the prime suspect for a short time in 1969. Lindsey lived in the backroads just behind the murder site at Blue Rock Springs. Lindsey was later fired from the sheriff's office for mysterious reasons.

It was incredibly hard for a cop to get fired in the 1960s. Police departments routinely sent dirty, abusive, and even corrupt cops out on patrol without a second thought in those days. It was seen as the cost of doing business. Crooked cops operated openly. In order to get fired, you had to do something beyond the pale, such as being credibly accused of statutory rape, as in Buzz Gordon's case. Somehow, Darlene managed to find two men bad enough to get canned from the police force in the '60s. That says an awful lot about the type of dangerous person Darlene sought out in a romantic partner and kept in her orbit.

In 1972, a woman named Marjorie Lynn Lubbers was shot and killed with Lindsey's .357 magnum service weapon at his home. Lindsey dated Marjorie for about a month, during which she spent a lot of nights at his place. She had a three-year-old and a five-year-old. The story is that after an argument with Lindsey, while her children were in the next room, she was shot to death through the heart. The gun was found under a bed. The coroner, Dan Horan, and Det. Sgt.

Les Lundblad (remember him from the Lake Herman Road botch job?) ruled the death a suicide.[77] Of course they did! Lundblad's Razor was back in action.

In the 1970s, suicide by gunshot was an extremely rare way for a woman to die. Mothers of small children don't just shoot themselves with high-powered .357 magnums in the heart with their kids a few feet away. Guns don't just slide themselves under beds. Domestic violence is a far more common way for a woman to die. And almost 50% of female murder victims are killed by a former or current intimate partner.[78]

Looks like two awful men covered for another awful man. Another woman was the victim of a homicide in Vallejo and the cops, specifically Les Lundblad, did nothing to solve the case or bring her killer to justice. Honestly, I'm surprised that one of the Zodiac fanboy ghouls hasn't released a calendar featuring the pretty unsolved murder victims of Vallejo in the Zodiac era. Darlene Ferrin could be Miss July.

CHAPTER 8: STABBING AT LAKE BERRYESSA

BRYAN HARTNELL. *ROCK ISLAND ARGUS*, OCTOBER 17, 1969. CECELIA SHEPARD. *LONGVIEW DAILY NEWS*, OCTOBER 17, 1969.

THE ZODIAC'S NEXT KNOWN ATTACK TOOK PLACE during a picnic date at picturesque Lake Berryessa in Napa County, California. The lake, a man-made reservoir, was named after the Berryessa family, who had emigrated from Spain's Basque Country to Sinaloa, Mexico, in the early eighteenth century. In 1735, eighteen-year-old José de Jesus Berryessa married a ten-year-old local girl named Maria. After nineteen years, they had a daughter, Ana Ysabel. Seven years later, they had a son, Nicolas.

In 1775, the Spanish government intended to settle what is now California. Ana Ysabel, at twenty-one, and her kid brother Nicolas, at just fourteen, joined a group of colonists and made their way north. The Berryessas settled, married fellow colonists, had heaps of kids, and accumulated massive Mexican land grants for their family in the San Francisco Bay Area. They got very rich from mining and ranching.

However, their wealth was built on exploiting Indigenous men and women. In 1854, the Bureau of Indian Affairs reported that 150 Indigenous people were enslaved in the Berryessa Valley—and that was just one of many groups of people captured and forced into slave labor on Berryessa land from the Indigenous Pomo nation. That's the dirty secret of their riches. The Berryessas' mining and ranching operations were profitable because they had zero labor costs. The Berryessas were wealthy because they captured and sold human beings for slave labor.

By the late 1850s, Anglo settlers started encroaching on Berryessa land. Eight Berryessa men were murdered by the gringos. The family fled, and the land was re-colonized by Anglo-Americans armed to the teeth with guns and lawyers.

Rancho Las Putas belonged to José Jesus Berryessa until one day it didn't anymore. The gringos didn't bother to take the Berryessa name off their lake. José's still buried under the lake that bears his family's name.

The population exploded when Gold Rush gringos flooded the area in search of fortune. Their families hung around and established themselves as ranchers. In 1953, the U.S. government launched the Monticello Dam Project. This involved damming Putah Creek and flooding the valley, which displaced the ranchers. Dorothea Lange photographed the whole sad ordeal in her project *Death of a Valley*. By 1963, the entire area was submerged, creating Lake Berryessa, now the second-largest reservoir in California.

The lake, originally fenced off and not intended for public use, quickly became a hotspot despite the barriers. (Nobody gave a shit about the fence and everyone jumped in the water anyway.) Authorities abandoned the fence idea and began selling recreational concessions. The area soon became a popular destination for fishing, swimming, boating, sunbathing, hiking, bird-watching, and, yes, picnicking.

On September 27, 1969, two college students, twenty-year-old Bryan Hartnell and twenty-two-year-old Cecelia Shepard, were doing just that at Twin Oak Ridge. The views of Lake Berryessa and the surrounding hills were stunning. More importantly, their little picnic area was secluded.

Bryan and Cecelia used to date one another but, according to Bryan in a 1969 police report, they went to Lake Berryessa as old friends catching up—nothing more. The two of them were Seventh-Day Adventists, a form of evangelical Christianity that dates to the mid-nineteenth century. Seventh-Day Adventists observe kosher dietary law and are often strict vegetarians.

They live about ten years longer than the average Californian, probably because they adhere to a low-fat vegetarian diet, have strong social bonds through their church, enthusiastically participate in exercise and physical activity, and don't smoke or drink alcohol. Or maybe it's due to Kellogg's Corn Flakes, Rice Krispies, and soy-based meat alternatives, the most well-known culinary contributions of the movement.

Everybody lies to the cops, even fine, upstanding church folk. As for what Bryan and Cecelia were doing there, in a 2019 email interview with *Shadow of the Zodiac,* Bryan admitted he was hoping they could become more than friends again:

> **Q. When you went out to the lake were you hoping to rekindle your relationship with Cecilia?**
> **A. i loved Cecilia and yes i was hoping we could rekindle our love for each other, and you know maybe we would've got married and had kids. Funny thing is about i say 20 minutes before the attack Cecilia asked me what i thought about having kids. no one knew this, and this is the first time i actually say anything about it.**[79]

The thing was, Bryan already had a girlfriend in September of 1969. She was back home in Oregon. Cecelia was from Loma Linda, an area of California with a large Adventist population that is considered a longevity "Blue Zone"—there's a large population of thriving seniors and a high concentration of people living well beyond the age of 100. She was leaving town in a couple of days, going south to the University of California, Riverside, where she was a music major. Bryan helped her pack.

Bryan wanted to be with Cecelia, but he didn't want his girlfriend to know about it. In fact, when Bryan became momentarily famous for being a Zodiac victim, he was really focused on getting to a phone to call his girlfriend. He wanted to spin a story and do some damage control before the newspapers came out and she read about how the Zodiac ruined his picnic with an ex.

On the day of the attack, Bryan and Cecelia left Pacific Union College, an Adventist college in Napa County, with their friend Judith around 1:00 p.m. They stopped by a rummage sale in St. Helena, where Bryan bought a television set. Towering at six-foot-seven, he drove a comically small 1956 Volkswagen

BRYAN HARTNELL IN THE HOSPITAL. *VALLEJO TIMES-HERALD*, OCTOBER 8, 1969.

Karmann Ghia—a sporty version of the VW Beetle. He couldn't fit himself, both girls, and the television set in the car simultaneously, so he left the girls at the rummage sale and drove the TV back to his college housing. Bryan returned an hour later and picked up Cecelia. They told third-wheel Judith they were heading to San Francisco and dropped her off at her home in St. Helena before continuing on their way.

When Bryan and Cecelia dated two years earlier, they spent a lot of time at Lake Berryessa. It was about an hour away from Pacific Union College. More importantly, it was an hour away from the prying eyes of religious busybodies from their church and Bryan's school.

They shelved their San Francisco plans and instead enjoyed a romantic lakeside picnic. As they sat on a blanket and looked at the water, they talked about whether they wanted to have kids—you know, one of those conversations that typically comes up between totally platonic friends who haven't seen each other in a while.

Just before 6:30 p.m., Cecelia spotted a man coming down the hillside about 200 to 300 yards away. He paused and seemed to watch the couple. Cecelia didn't think much of it and returned her attention to Bryan. After a while, she glanced over again, and this time the man—described as a brown-haired white guy—was only 75 to 100 feet away. She mentioned it to Bryan. He figured the guy was taking a leak behind a tree because there weren't any toilets nearby.

When the man emerged from behind the trees, he was wearing a black hood made of cotton over his head and shoulders, kind of like an executioner's mask. The hood featured a large white embroidered emblem, which resembled a Celtic cross, a crosshair symbol, or the strange symbol the Zodiac Killer from Vallejo used to sign his letters. The Zodiac had been a local news story in the North Bay, but Bryan and Cecelia had never heard of him. They didn't recognize the symbol.

The man approached, and Cecelia shouted, "Oh my god, he's got a gun!"[80] The guy in the homemade supervillain costume nervously claimed he was an escaped prisoner who had just killed a prison guard and stolen a car. There were sunglasses clipped to the hood. He looked ridiculous. His brown hair "hung down across his forehead and was showing through the eyeholes."[81]

He demanded Bryan's wallet and keys, insisting that he needed to escape to Mexico. Bryan complied and then spoke to the guy for a couple of minutes. He asked the guy if he'd accept a check. He offered to give the guy his contact info. He told the guy he studied sociology in college and asked if there was any way he could help the masked man. Bryan acted completely unbothered by the masked man pointing a gun at him. It might have been an attempt to understand the criminal's mindset or just an effort, for self-preservation, to build rapport with a man holding a gun. Whatever it was, it was weird that Bryan wasn't afraid of the man with the gun and treated him more like a curiosity than a threat. Bryan took being held at gunpoint as an opportunity to question a real criminal and determine if what he'd read in *Reader's Digest* checked out with the reality of what he believed to be an armed robbery.

The masked man then pulled lengths of clothesline from his belt and ordered Cecelia to hogtie Bryan. She tied the ropes loosely. Bryan believed he could overpower the shaky guy in the costume and grab the gun. He ran the idea by Cecelia, but she nixed it. She didn't want to risk it.

The hooded man tied Cecelia up, and Bryan, still trying to make small talk with the masked man, asked if the gun was really loaded because he had read that criminals sometimes use unloaded guns just to scare people. The guy showed him that it was loaded. Then, he pulled a long knife out of a sheath on his belt and started stabbing the couple. Bryan was stabbed six times in the back and Cecelia was stabbed ten times in the abdomen. She fought and squirmed during her attack, but Bryan played dead.

It worked. The masked maniac left, walking back up a trail in the hills. Once he was gone, Bryan and Cecelia worked like hell to untie each other while losing blood by the minute. Bryan used every ounce of strength in his body to drag himself 300 yards towards help. He screamed bloody murder until he encountered a man named Ronald Fong in a speedboat on the lake. Fong went to call for help at the Rancho Monticello resort where he was staying. Bryan crawled his way to the road.

When a park ranger named Dennis Land arrived in his pickup truck at 7:10 p.m., flashlight in hand, Bryan initially feared it was the masked attacker returning to finish him off. Fortunately, it was one of the good guys. Ranger Land quickly got Bryan into his truck, addressed his wounds, and drove off to find Cecelia, who was being treated by another park ranger. Bryan collapsed in the truck, exhausted and in shock. Ranger Land left Bryan at the crime scene and covered him with a blanket, then went back on patrol, ready to answer calls in his truck and offering to escort the police and ambulance to the crime scene.

Lake Berryessa is an isolated location. Cops, coming from Napa and St. Helena, got there at about 7:40 p.m., and the ambulance, also coming from Napa, arrived at 7:55 p.m. It took another hour for the ambulance to get to Queen of the Valley Hospital.

Though the attack happened at 6:30 p.m., Bryan and Cecelia, both in critical condition, didn't receive treatment at the hospital until around 9:00 p.m. Bryan survived the ordeal. Cecelia lived for two more days before succumbing to her injuries.

At 7:40 p.m. that night, the Napa Police Department got a call, saying, "I want to report a murder, no, a double murder. They are two miles north of Park Headquarters. They were in a white Volkswagen Karmann Ghia. I'm the one that did it." The call came from a payphone near the Napa Car Wash on Main Street, about twenty-seven miles from the crime scene. This Zodiac called the wrong cops. Instead of calling the Napa County Sheriff's Office, just a few blocks away from the payphone he was using, he called the Napa (City) Police. The Vallejo Zodiac called police from the correct jurisdiction, seemed to be familiar with police procedure, and could quote from police reports and accurately give cardinal directions. The San Francisco Zodiac was hyper-aware of the mistakes the police made in their response to the Paul Stine murder. The Lake Berryessa Zodiac goofed and called the wrong agency. Napa P.D. contacted Napa County Sheriff's Office and informed them about the call.

Deputy Dave Collins of the Napa County Sheriff's Office was at the crime scene. "I began a search for evidence and discovered a footprint that led from Berryessa Knoxville Road to the victims and back again, which was totally separate from the shoes that they were wearing," he said. "When I went to the roadway, I saw the white Karmann Ghia and I saw tracks leading away from it. . . . I looked at the Karmann Ghia, and on the passenger door the circle with the vertical and horizontal line through it was displayed on the door and there were several dates, and then it ended with September 27th 1969, 6:30 pm, by knife, which was our crime, so he had left his calling card, which is what he had done. I recognized the symbol on the door as being the same symbol she had described on the hood."[82]

Either the Zodiac had struck at Lake Berryessa or someone really wanted to make it look that way. Instead of a letter, this Zodiac Killer wrote his message on Bryan's car door. It began with the Zodiac symbol and continued:

> Vallejo
> 12-20-68
> 7-4-69
> Sept 27, 69-6:30
> By knife

"12-20-68" and "7-4-69" are the dates of the Lake Herman Road and Blue Rock Springs murders. The person who wrote this message wanted the authorities and the media to associate the attack at Lake Berryessa with the earlier Zodiac murders.

Unlike the Zodiac letters to the newspaper that were written using a blue felt-tipped pen—because blue photographs as black in newsprint—the message on Bryan's car was scrawled in black ink. Unlike previous (and future) Zodiac attacks, this Zodiac used a knife instead of a gun. This Zodiac attacked in broad daylight instead of under the cover of darkness. The previous Zodiac attacks were quick, brutal executions or blitz attacks. This Zodiac tied up his victims and hung around, talking with them for around fifteen minutes. This Zodiac called the wrong cops. This Zodiac didn't write a letter; he wrote on a car door.

This Zodiac Killer took his time. He wore a spooky homemade costume, made small talk, and even had a backstory. Physically, this Zodiac was up to sixty pounds heavier than the one who had struck at Blue Rock Springs. This Zodiac seemed to be influenced by the Tate–LaBianca murders in August of 1969. Instead of writing a letter, he scrawled a message on a car door for authorities to see. All of this suggests that it may be the work of a copycat influenced by both the Zodiac and the Manson murders. And Helter Skelter and Zodiac were both bullshit.

Bryan Hartnell described his attacker as having brown hair and weighing 225 to 250 pounds, which is itself notable since that was a massive man in 1969. Remember, the average adult American man was 166 pounds in the 1960s. This dude is about the size of the average NFL lineman at the time—

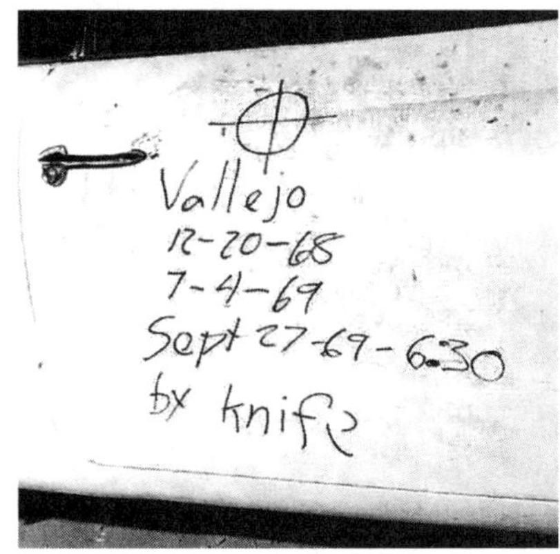

BRYAN HARTNELL'S CAR DOOR. SEPTEMBER 27, 1969.

outweighing the heavyweight boxers Muhammad Ali, George Foreman, and Joe Frazier. Bryan was no help with height—at six-foot-seven, everyone was short to him.

At least Bryan understood his limitations when giving an eyewitness description—most people are terrible at it but are convinced they're doing a great job. Bryan also said the man wore "sloppy clothes. And he had on this old pair of pleated pants. Well, like I say, he was dressed kind of sloppily, you know. His pants real tight up here and his stomach kind of pouched a bit." Cecelia saw his face from far away, but since he was wearing a mask by the time Bryan spotted him, he never saw his face.

The footprints that Deputy Collins discovered leading from Hartnell's car to the crime scene were made by size-10½ Wing Walker boots. These boots were commonly worn by Navy and Air Force personnel working on aircraft and civilian airplane maintenance workers. Plaster casts were taken of the boot impressions, and analysis determined that the man who left them weighed approximately 240 pounds.

Seems Bryan Hartnell could have had a successful career at the Guess-My-Weight booth at the carnival. His estimate of his attacker's weight was right in line with the boot impression. This Zodiac was a very big man.

Sgt. Hal Snook, the head of the Napa County crime lab and a seasoned forensics expert, photographed the footprints and combed through the crime scene. He discovered a bottle with latent prints and found multiple prints on the car-wash payphone, including a palm print that was so fresh he had to dry it himself to get a proper impression. Snook also examined items inexplicably removed from the crime scene by Ranger Land and placed them in an evidence locker, including Bryan's wallet and car keys. Although the killer had taken Bryan's wallet and keys, he had left them at the scene. Bryan wasn't robbed.

Sergeant Snook also found tire treads at the scene that revealed two different tread patterns. He believed the Zodiac was driving a vehicle with mismatched

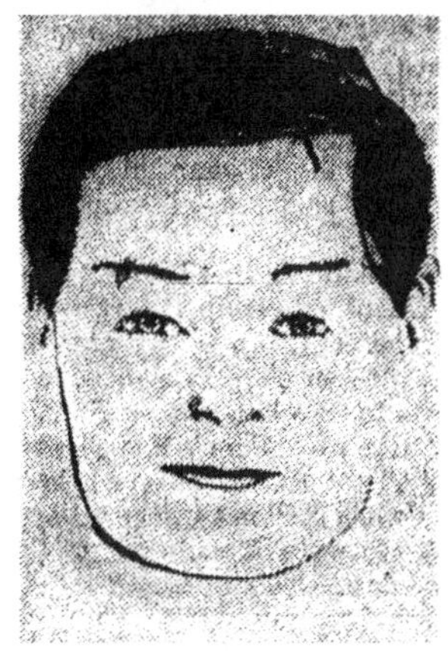

SKETCH OF THE LAKE BERRYESSA PERSON OF INTEREST.

tires. The measurements Snook took suggested that it was a small car. This is not the same type of large, boat-sized, American-made car typically associated with the earlier Zodiac murders at Lake Herman Road and Blue Rock Springs. It seemed that this Zodiac was also a huge guy in a tiny clown car.

The caller who took credit for the "double murder" gave the location of the crime scene as "two miles north of park headquarters." Police determined that it was a little over a half mile north of the park headquarters. This Zodiac, unlike his Vallejo counterpart, sucked at estimating distances.

There were other witnesses around that night. Dr. Clifton Rayfield and his sixteen-year-old son, David, came forward to tell police about a man they saw at Lake Berryessa around 6:30 p.m. just north of park headquarters.

Rayfield and his son described the man as a five-foot-ten heavyset white male wearing dark trousers and a dark long-sleeved shirt with some red on it. The guy wasn't carrying anything and seemed to be out for a walk. Over the years, many Zodiac enthusiasts have speculated that Dr. Rayfield and his son encountered the Zodiac, and that the red on the shirt was blood. Maybe that's the way it works in television police procedurals, but in real life a blood-soaked black or navy shirt wouldn't register as having red on it. The blood would appear dark on a dark shirt. Blood would appear bright red only on a light-colored shirt.

David told cops that when the guy saw him and his dad he "turned and walked up a hill in a southerly direction." The doctor also reported seeing a man in the area shooting BB guns with two young boys. This may or may not have been the same man.

Three young women, students at Pacific Union College, also came forward, telling police about encountering a "nice looking," six-foot-or-taller white man, conservative, with side-parted black hair. They put him between twenty-eight and forty years old, weighing about 200 to 225 pounds with a "muscular build," and said he was wearing a short-sleeved sweater and dark clothing. Allegedly, he watched them sunbathe for up to forty-five minutes sometime between 3:00 and 4:30 p.m. The women believed the guy, who drove a late-model blue Chevy with California plates, followed them to the beach. The details provided by the women were used by police to generate an Identikit sketch image of the man.

These descriptions do share some commonality with the masked man who attacked Bryan and Cecelia. Maybe it was the guy. Maybe it wasn't.

Investigators made finding the man with the blue Chevy a priority. He was considered a witness to the crime or a person of interest.

Napa County detectives along with agents from the California Department of Justice hightailed it to Travis Air Force Base to learn more about the Wing Walker boots. They worked the shoe angle hard, hitting a targeted list of civilian shoe stores and military orders attempting to identify the perp by his Wing Walkers.

Meanwhile, Sherwood Morrill, the head of the Questioned Documents Section of California's Criminal Identification and Investigation Bureau, determined that the writing on Bryan Hartnell's car door and the writing from the Zodiac letters came from the same individual. Forget that it's nearly impossible to match a writing sample on a piece of paper and one written on a car door with any degree of accuracy–Morrill compared apples to oranges and came up with Zodiac.

Investigators immediately dropped the Wing Walker angle and put a halt on trying to locate the nice-looking man with the blue Chevy who enjoyed watching young women in bikinis. Now that the circus had come to Napa, local investigators were forced to play catch-up on the Zodiac case, conferring with Solano, Vallejo, and California Department of Justice authorities.

If the cops really believed there was a Zodiac Killer, and that the Vallejo and Lake Berryessa murders were committed by the same man, why didn't they take another look at Vallejo's first and best suspect, George Waters? If they had, they would have realized that George Waters drove a blue Chevy like the one the Napa cops were looking for. They would have also realized that George Waters looked nearly identical to the Identikit sketch provided by the three sunbathing college girls of the "nice looking" dark-haired man who was a person of interest in the Lake Berryessa murder. If someone noticed how similar George Waters looked to the sketch, they might have checked out where he hung out. At the time, George Waters lived and worked in St. Helena—precisely where Bryan Hartnell and Cecelia Shepard had been the afternoon before they were attacked at Lake Berryessa. George Waters, a man with a history of abusing women, who had harassed Darlene Ferrin, broken into her apartment, threatened to rape her, then bragged about killing her, was based in the same town visited by the victims of another Zodiac attack on the day they were assaulted. How did this guy slip through the fingers of the investigators again? Why was nobody looking into any of this?

If any of the detectives working the Zodiac as a cold case had taken a proper look into George Waters, red flags would have gone up as soon as they learned that a man named George Waters was a prolific author of letters to the editor in the *Napa Valley Register* throughout the 1970s and 80s. He wrote letters about everything from libertarian politics to complaints about the comic strips. If there was a Zodiac, writing letters to the newspaper sounds like something he'd do, right? It's the kind of thing investigators should follow up on. I know for a fact that no police and civilian Zodiac researchers pursued the letter-writing angle because I spoke to the George Waters who wrote the letters to the editor, and he'd never been contacted by police or Zodiac internet sleuths before speaking with me. To clarify, this George Waters was not the Zodiac suspect; he was a well-liked and prominent businessman in Napa who happened to share his name. He was also a member of numerous fraternal organizations and an avid supporter of local charities. No one looking into the Zodiac case took the time to investigate why an individual who shared a name with Vallejo's prime suspect in the Ferrin murders—and also lived in Napa County—was writing letters to the editor of the local newspaper. No one cared enough to follow up.

One final word on the investigation at Lake Berryessa: Sergeant Lynch of the Vallejo Police Department contacted a subject named Arthur Leigh Allen, who was a little over six feet tall and weighed about 250 pounds. He asked Allen a few questions to determine his whereabouts during the Lake Berryessa attack. Nothing came of the initial conversation, and Lynch even forgot what information prompted him to question Allen in the first place. Lynch told Robert Graysmith in *Zodiac Unmasked,* "I like him the least [as a suspect]. I was positive it wasn't Allen. The minute I looked at him, I said mentally that isn't Zodiac. I only typed in five or six lines on the report . . . Only in order to get Allen's name in."

His name would come up again. ⌖

CHAPTER 9: WHO IS SUSPECT ARTHUR LEIGH ALLEN?

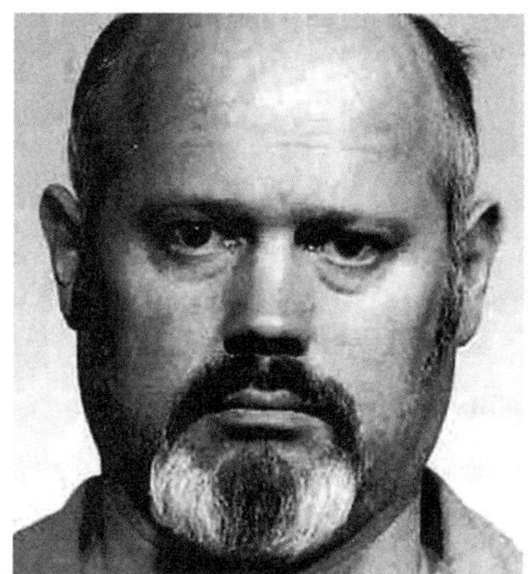

ARTHUR LEIGH ALLEN.
UNDATED FILE PHOTO.

IF YOU'VE EVER READ A BOOK ABOUT THE ZODIAC, visited a true-crime forum, or watched the movie, you know that Arthur Leigh Allen was considered the prime suspect by police. In fact, he was the only person ever officially named as a suspect in the Zodiac murders.

Arthur Leigh Allen has got to be one of the most "serial-killer-sounding" names of all time. He has three first names—and the middle one is *Leigh*. There's a theory called nominative determinism that suggests that people tend to fulfill the destiny of the names given to them, often gravitating towards jobs or hobbies that align. If you name your kid Storm Field or Amy Freeze, they'll likely be television meteorologists. If your son's name is Tyson Fury, he'll probably be a professional boxer. If you wanted your daughter to work a neon-lit pole at an '80s strip club, you'd name her Heather or Crystal. With a name like Arthur Leigh Allen, his destiny was sealed. One day, he was going to be sitting across a table from the cops, questioned about a series of serial killings.

Following the attack at Lake Berryessa, Napa and Vallejo cops, working together, looked for leads wherever they could find them. One of the leads that came up was the name Arthur Leigh Allen. Books and websites about the Zodiac case have a blind spot when it comes to the origins of Allen as a suspect. I knew that the Zodiac researcher Max Daley was able to get to the bottom of how Arthur Leigh Allen ended up on the police radar during his work on the film *Zodiac* and for a piece he wrote for *Vanity Fair.* Mr. Daley told me:

> **According to Bob Luce, Arthur Leigh Allen's boss in early 1969, he was the first person to report Allen as a potential Zodiac suspect in the first days of October 1969. Luce's identity as the first person to report Allen had been lost by 1971, and it was still unknown to detectives in 1991. Cut to 2007, when I was working as a researcher on the Paramount film, *Zodiac,* and I cold called Mr. Luce while trying to dig up information about all the cars Allen drove in 1969. It was during this call that Luce recounted for me how he'd reported Allen, and both of Luce's sons verified their father's story.**
>
> **Luce owned and operated an ARCO gas station on the northwest side of Vallejo, on the corner of Broadway and Nebraska Street, and this was where Allen had worked from approximately February to April of 1969. Allen was fired from the job because he'd repeatedly arrived late, sometimes drank on the job, but primarily because there had been numerous complaints from customers about the way Allen would leer at their young children.**
>
> **Five or six months after Allen was fired, in the days immediately following the September 27th attack at Lake Berryessa, a Vallejo Police Detective stopped by Luce's gas station. Given its location on the edge of town, right along the road leading up to Napa, the detective thought the attacker might have fueled up at Luce's station on his way up to the lake, so he asked Luce if any customers had come through on the day of the attack that fit the descriptions of the suspect and his vehicle.**
>
> **Luce was told the Lake Berryessa suspect was around 6 feet tall, and weighed roughly 225-250 pounds, and the suspect's vehicle had a track-width of "approximately 52 inches," which meant it was a very small car, and this car also had narrow tires that were mismatched in both size and tread pattern, and these treads were also very worn-down.**

> **"You've got this big guy," Luce said, "but he's driving this tiny car with poker-chip tires, and you don't often see big guys driving small cars, they're usually driving something like a full-sized sedan or truck, so a big person in a small car would stand out."**
>
> **None of Luce's customers came to mind, but his former employee, Arthur Leigh Allen, did cross his mind. This was because Allen was a big guy, 6 feet tall and around 240 pounds, and according to Luce, back in 1969, Allen drove a ramshackle, multi-colored, cobbled together Volkswagen Beetle, and those cars have a track-width of 52.5 inches and ride on narrow tires.**
>
> **"He was the only guy I knew who was that big, but drove a car that small," Luce added."**

This was a serious lead. Allen matched the description of the attacker at Lake Berryessa and his compact car with mismatched tires fit the description of the car associated with the crime. The Vallejo detective who talked to Luce relayed the information to his superiors and on October 6, 1969, Sergent Lynch of the Vallejo Police Department contacted Arthur Leigh Allen. According to Daley, "Days later, John Lynch interviewed Allen, this was on October 6th at the elementary school where Allen worked as a janitor. It appears Allen had driven a different car to work the day Lynch visited him, so unfortunately Lynch dismissed Allen as suspect. Lynch also failed to note in his report the name of the person and reason he was led to Allen." Lynch asked Allen a few questions to determine his whereabouts during the Lake Berryessa attack, but nothing came of the initial conversation.

Sergeant Lynch dropped the investigation into Arthur Leigh Allen before it even started. Lynch took one look at Allen, and told himself, "That isn't Zodiac," and that was the end of it. Allen told him that he had gone skin-diving the day before the Lake Berryessa attack and had spent the afternoon and evening at home in Vallejo on the day of. Lynch wrote that down, didn't follow up with the alibi witnesses, and forgot all about it. Lynch didn't even follow up on the initial tip that led him to Allen—he didn't ask to see Allen's Volkswagen or take measurements, photos, or tire impressions from the car to see if it matched the crime-scene evidence. It would have been nice if he had asked Allen, a former Navy man, if he owned a pair of Wing Walker boots, but he didn't do that either. He didn't even ask for his shoe size, which happened to be 10½, the same size as the boot print of interest at Lake Berryessa.

SGT. JOHN LYNCH. *VALLEJO TIMES-HERALD*, APRIL 4, 1972.

This is the same Sgt. John Lynch who dismissed George Waters, the man who broke into Darlene Ferrin's home, threatened to rape her, stalked her, whom she was "deathly afraid of," according to her family, and had a police record for beating women and violating orders of protection, as a suspect in her murder based on a flimsy alibi.

Lynch probably wasn't thinking about the Lake Berryessa leads—a small car with mismatched bald tires and a suspect around 240 pounds—as a guideline when talking to Allen. Lynch was likely thinking about the attacks his department was investigating in Vallejo when he dismissed Allen, since his ramshackle car didn't resemble the Impala or the blue sedan seen at the Lake Herman Road crime scene and the brown Corvair-type car from the Blue Rock Springs murder site. Allen's VW sure as hell fit in with the evidence at Lake Berryessa, but Lynch had a blind spot. He was looking for the Vallejo Zodiac, not the Napa County Zodiac.

To make matters worse, Lynch didn't bother asking if Allen had access to a brown Corvair, a description of the Zodiac's vehicle given by Mike Mageau and a lead developed by his own department. It turns out that Allen's friend Phillip later claimed he was trying to sell his brown Corvair and parked it with the key in its ignition, at Bob Luce's service station, where Allen worked.

It should come as no surprise that Lynch didn't inquire whether Allen drove an Impala or a blue sedan like the cars associated with the Lake Herman Road murders. Allen didn't have access to an Impala, but he owned a blue and white Ford, and he often drove his father's sky-blue Buick. Lynch completely dropped the ball with his initial investigation and Arthur Leigh Allen has been in Zodiac suspect limbo ever since. If Lynch had taken the lead a bit more seriously, he might have discovered he had a viable murder suspect, or he might have been able to clear Allen way back in 1969.

Allen didn't match the physical description of the shooter from Blue Rock Springs. Lynch was working with local bias, focused on finding a suspect that matched the description Michael Mageau had provided: "WMA, short, possible 5'8", was real heavy set, beefy build . . . not blubbery fat . . . 195 to 200 [lbs.] or maybe even larger . . . short curly hair, light brown almost blond . . . with a large face." But Allen was middle-aged, six feet even, bald, and extremely overweight. There was no way anyone would confuse a six-foot, 250-pound bald man with the short, heavyset man with a full head of curly hair described by Mageau. And that's why the top Zodiac suspect was blown off the first time police interviewed him.

This is the folly of trying to match one suspect to every Zodiac crime scene. Arthur Leigh Allen didn't do the murders at Lake Herman Road. Solano and Vallejo cops, including Sergeant Lynch, believed David Magris and another member of his drug gang did that one. And it's also clear that Arthur Leigh Allen wasn't the forty-something crew-cut guy with the horn-rimmed glasses from the San Francisco composite sketch. Officer Donald Fouke, a possible witness to the aftermath of the Presidio Heights Zodiac murder, laughed when shown a photo of Allen, saying the man he encountered in Presidio Heights was "100 pounds lighter than Allen." That said, Allen remains an intriguing suspect—but only for the Lake Berryessa murder.

If each Zodiac crime had been investigated as an individual case rather than as part of a serial, police could likely have solved some, or even all, of the murders.

Two years went by. Another confirmed Zodiac murder occurred, along with half a dozen (or more) other possible Zodiac-linked killings that were either claimed by the killer or reported in the news. A 1966 murder in Riverside was also attributed to the Zodiac, and a whole bunch of letters, supposedly from the killer, arrived at the newspapers. The cops were no closer to solving the case than they were on the day they first talked to Arthur Leigh Allen.

Then, in 1971, Allen's name came up again. Donald Lee Cheney, a former friend who had been close to Allen from 1962 until Cheney moved to Southern California in 1969, informed Manhattan Beach police that he had information about a possible Zodiac suspect. Cheney said that during a conversation on New Year's Day, Allen had talked about wanting to "kill couples at random," claimed he would "call himself Zodiac," and said he "would use a flashlight attached to his gun to aid hunting at night." He also said he'd like to try his hand at "shooting tires on the school bus and picking the little darlings off as they come bouncing out of the bus."

Every bit of this information provided by Cheney was found in Zodiac letters printed in the newspaper years earlier. Cheney just regurgitated the legend. He offered no specificity or insight into Allen apart from what was already floating around the news media. The Zodiac existed in the pages of the newspaper, not in real life. Cheney gave the police recycled information from a letter-writer they already knew to be a proven liar—someone who had taken credit for crimes he didn't commit and got details wrong when he boasted of his crimes. Life imitates art. The informant was (mis)quoting the crank letter-writer in what seemed to be more bullshit.

Cheney seemed to have an axe to grind and was determined to pin a crime on Allen. Before going to the Manhattan Beach police, Cheney had already approached the Pomona Police with his Allen-is-Zodiac story, only to be dismissed. Cheney's story also changed whenever new information came out that pointed away from Allen. When Allen's DNA was a bust, Cheney revised his story, claiming that Allen had asked him to lick envelopes and stamps because he didn't like the taste of the adhesive—that's why his DNA wasn't on the letters. When Allen's fingerprints didn't match, Cheney claimed he had asked him to leave a fingerprint on a ball of paraffin wax. When the handwriting didn't link Allen to the letters, Cheney's buddy Sandy Panzarella told police that Allen was ambidextrous and could write with both hands.

Allen's brother Ron, who used to live with Don Cheney, told Inspectors Toschi and Armstrong "that he had received a complaint from Cheney that his brother had made improper advances towards one of his children." This complaint happened in 1966 or 1967, which means Cheney stayed friends with a guy who he believed had inappropriate sexual contact with his daughter for years after the incident. This isn't just unreliable information; Cheney might have been floating the Allen-is-Zodiac story to police for revenge in an attempt to get Allen punished for an unrelated crime involving inappropriate sexual conduct between Allen and his daughter.

It's important to remember that everybody lies to the cops. Sometimes, they lie out of concern for their young daughter if they think something might have happened with their pedo friend. The Cheney lead was a shit lead, but at least it was something. The case had gone completely cold before Cheney came calling. The information prompted Sergeant Mulanax, Inspector Armstrong, and Inspector Toschi to pay Allen a visit at his place of employment, an oil refinery in Pinole, California.

The investigation picked up where Lynch had left off two years earlier, with police following up on some of the details Allen had provided. Allen

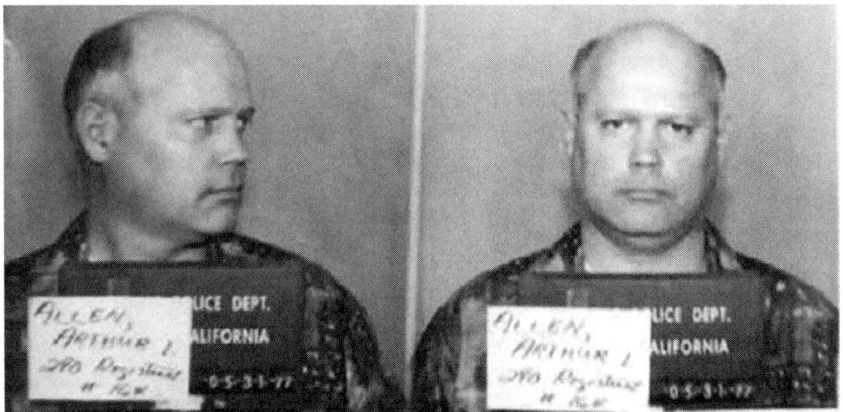

ARTHUR LEIGH ALLEN MUGSHOT. ATASCADERO STATE HOSPITAL, MAY 31, 1977.

claimed that on the day before the Lake Berryessa murder he got friendly with a serviceman stationed at Treasure Island and his wife on a diving trip. He said the couple could vouch that he was there, but he forgot the guy's name. He also mentioned that he had told Sergeant Lynch about his neighbor, an elderly man named William White, who could confirm that Allen had returned to Vallejo at around 4:00 p.m. on the day of the Lake Berryessa murder. But, oops—Allen told Toschi, Armstrong, and Mulanax that he had forgotten to inform Sergeant Lynch that White had died about a week after Lynch questioned him.

Then, without any prompting, as if he were trying to make himself seem more suspicious, Allen told cops, "The two knives that I had in my car with the blood on them, the blood came from a chicken that I had killed." The cops had never mentioned knives or blood.

The investigators then noticed that Allen was wearing a Zodiac brand diving watch with the same logo the Zodiac Killer signed his letters with. But this was not a rare watch—it was a model popular with divers in the '60s and '70s and Allen was a diver. The watch was a Christmas gift from his mother in 1967; his brother Ron got an identical Zodiac watch that Christmas.

Allen also told the investigators that he loved the short story "The Most Dangerous Game," which was referred to in a Zodiac letter and cipher. He eagerly volunteered that he had been in Riverside, California, around the time of the 1966 murder of Cheri Jo Bates—an incident that had been linked to the Zodiac during the time of Allen's questioning in 1971 but was later ruled out by Riverside police and no longer considered a Zodiac murder. Allen was

ZODIAC SEA WOLF WATCH AD. *THE HERALD-TIMES,* APRIL 26, 1972.

trying desperately to insert himself into the Zodiac legend.

What the "top suspect" in the Zodiac case gave the police was Zodiac information straight out of the media narrative. Allen didn't provide a single detail that hadn't already been supplied by the Zodiac-industrial complex. Half a century later, the whole thing seems absurd—Allen came off more like a Zodiac fan than a Zodiac suspect. But at the time the cops left the interview feeling as though they had just met the Zodiac Killer.

That may have been Allen's intention. Maybe Allen preferred to be thought of as the mastermind Zodiac Killer, the guy who outsmarted the cops, rather than what he really was—a sad, alcoholic child molester who lived in his mother's basement and couldn't hold down a job.

Cops continued their investigation of Allen. His criminal history was troubling. In 1958, Allen had been arrested for disturbing the peace after an incident involving a seventeen-year-old kid named Ralph Spinelli. According to Max Daley,

Arthur Leigh Allen and Ralph Spinelli crossed paths for the first time back in the early summer of 1958. Spinelli had just finished his junior year of high school, and Allen was 24 years old and in the Navy. The reason they met involved another Vallejo teen, Larry Bianci, who had heard Spinelli danced with his girlfriend at a party. Later that night, Bianci was driving around Vallejo looking for Spinelli so he could confront him about this dance, and along the way he ran into Allen, who then offered to serve as back-up during the fight. When Bianci confronted Spinelli at his home and things escalated, Allen kicked in the door to Spinelli's house while carrying a knife, and for this he was

> **later arrested by the Vallejo Police. Allen's parents became involved to help smooth things over for their son, and after they quickly paid for the Spinelli's replacement door and all the repair work, the Spinellis then agreed to drop charges. Allen's arrest, along the notation DP [Declined Prosecution], still appeared on his record. This was a lucky outcome for Allen, because if charges had been filed it would likely have meant a dishonorable discharge from the Navy.**

This is unhinged behavior from Allen. He was a grown man who knocked down a mobster's door and threatened his teenage son with a knife.

Allen served eight years in the Navy and was honorably discharged at the end of his contract, despite being court-martialed for bringing a loaded .45 caliber pistol onto the base at Treasure Island. His father—Ethan Allen, a living legend in the Navy who had run the dive-bomber program pivotal to winning the Battle of Midway—likely pulled some strings to clear that mess up. Allen was fired from a teaching job in Fairfield in 1962 for having a loaded gun on school grounds, then he was fired from his job as a teacher at Valley Springs Elementary School after allegations of child molestation in 1968. He lived one block from the International House of Pancakes, where Darlene Ferrin once worked, and about a ten-minute walk from the payphone the killer used after Darlene's murder.

After a year of looking at Allen as a suspect, cops got a warrant for his trailer in Santa Rosa. They executed the search and found nothing that tied Allen to the Zodiac murders or letters, but they did find a giant dildo, a bunch of porn, and a refrigerator full of dead squirrels. Cops also ran his fingerprints against the fingerprints associated with the Zodiac case they had on file—no match. Cops compared a sample of his handwriting to the Zodiac letters—no match.

Decades later, Allen's DNA was compared to what was believed at the time was a Zodiac DNA sample—no match. Allen was arrested again for child molestation in 1974 and sent to the Atascadero State Hospital for the Criminally Insane.

Handwriting analysis is junk science, and it's entirely possible that none of the fingerprints taken from the Zodiac crime scenes belonged to the killer. Maybe the killer wore gloves. As for comparing Allen's DNA to that associated with the Zodiac case in the 1990s and early 2000s—it was a botched job from the start. The lab tested a fake letter from 1978 and attempted to match Allen's palm print to the questionable 1974 "Exorcist" letter. Worse, the chain of custody was broken when two of the letters tested were kept as souvenirs in an SFPD cop's home instead of in a secure evidence locker. Plus, the lab tested the outside of the envelope, not under the flaps and stamps. It was a made-for-television mess.

All the "hard evidence," as well as an analysis of Allen's handwriting, indicated that Arthur Leigh Allen was not a match for any of it. Allen was dropped as a Zodiac suspect in 1972 and cops moved on.

In 1986, Robert Graysmith's book *Zodiac* became a sensation, sparking a renewed interest in the case. Graysmith, who was convinced that Arthur Leigh Allen was the Zodiac killer—he used the alias Bob Hall Starr in his book—presented a compelling, somewhat embellished, circumstantial case against him. The book brought Allen into the spotlight as a suspect with the public and the police.

Then, in late 1990, a half-assed wiseguy called Ralph Spinelli (the same Ralph Spinelli whom Allen got arrested for breaking down a door and attacking in 1958) found himself facing thirty years in prison for a series of armed robberies. Spinelli wasn't too keen on the prospect of a prison term that would end when he was eighty years old, and he was looking to deal.

Spinelli told cops he'd give them the name of the Zodiac if "some type of deal is made regarding his offenses." In 1991, Det. George Bawart, who had retired from the police force, was brought back by the Vallejo Police Department on a consultant's contract to investigate Zodiac leads. Bawart and Captain Conway, another Zodiac-era cop, were given a heads-up about this possible Zodiac informant.

They knew the fifty-year-old Spinelli from his family's organized-crime links in the strip-club and vending-machine business. The Spinellis weren't exactly the Gottis in New York, but in a place like Vallejo they passed for guys with mob ties. The real-deal Mafioso Jimmy Duardi lay low in Vallejo for a little over a decade from the early '50s to the early '60s after being linked to the murders of a Kansas City mob boss, a Mafia soldier, and a service-station attendant. Lying low for a guy like Duardi meant hijacking truckloads of liquor, running nightclubs, and stealing everything of value from Terry's Waffle Shop.[83] Young Ralph Spinelli looked up to the gangster and in turn Jimmy D. mentored the kid from Vallejo. Spinelli was a quick study and soon found himself as a member of Duardi's robbery crew and set himself up in the strip-club business, running the Crazy Horse Saloon in Fairfield.

When Bawart and Conway talked to Spinelli, he refused to give the name until all charges against him were dropped. They politely told him to go fuck himself because that wasn't happening, but they kept pressing him. Spinelli told them his mystery Zodiac man "said he was going to San Francisco [to] kill a cab driver. The next day or so, a cab driver was killed in San Francisco, and the Zodiac took credit for it."

Another informant with details straight out of the newspaper. No matter how hard they pressed, Spinelli wouldn't give a name without a deal. This went on for a month until Spinelli's lawyer Craig Kennedy called Captain Conway. "He indicated that the name given to him by Ralph Spinelli was Lee Allen." The Arthur Leigh Allen Zodiac investigation was back on, twenty years after it began.

Spinelli added one very important element to the Allen story: motive. According to Spinelli, Allen approached him at the Crazy Horse Saloon in October of 1969 asking for work as a hitman. Allen tried to impress the gangster by laying out his résumé as a cold-blooded killer. He told Spinelli he was responsible for the first four Zodiac murders and the letters to the newspapers. Allen allegedly told Spinelli that he invented the Zodiac character as a cover scheme to distract cops into looking for a madman killing strangers instead of him. This ruse would allow Allen to carry out targeted hits for Spinelli while Zodiac took the blame.

Spinelli didn't believe any of this nonsense and threw Allen out of his club. It was an absurd story from an absurd person with an absurd request. Allen returned and, to prove his bona fides, he told Spinelli he was going to kill a cab driver in San Francisco and make it look like a Zodiac crime. Paul Stine was murdered in San Francisco shortly after their meeting and the Zodiac wrote a letter to the *Chronicle* taking credit for the kill two days after the murder.

If this meeting ever actually happened, it makes me feel sad for Arthur Leigh Allen. Here he is, this overgrown man-child living in his mother's basement, unable to hold down a job because of drunkenness and child molestation, trying to impress a local dirtbag he got arrested for fighting a decade earlier, telling fantastical tales about how he's the Zodiac Killer, and begging to get hired as a hitman. It reeks of desperation. It reeks of naivety about how the underworld works, just like the high-school drug dealer Johnny Doyel telling David Magris that if somebody killed the vicious guard dog at the Dairy Farm, "the Mafia" might notice and hire them. It's one thing for a teenager to believe the fairy tale that mob bosses sit around reading the newspaper and just hire random psychos off the street based on particularly brazen crime stories in the paper, but it's something far more pathetic when a middle-aged man walks into a strip club and tells the gangster running the joint he's the Zodiac Killer for hire.

As interesting as Spinelli's story was, and as much as his mob ties glamorize the whole affair, he offered nothing of consequence that wasn't reported in the press or Graysmith's book to link Allen to the Zodiac murders. A well-crafted bullshit story is still bullshit. Spinelli offered all style and no substance. But it was compelling, and investigators ran with it.

The cops got another search warrant for Allen's property approved on February 13, 1991. Allen was present for this search. According to the Zodiac expert Michael Butterfield, "He [Allen] told investigators he was a 'nice guy,' although he did receive cruel pleasure from sadistic type pornography."[84]

The police found an audio tape that Allen claimed "was a tape in which he is spanking a young boy who was feigning pain."[85] He said he found it sexually stimulating.

They also found a bomb-making recipe, four pipe bombs, black powder, bottles of potassium nitrate and sulfur, a Ruger .22 revolver, a .22 pistol, a Ruger .44 Black Hawk, a Colt .32 automatic, a Marlin .22 rifle with scope, an Inland .30 caliber rifle, a Stevens Model 835 twelve-gauge double-barrel shotgun, a Winchester Model 50 twenty-gauge automatic shotgun, and a large hunting knife.

Allen's arsenal was wild, but nothing they found at his place could be linked to the Zodiac case. Cops already knew that Allen liked kids and guns—all they found was evidence of that. They could have arrested him for the weapons and bombs, since, as a convicted felon, that stuff was illegal for him to possess. California Penal Code 29800 prohibits felons from owning, possessing, or purchasing firearms. It applies to felonies committed in California, other states, or under federal law. But the cops didn't even bother taking him in for the weapons or the tape of the young boy being spanked. According to Max Daley, "in 1991, Allen was asked by Detective Bawart if he knew why he'd become a person of interest back in 1969, just after the attack at Lake Berryessa. Allen responded, 'Perhaps because I drove a Volkswagen with one blue fender and one green fender.' This comment about the Beetle was lost on Bawart at that time because there was no record in Lynch's report about Bob Luce's tip involving a ramshackle, multi-colored Beetle. When I read Allen's response to Bawart, it seemed clear to me that Allen suspected someone had seen his Beetle up at the lake on the day of the attack, and he suspected this was the reason he had been reported."

Bawart tracked down Michael Mageau, who had been on a two-decade-long drug and alcohol bender, and presented him with a photo lineup. The lineup was hardly legit. California photo lineup procedure dictates that "an identification procedure shall be composed so that the fillers generally fit the eyewitness' description of the perpetrator. In the case of a photo lineup, the photograph of the person suspected as the perpetrator should, if practicable, resemble his or her appearance at the time of the offense and not unduly stand out." One of the photos was an obvious mug shot—cops aren't supposed to use those. Another photo is of an old man. Another one looks like it's from the 1940s. Some of the guys were skinny. The men didn't look similar at all. Allen was the only one with a round face, and the photo of Allen was much brighter and higher quality than the other five. Like a magician influencing a mark to pick a card, Bawart got Mageau to pick Allen out of the lineup. Mageau said he was "pretty sure" because "the guy responsible had a round face."

Allen was surveilled for months and questioned multiple times by Vallejo police following the search warrant. He cooperated with them, yet they got nothing. Allen's story made it to the newspapers and television news, and he appeared on tabloid programs proclaiming his innocence. On August 26, 1992, fifty-eight-year-old Arthur Leigh Allen was found on the floor in the basement of his mother's house, dead from natural causes linked to atherosclerotic heart disease and diabetic kidney failure, according to the coroner's report.

Not one single piece of credible evidence links Arthur Leigh Allen to the Zodiac murders or Zodiac letters. The Zodiac is bullshit, and Allen was a bullshit Zodiac suspect. Allen might have actually had something to do with the murder at Lake Berryessa but, because Sergeant Lynch didn't take the Allen tip seriously in 1969, no one investigated him or his connection to the Lake Berryessa murder properly.

Still, the police and the public just can't let him go. In 2018, a Vallejo police detective named Terry Poyser was working on the Zodiac as a fifty-year-old cold case leveraging DNA evidence. Vallejo P.D. still had three of the original 1969 Zodiac letters—sent to the *Chronicle, Examiner, and Vallejo Times-Herald*—as well as two of the envelopes from the letters in their evidence locker. Meanwhile, the SFPD had effectively stopped working the Zodiac case in 2004, and Solano County seemed to have given up on the matter as far back as 1970. The FBI was never even officially on the case—they assisted only when directly asked for help running a suspect's prints and providing background information for investigative agencies. For decades, no one in an official capacity had been actively pursuing the case—until Detective Poyser submitted the envelopes to a private lab for DNA testing, hoping to obtain a profile from under the envelope flaps and stamps.

According to the *Sacramento Bee,* "Poyser said he believes the Zodiac Killer is no longer alive. Arthur Leigh Allen, a former elementary school teacher and convicted child molester who lived in Vallejo, was considered a top suspect. Allen died in 1992 at the age of 58. . . . 'Our Vallejo suspect is probably still the best lead,' Poyser said of Allen. 'There are probably 30 different circumstantial things that point to him. . . . He was extremely intelligent but a deviant dude.' . . . Even if Allen doesn't prove to be the Zodiac, Poyser said he believes it was someone familiar with Vallejo, and perhaps with a law enforcement or military background."[86]

Nothing came of the DNA testing.

And yet, in 2024, Netflix released a documentary called *This Is the Zodiac Speaking* that focused on Allen as a suspect. Apparently, for the Zodiac-industrial complex, there's still milk to be squeezed out of that cash cow, Arthur Leigh Allen.

CHAPTER 10: DEATH IN PRESIDIO HEIGHTS

ON OCTOBER 11, 1969—JUST TWO MONTHS AND TWO days after the Manson Family's brutal Helter Skelter spree spooked Los Angeles, marking the last gasp of the idealized peace-and-love spirit of the '60s counterculture with the murders of actress Sharon Tate, her unborn child, and four non-celebrities—a twenty-nine-year-old taxi driver named Paul Lee Stine was shot and killed inside his cab. The crime happened on the northeast corner of Washington and Cherry Streets in the wealthy Presidio Heights neighborhood of San Francisco. A few hours after Paul Stine's murder, Charles Manson was arrested at Barker Ranch in Death Valley.

At first glance, the cases don't have much in common. Paul wasn't rich or glamorous—he was a San Francisco State College graduate student, just three months shy of earning a Ph.D. in English. He drove a cab from 9:00 p.m. until 5:00 a.m. to pay the bills. But Paul Stine and Sharon Tate are forever linked for one reason: their murders were attributed to two of the late 1960s' most notorious monsters.

Driving a cab was a dangerous job. Eleven days earlier, another cabbie named Paul—Paul Hom—had been robbed at gunpoint and forced into the trunk of his cab in the Presidio, a park and U.S. Army post a short distance from where Paul Stine met his demise. Paul's murder didn't get its first brush with Hollywood until a media-savvy cop, Inspector David Toschi, arrived on the scene as the lead investigator. The Hollywood legend Steve McQueen used Toschi's style and swagger as inspiration for his character in the film *Bullit*. The big-time murder

PAUL STINE.
VENTURA COUNTY STAR,
OCTOBER 19, 1969.

cop caught a small-time case. Paul's story was cut and dried—a cabbie picked up a fare and the rider pulled a gun before robbing him of a couple of bucks and putting a bullet in him.

Fortunately, there were witnesses—though, unfortunately, they were children. Lindsay Robbins (sixteen), Rebecca Robbins (fourteen), and their thirteen-year-old brother Trevor spotted suspicious activity. Even more unfortunately for investigators, the Robbins kids didn't witness the murder or even hear a gunshot. They did, however, see a man in the front seat of Paul's cab, rooting through his pockets while the driver's body was slumped on his lap. The children watched as the man wiped down the interior of the cab with a rag or handkerchief and exited the cab through the passenger door. He then walked to the driver's side and wiped down the exterior of the door before calmly walking away, north on Cherry Street towards the Presidio.

The Robbins kids described the suspect as a white male in his early forties with a reddish-blond crew cut. He wore eyeglasses, dark brown trousers, a parka, and dark shoes. This version of the Zodiac was different from the others—the physical descriptions were not a match to the earlier eyewitness accounts. This clearly wasn't the 225-250-pound man dressed like an executioner with dark, greasy hair peeking out of his hood who attacked Bryan Hartnell at Lake Berryessa. It also wasn't the short, fat-faced guy with curly brown hair between twenty-six to thirty years old who shot Mike Mageau and Darlene Ferrin at Blue Rock Springs. This Zodiac was much older than the Blue Rock Springs Zodiac. He was between thirty-five and sixty pounds lighter than the Zodiac in the Halloween costume at Lake Berryessa, and he didn't use a knife. This Zodiac, unlike all the others, robbed his victim of his wallet. This Zodiac, unlike all the others, attacked a solo man, not a couple. This Zodiac, unlike all the others, struck in a major city, not in a secluded lover's lane in the North Bay.

The Presidio Heights crime scene was confusing. A smeared bloody partial fingerprint was found on the exterior of the cab between the driver's-side front and back doors—a strange place for a killer to leave his mark, especially since witnesses saw him exit through the passenger side and wipe down the driver's side. The print could have belonged to the killer, but it could just as easily have been left by a cop, an EMT, or a concerned passer-by checking on Paul. It could have even come from one of the kids who called the police. Lindsay Robbins, one of the young witnesses, claimed to have followed the perp to the corner of Cherry Street and watched the killer stroll to the intersection of Jackson and Cherry. If Lindsay was the kind of kid who'd follow a suspect, wouldn't it make sense that he'd be the kind of kid to check on the victim and attempt to render aid? Did Lindsay peek inside the cab and inadvertently leave a bloody print on the driver's side? The Zodiac expert Tom Voigt reported that, according to Lindsay's son Patrick, that's exactly what happened.[87]

When the police arrived, the situation quickly devolved. Officers Armand Pelissetti and Frank Peda were the first on scene. Pelissetti responded to an assault-in-progress call and came upon a murder. Pelissetti was told the direction of flight of the suspect. Instead of following in his patrol car, he chose to pursue on foot. The suspect had about a forty-second head start, but Pelissetti was careful not to blindly give chase as though he were in *Mission: Impossible*. The shooter was armed and dangerous and had already shot one man to death. Pelissetti approached cautiously and by the book in case the killer was lying in wait. The guy got away. Pelissetti returned to the witnesses, got a description, and put it over the radio. This prompted additional units to flood the area in search of the killer. An ambulance arrived, plus K-9 units and a fire-department spotlight.

Meanwhile, moments before Pelissetti's radio transmission, Officers Donald Fouke and Eric Zelms were two blocks from the crime scene when they spotted a white male walking east on Jackson Street, near the intersection of Maple. The man more or less matched the description given by the Robbins kids. He was walking alone before he may have dipped into the doorway of a house (Fouke's story changed almost every time he told it). So why didn't they stop and question him? In the documentary film *This Is the Zodiac Speaking,* Officer Fouke claimed they hadn't yet received the witnesses' description: "The initial radio description of the suspect was that of a Black male, five-foot-ten or something like that," he said. "Seeing that it was a white male in an affluent neighborhood walking alone along a street, we didn't think it was a suspect. So, we proceeded to the next block."

Fouke's claim that the initial radio dispatch indicated a Black male suspect has never been substantiated by an official record independent of

WANTED

SAN FRANCISCO POLICE DEPARTMENT

NO. 90-69 | WANTED FOR MURDER | OCTOBER 18, 1969

ORIGINAL DRAWING

AMENDED DRAWING

Supplementing our Bulletin 87-69 of October 13, 1969. Additional information has developed the above amended drawing of murder suspect known as "ZODIAC".

WMA, 35-45 Years, approximately 5'8", Heavy Build, Short Brown Hair, possibly with Red Tint, Wears Glasses. Armed with 9 MM Automatic.

Available for comparison: Slugs, Casings, Latents, Handwriting.

ANY INFORMATION:
Inspectors Armstrong & Toschi
Homicide Detail
CASE NO. 696314

THOMAS J. CAHILL
CHIEF OF POLICE

ZODIAC WANTED POSTER.
SAN FRANCISCO POLICE DEPARTMENT, OCTOBER 18, 1969.

Fouke's intradepartmental memo to Toschi and Armstrong a month after the fact. Is it possible that Fouke just assumed that the suspect was a Black man because of bias, and that that's why he didn't view the middle-aged white man walking down the street in a rich neighborhood suspiciously? Isn't that the gist of what he told David Fincher's documentary crew? Fouke thought the white guy walking in Presidio Heights looked like he belonged in an affluent neighborhood. Fouke didn't think the guy looked like a criminal and allowed him to walk away. Fouke might have heard a taxi robbery call come over the radio and assumed the perp was a Black man. There's no record of a radio transmission indicating the suspect was a Black man. There is no record of an incorrect description in Officer Pelissetti's incident report. That may have happened in Fouke's imagination. Paul Stine's murderer may have casually walked by two cops rushing to the scene because one of those cops assumed crimes like taxi robberies weren't committed by average-looking white men.

On the next block, Fouke and Zelms crossed paths with Pelissetti. According to Fouke, they informed him that they had seen a white guy, not the suspect they were originally looking for. At that point, Fouke claims Pelissetti gave them a revised description of the suspect, as provided by the Robbins kids. But none of this appears in Pelissetti's report on the Stine murder. There was no mention of the wrong description coming from dispatch, no record of Pelissetti correcting the error and issuing a revised description over the radio, and no documentation of his encounter with Fouke and Zelms. Decades later, in the 2007 documentary *This Is the Zodiac Speaking,* Pelissetti stated that Fouke "did not mention to me that he has seen anybody at that point or had stopped anybody."[88]

It's fairly obvious that Pelissetti, in cop parlance, "did the right thing" by Fouke and Zelms. In corroborating Fouke's story of dispatch putting out an incorrect description of a Black male suspect, he saved them the embarrassment of being the guys who let the Zodiac Killer walk away because of racial bias.

Two days after his death, Paul Stine's murder became a Zodiac case when the following letter, accompanied by a bloody piece of Stine's shirt, was sent to the *San Francisco Chronicle*:

This is the Zodiac speaking.

I am the murderer of the taxi driver over by Washington St + Maple St last night, to prove this here is a blood stained piece of his shirt. I am the same man who did in the people in the north bay area.

The S.F. Police could have caught me last night if they had searched the park properly instead of holding road races with their motorcicles seeing who could make the most noise. The car drivers should have just parked their cars and sat there quietly waiting for me to come out of cover.

> School children make nice targets, I think I shall wipe out a school bus some morning. Just shoot out the front tire + then pick off the kiddies as they come bouncing out.

The Zodiac was threatening to kill kids coming off a school bus. Things had escalated. Officials kept this news quiet initially, not wanting to cause a widespread public panic, but people began to notice armed officers riding on school buses, police cars providing escorts, and helicopters hovering overhead. The news broke and people were justifiably terrified. The Zodiac had finally figured out a way for the public at large to notice him. He never did shoot any children on school buses. Another letter, another lie.

If the bloody shirt belonged to Paul Stine, it would be the first time a piece of evidence could tie a Zodiac letter and a Zodiac crime scene together. This had investigative merit.

Someone had cut a large rectangular piece out of the back of Paul's shirt. Despite the obvious missing fabric, every single police officer and EMT who encountered Stine's body, Deputies Schultz and Kindred from the Coroner's Office who took possession of Stine's body, the coroner who declared him dead, and the medical examiner who carefully examined his belongings as part of the autopsy and found $4.12 in change (that wasn't mentioned in Pelissetti's report) on his person, all somehow failed to notice the big hole in his shirt. The coroner who was required to examine Stine's clothing as part of a postmortem didn't note anything irregular about the shirt. The officers who vouchered Stine's personal property somehow missed it too. Then, from that missing rectangle, the Zodiac mailed a piece of Paul's bloody shirt to the *San Francisco Chronicle*—and the SFPD tested it and confirmed it was part of Stine's shirt and the blood matched Stine's blood type.

It wasn't until Toschi opened the evidence bag containing Paul's shirt that it became apparent that someone had tampered with it, and worse still, no official report or personal account reflects that anyone noticed until the Zodiac letter arrived. It's almost impossible to believe that all those experienced professionals, including those who interacted with his shirt as part of their job, could have missed a gaping hole. The logical, yet cynical, conclusion is that the shirt was tampered with after it was in evidence.

The Zodiac mailed in another piece of the shirt three weeks later, along with another letter to the *Chronicle*:

This is the Zodiac speaking

Up to the end of Oct I have killed 7 people. I have grown rather angry with the police for their telling lies about me. So I shall change the way the collecting of slaves. I shall no longer announce to anyone. When I comitt my murders, they shall look like routine robberies, killings of anger, + a few fake accidents, etc.

The police shall never catch me, because I have been too clever for them.

1. I look like the description passed out only when I do my thing, the rest of the time I look entirle different. I shall not tell you what my descise consists of when I kill.
2. As of yet I have left no fingerprints behind me contrary to what the police say in my killings I wear transparent finger tip guards. All it is is 2 coats of airplane cement coated on my finger tips—quite unnoticible + very efective.
3. My killing tools have been bought through the mail-order outfits before the ban went into effect. Except for one + it was bought out of the state.

So as you can see the police don't have much to work on. If you wonder why I was wipeing the cab down I was leaving fake clews for the police to run all over town with, as one might say, I gave the cops som bussy work to do to keep them happy. I enjoy needling the blue pigs. Hey blue pig I was in the park—you were useing fire trucks to mask the sound of your cruzeing prowl cars. The dogs never came with in 2 blocks of me + they were to the west + there was only 2 groups of parking about 10 min apart then the motor cicles went by about 150 ft away going from south to north west.

Must print in paperps. 2 cops pulled a goof abot 3 min after I left the cab. I was walking down the hill to the park when this cop car pulled up + one of them called me over + asked if I saw anyone acting suspicious or strange in the last 5 to 10 min + I said yes there was this man who was runnig by waveing a gun + the cops peeled rubber + went around the corner as I directed them + I disappeared into the park a block + a half away never to be seen again.

Hey pig doesnt it rile you up to have your noze rubed in your booboos?

If you cops think I'm going to take on a bus the way I stated I was, you deserve to have holes in your heads.

Take one bag of ammonium nitrate fertilizer + 1 gal of stove oil + dump a few bags of gravel on top + then set the shit off + will positivily ventalate any thing that should be in the way of the blast.

The death machine is all ready made. I would have sent you pictures but you would be nasty enough to trace them back to developer + then to me, so I shall describe my masterpiece to you. The nice part of it is all the parts can be bought on the open market with no questions asked.

- 1 bat. pow clock—will run for aprox 1 year
- 1 photoelectric switch
- 2 copper leaf springs
- 2 6V car bat
- 1 flash light bulb + reflector
- 1 mirror
- 2 18″ cardboard tubes black with shoe polish in side +
- the system checks out from one end to the other in my tests. What you do not know is whether the death machine is at the sight or whether it is being stored in my basement for future use. I think you do not have the manpower to stop this one by continually searching the road sides looking for this thing. + it wont do to re roat + re schedule the busses because the bomb can be adapted to new conditions.

Have fun!! By the way it could be rather messy if you try to bluff me.

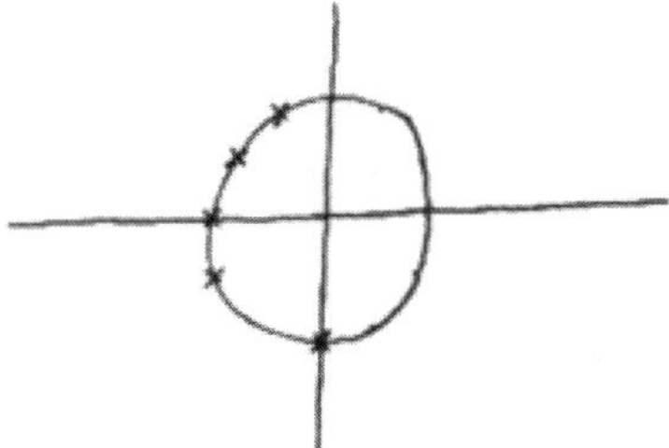

PS. Be shure to print the part I marked out on page 3 or I shall do my thing.

To prove that I am the Zodiac, Ask the Vallejo cop about my electric gun sight which I used to start my collecting of slaves.

Zodiac must have enjoyed the fear his letter threatening the schoolchildren caused. In this letter, he threatened to detonate an ammonium nitrate bomb. He never did that either. Another letter, another lie.

Two days after the Zodiac letter that said, "2 cops pulled a goof," Officer Fouke wrote an intradepartmental memo to Toschi and Armstrong about the night of the Presidio Heights murder:

> **I respectfully wish to report, that while responding to the area of Cherry and Washington Streets a suspect fitting the description of the Zodiac killer was observed walking in an easterly direction on Jackson Street and then turn north on Maple Street. This subject was not stopped as the description received from communications was that of a negro male. When the right description was broadcast reporting officer informed communications that a possible suspect has been seen going north on Maple Street into the Presidio, the area of Julius Kahn playground and a search was started which had negative results. The suspect observed by Officer Fouke was a WMA [white male adult] 35-45 Yrs., about 5'10", 180-200 lbs., Medium-heavy build, barrel-chested, light colored hair possibly greying in rear (may have been lighting that caused this effect), crew cut, wearing glasses, dressed in dark blue waist length zipper type jacket (navy or royal blue) elastic cuffs and waistband, zipped part of the way up. Brown wool pants, pleated type, baggy in rear (Rust brown). May have been wearing low cut shoes. Subject at no time appeared to be in a hurry walked with a shuffling lope. Slightly bent forward head down. The subject's general appearance to classify him as a group would be that he might be of Welsh ancestry.**

Sometimes, even the cops lie to the cops.

Fouke's account of his encounter with the barrel-chested Welshman didn't come until a month after Paul was murdered, and it might be the most cover-your-ass cop memo in the history of cover-your-ass cop memos. It came as a direct reaction to the Zodiac calling out Fouke and Zelms for letting him get away. Fouke even busted out the "blame the Black guy" trope.

Unless Fouke had a photographic memory, the level of detail in the memo is absurd. For us to believe that Fouke's written recollection was sincere, we'd have to believe that, on a hot call while looking for a Black assailant, he drove past a white dude at around forty miles per hour and remembered all those details.

Somehow, this brief encounter left such an impression on Fouke that he could guess his ethnicity and recall, with total accuracy, what he was wearing and how he walked. He was able to preserve this information in the front of his mind for a full month. All this, even though, as a busy SFPD officer in a sector car, he'd likely had hundreds of similar encounters since then.

The Zodiac was leading the SFPD around by the nose. Fouke's memo was a direct reaction to the Zodiac letter. The letter-writer was manipulating the situation and the SFPD was scrambling to regain some sense of authority by producing ridiculous interdepartmental memos.

Luckily for everyone, the homicide super-cop Inspector Toschi was on the case, though he made some unusual investigative choices. Instead of using a trained sketch artist, he relied on a random San Francisco cop named Juan Morales to talk to the child witnesses and nail down a composite sketch of the man they had seen in Paul's cab after the murder. Toschi never bothered to speak with the witnesses himself—he didn't interview the Robbins kids.

According to Fouke, Toschi never talked to him either. On October 13, 1969, the sketch was released and cops distributed it to local cab companies and drivers. At that point, they were searching for a perp who committed gunpoint robberies of cabbies and murdered Paul Stine. The wanted poster gave the case number for the robbery of that other Paul—Paul Hom—meaning the cops believed the cases were connected. It presented a description of a suspect who was a confusing mix between Paul Hom's robber and Paul Stine's killer.

The cases were similar but certainly not identical. The details of Hom's case are as follows. On September 30, 1969, eleven days before Paul Stine was murdered, Paul Hom picked up in his yellow cab a passenger he believed to be a cook or restaurant service worker from the cab line at the Fairmont Hotel, the same general area where Stine was later to pick up the Zodiac. The passenger sat in the front seat, just like the man spotted by the Robbins kids in the front seat of Stine's cab on the night he was murdered. Hom's passenger asked to be taken to one location in Presidio Heights (Washington and Locust Streets), then changed his mind at the last minute and requested to be taken to another spot nearby, into the Presidio, saying, "My girl left my car there." According to Paul Stine's trip sheet, his passenger also asked to go to one location (Washington and Maple Streets) but ended up at another (Washington and Cherry Streets). Once inside the gate of the Presidio, Hom's passenger pulled out a revolver, ordered the cabbie to stop, and robbed him. Then he forced the cabbie into the trunk of his car and locked him inside.

Hom described his robber as a white man in his twenties, around five-foot-nine, weighing between 130 and 140 pounds, with dark hair, wearing a blue denim jacket and dark trousers. When Hom saw the composite drawing from Paul Stine's murder, he said his robber was thinner than the man in the drawing and didn't wear glasses. Capt. Martin Lee of the SFPD believed that Hom's robber and Stine's killer were the same guy. Lee, not the most politically correct of officers, suggested that Hom, an Asian man, was unable to tell white people apart because "all Occidentals look the same to an Oriental." This, according to Lee, is why Hom couldn't match the perp to the sketch. Oof.

With his involvement in the Paul Stine murder, Toschi finally found himself at the center of the action. San Francisco's super-cop was ready to do battle with the Zodiac, the Bay Area supervillain. Toschi and the Zodiac made the big time together—the case of the quirky letter-writing killer in the North Bay was local news, but when the Zodiac landed in San Francisco, he became a national news story. The papers of record on both coasts, the *New York Times* and the *Los Angeles Times,* covered the story.

With a couple of letters to the newspaper and a piece of the victim's bloody shirt, Paul Stine's murder was no longer being investigated as a taxi robbery turned murder. Now, the cops were chasing the Zodiac Killer.

Even after Paul's murder became a high-profile media case, Toschi didn't deign to speak to the witnesses or find a proper sketch artist. He was way too sharp of an investigator for this negligence to make sense. Instead of investigating Paul's death, Toschi and Armstrong drove to Napa County and consulted with cops from Vallejo, Napa County, and the California DOJ to learn about Zodiac. Just as in the Cecelia Shepard murder case, once the Zodiac connection was made in the Paul Stine case, the investigation and all the early leads were dropped for Zodiac fairy tales. Toschi wasn't looking for a homicidal taxi bandit anymore, he was chasing the Zodiac. When Toschi returned to San Francisco he flooded the FBI with fingerprints and handwriting samples from

INSPECTORS TOSCHI AND ARMSTRONG. *DAILY ITEM*, FEBRUARY 8, 2007.

the city's usual creeps and weirdos, looking for a match. The FBI had thirty-eight different prints on file from the Zodiac crime scenes, but not a single print was present at multiple Zodiac crime scenes. The feds pulled fingerprints from the letters, but none of the prints associated with the letters matched any prints from the crime scenes either. Toschi was very interested in a possible link between the celebrity Manson murders in Los Angeles and the Zodiac murders in the Bay Area. He had every male member of the Manson Family checked out and had their prints and handwriting compared to the evidence he was working with. None of them matched his Zodiac evidence.

While Toschi waited for print and handwriting matches and Manson links, the cabbie killings continued. There was a serial offender robbing cabbies at gunpoint and shooting them in low-crime Presidio Heights. On January 25, 1970, Charles Jarman was robbed, shot in the head, and murdered in his yellow cab on a Presidio Heights street—just nine blocks from the spot where Paul Stine had been robbed, shot in the head, and killed in his cab on October 11, 1969.

Toschi and Armstrong, two inspectors who couldn't find a Jew in Jerusalem when it came to Paul Stine's murder, were somehow able to perform a miraculous feat of exceptional police work in the Jarman case. Toschi had a hunch to check for fingerprints on a crumpled-up letter in Jarman's pocket. He rushed the letter to the crime lab where Inspectors Kirkendall and Wright immediately recognized a match—by sight, without the aid of computers—between the fingerprint on the letter and one belonging to a man arrested by the SFPD on January 12th for drug charges. That man was Robert Bromell, a twenty-two-year-old busboy and addict, living at 610 Geary Street, just two blocks from where Paul Stine picked up his murderer.

Bromell was booked on robbery and murder charges. His twenty-year-old girlfriend Anita Runyan was arrested with him on a warrant from a Mickey Mouse marijuana arrest. Toschi and Armstrong bent the truth to convince Bromell that his girlfriend was being charged as an accomplice in the Charles Jarman murder. They offered Bromell a deal: they'd let his girlfriend go, free and clear, if he owned up to the cabbie's murder. Minutes later, he confessed to the taxi robbery, saying that an accidental gun discharge led to the death of Jarman. His motive? He was $23 short on rent, and Runyan was hassling him.

Toschi and Armstrong cracked the case with remarkable speed—they followed a hunch, found evidence, arrested the perp, got a confession, and closed the case within a matter of hours. Impressive. Especially since this was the same Toschi who never had never spoken to the witnesses in the Paul Stine case. The same Toschi who had sent a patrol cop instead of a trained sketch artist to get the composite drawing. The same Toschi who had failed to order elimination prints taken from the witnesses seen by the first responding officer near Paul Stine's cab. The same Toschi who hadn't sent a sketch artist to draw the possible Zodiac suspect Officer Fouke encountered. The same Toschi who, according to Fouke, had never even asked him about the suspect he'd seen. Where was this investigative energy and competence when it came to the Stine murder?

If Bromell believed that taking a cab to a quiet, upscale part of the city and robbing the driver at gunpoint was a reasonable way to make a few bucks, he should have been a suspect worthy of investigating for Paul Stine's robbery-turned-murder. Bromell had arrived in San Francisco in the fall of 1969, after abandoning his wife and six-month-old child back in Pendleton, Oregon. That timing coincides with the start of a series of gunpoint taxi robberies which began at hotels in the theater district and ended near the Presidio.

Robert Bromell's robbery and murder of Jarman mirrors the gunpoint robberies of Paul Stine and Paul Hom. The similarities in the three crimes are impossible to overlook. Not only does it look like a pattern of crimes committed by the same criminal, but Bromell fits the description of Hom's robber. He was, in fact, a restaurant worker, and likely responsible for that crime, but he's probably not the man in the sketch from the Paul Stine murder.

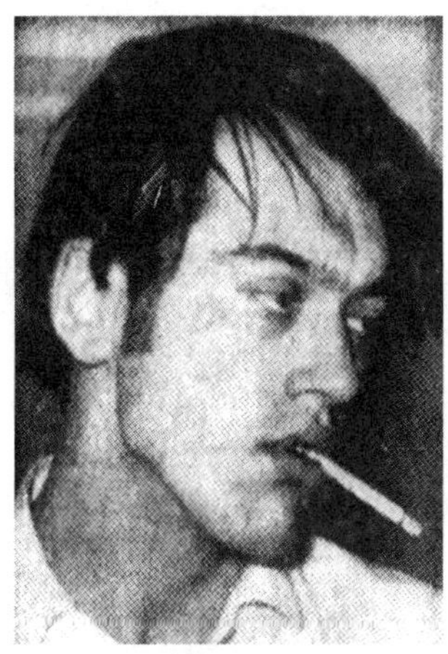

ROBERT BROMELL.
SAN FRANCISCO EXAMINER,
JANUARY 29, 1970.

Still, the Robbins kids didn't witness Paul Stine's actual murder. They only saw a man sitting in the front seat of Paul's cab, going through his pockets, and propping his body up. The children initially believed Paul was drunk and the other man was helping him. They thought they were watching some comedic street theater. They also saw the man wiping down the area near the door handle. As for whether they saw the killer, it's possible that the older man with a crew cut and glasses was a good Samaritan trying to help Paul. He could have been a criminal opportunist trying to roll a corpse for a few bucks. They didn't witness a killing. They didn't hear a gunshot. In fact, no one in the area reported a gunshot.

Was the Zodiac-style murder of Charles Jarman committed by the same man who killed Paul Stine and robbed Paul Hom at gunpoint? The cases were understandably linked in the news media. The *Los Angeles Times* picked the story up and put it on the front page. The *Times* went big on the Zodiac links. They mentioned that, oddly, four men's shirts were found in the vicinity of the crime.[89] Before police even had a suspect, Inspector Armstrong told the *Oakland Tribune* on January 26, 1970, that he didn't believe the Jarman case was the work of Zodiac—but "there is always a possibility." Toschi was quick to tell the press that, although the cases were eerily similar, there was a major difference: Jarman's shirt hadn't been ripped. Toschi said this as though the Zodiac ripped every one of his victim's shirts and that was some kind of signature. Toschi knew better.

The day after Armstrong's comment to the *Tribune,* Toschi requested that the FBI compare Bromell's handwriting from his 1965 Army enlistment forms to the Zodiac letters. No match. Of course not. Bromell wasn't the Zodiac Killer from the North Bay—he was neither clever nor sober enough to write cryptograms and taunting letters. He was a dope fiend who had lived in Oregon during most of the Zodiac murders. Toschi knew this. While Bromell seemed like the right guy for Paul Stine's murder, he was clearly not the man behind the Faraday, Jensen, Ferrin, and Shepard murders. Toschi knew that better than anybody. So why go through this dog and pony show with handwriting analysis? Why bother clearing Bromell as a Zodiac suspect without narrowing the investigation into Paul Stine's murder independently of the Zodiac killings? The news media were starting to buzz that Toschi and Armstrong had caught the Zodiac Killer.

Toschi and Armstrong got Bromell's confession for the Jarman murder in minutes—so why not hang around a little bit longer and see if he could get him to talk about Paul Stine? It's inexplicable that they had this guy admitting to killing Jarman and didn't press him about the Stine murder or the Hom robbery. His description is a perfect match for the one Hom gave the police. This was a Les Lundblad–level fumble. Toschi and Armstrong were top-notch investigators. Robert Bromell was jonesing for a fix and badly overmatched by the detectives. It took a couple of minutes for Bromell's "accidental discharge" story to become "it was no accident, I shot that son of a bitch."[90] The detectives could have squeezed another couple of confessions out of Bromell and closed the Stine and Hom cases in the time it took to drink a cup of coffee. They chose not to. They had the guy, and he was folding under pressure. Did Toschi even care to solve the Paul Stine murder if it wasn't the work of the Zodiac?

If Bromell—a drugged-out transient just looking for a few bucks to score a fix—and not Charles Manson, Tex Watson, or the Zodiac, went down for Stine, it would no longer be a high-profile case and Toschi would no longer be heading the Zodiac investigation. The media would move on. The Zodiac would be proven to be a liar again. Inspector Toschi, who was enjoying the publicity, would have to move on to the nameless, faceless grind of San Francisco homicide, away from the spotlight.

Robert Bromell was a bad dude. According to his polar opposite half-brother Dale, a successful businessman and author, Robert "was a menace. He was a juvenile delinquent from the time he was in diapers on a tricycle." Robert was able to avoid a death sentence when he pled guilty for the Jarman murder and was sentenced to life with the possibility of parole. He was paroled in 1986 after serving sixteen years, and shortly after he was released he held up a liquor store with a knife. Robert told his brother he didn't think it was a big enough deal to get sent back to prison for. It was only a knife, and he didn't even kill the guy. Robert was in and out of prison until December 14, 1999, when he died of a drug overdose in Stockton, California.

At that time, the SFPD publicly believed the bloody partial print found on the cab belonged to the Zodiac. It was a smudged, low-quality print, but somehow Undersheriff Tom Johnson from Napa County jumped to a wild conclusion that based on preliminary analysis it appeared to the untrained eye to match a print from Lake Berryessa. Johnson announced this to the press, then quickly walked it back by telling them a day later that experts hadn't verified the print match yet. Two days after the initial announcement of the print match, Johnson told reporters the prints weren't complete enough for an identification of the killer and dropped the print-match angle.[91] The FBI assisted by comparing the partial print with thousands of persons of interest in the Zodiac case. Like every other suspect, Bromell was cleared when his fingerprints didn't match the bloody print. In the years since, that bloody print appears to be less than a sure thing. Investigators, including Inspector Armstrong, have expressed doubt that the print belonged to the Zodiac at all. In 2001, Inspectors Kelly Carroll and Michael Maloney, working Zodiac as a cold case for the SFPD, reinvestigated Arthur Leigh Allen as a suspect in the Paul Stine murder. Allen's prints did not match the bloody print or any of the twenty-nine other fingerprints found in Stine's car. These were sharp, twenty-first-century detectives. If they were looking at Allen after knowing his prints weren't a match, they must have known that the prints weren't considered a slamdunk anymore by police.

CHAPTER 11: THE DEVIL AND DAVID TOSCHI– FROM DIRTY HARRY TO DIRTY COP

Toschi: If the letter is a fake, I'm Zodiac.
—*San Francisco Examiner,* July 14, 1978

SFPD Chief Charles Gain called Toschi "a disturbed personality" because of his need for publicity. Such a craving might have impaired his work as an investigator, Gain said.
—*Oakland Tribune,* July 18, 1978

ONE OF THE MOST OFTEN OVERLOOKED ASPECTS OF the Zodiac case is the surprising lack of consistency not just in the killings themselves but in the letters that accompanied them. Like the murders, which vary in style and methodology, the letters read like they were written by different people. From differences in spelling to the addition of secret codes and changing voice, it seems the only thing the letters have in common is that they were all authenticated by Sherwood Morrill from the Questioned Documents Section of California's Criminal Identification and Investigation Bureau. Morrill relied on the pseudoscience of graphology to make his determinations. Handwriting analysis is not backed up by scientific evidence. It's about as legit as psychic mediums or tea-leaf readers.

In the 2023 documentary series *The Myth of the Zodiac Killer* Professor Thomas Henry Horan, the main proponent of the Zodiac hoax theory, asked two French computational linguistics experts to analyze all thirty-five Zodiac letters using artificial intelligence. Their analysis found "visible shifts in style throughout the letters" that were particularly noticeable before and after the murder of Paul Stine.[92]

One of the most intriguing aspects of these letters is that we know who wrote several of them: Inspector David Ramon Toschi, the lead investigator in the Zodiac case. Think about that for a second—the guy in charge of the Zodiac investigation was faking Zodiac evidence. This is not something that's talked about too much in the more than 100 books about the Zodiac Killer. This fact calls into question the validity of the entire case.

Toschi was pre-hippie San Francisco through and through. An Italian-American kid, he grew up in the gritty, working-class city before it became a destination for dropouts and rich kids looking to find themselves. He graduated from Galileo High School and joined the Army during the height of the Korean War, like a real American. After a year of fighting in Korea, he returned home and joined the San Francisco Police Department in the summer of 1953.

By 1960, Toschi had earned a promotion to homicide inspector. Big-city murder police will always be the glamour assignment for a young detective on the rise. If he wanted to make a name for himself in the media spotlight, he was in the right place. This was Toschi's opportunity to gain hero status in one of the nation's most high-profile cities.

There's no modern equivalent for what David Toschi meant to San Francisco at the height of his popularity. The city was ground zero for the counterculture, but to newspaper readers Toschi was the all-American hero who represented the way things used to be. He kept the city safe from the crazies of New America. Closing over 100 murder cases in his career, he worked on the big cases: the Zodiac, Patty Hearst, and the Zebra Killers. And while he might not have caught the Zodiac or the Zebra Killers, or even found Patty Hearst, he gave the newspapers good copy. A symbol of law and order, Toschi fought the good fight against hippies, dope fiends, maniac killers, and other agents of chaos in the epicenter of chaos.

The news media presented him as a swaggering, sharp-dressed super-cop who wore loud sport coats and bowties. His face and signature mop of curly hair were frequently shown on the pages of the daily newspapers. A larger-than-life San Francisco personality, he always had time to give a reporter a quote or pose for a photographer.

The three most famous San Franciscans in 1971 were Clint Eastwood's "Dirty" Harry Callahan (inspired by Toschi), Steve McQueen's Frank Bullit (also inspired by Toschi), and the Zodiac Killer (the archvillain to Toschi's

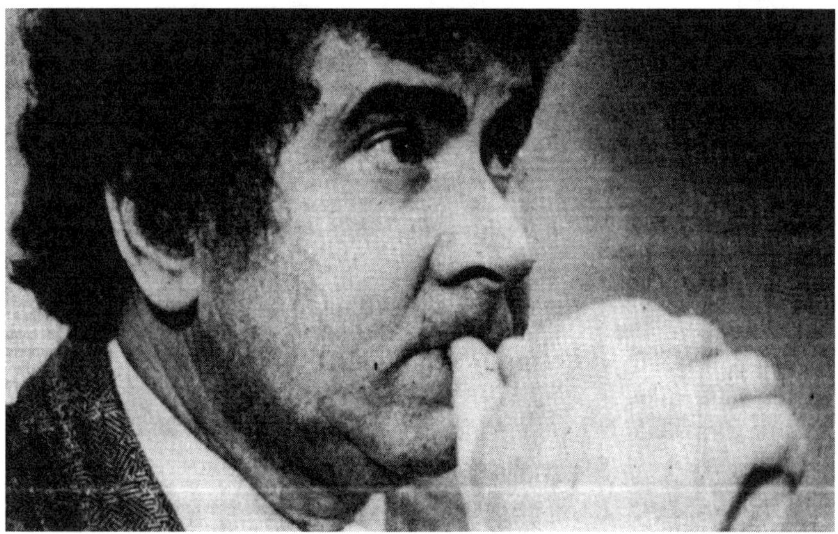

DAVID TOSCHI. *SAN FRANCISCO EXAMINER*, JULY 11, 1978.

heroic public persona). Funny thing is, none of these characters existed in real life, only in the media. All three were created, in large part, by the vivid imagination of someone who desperately wanted to be the most famous man in San Francisco. Toschi achieved his dream—for a while.

As it turned out, the lead investigator on the Zodiac case from 1969 to 1978, Inspector Dave Toschi, was a known hoaxer of Zodiac letters to the *San Francisco Chronicle*.

Don't take my word for it. Let the FBI tell you.

In a memo from August 23, 1978, the Special Agent in Charge of San Francisco wrote the FBI Director:

> **In light of recent news disclosures of 7/12/78, indicating that Det. David Toschi has authored one or more "Zodiac" letters which were subsequently sent to San Francisco local news media and is currently under investigation for same, psychological profiling of recent letter submitted by your division will be discontinued.**

On August 16, 1979, the Special Agent in Charge of San Francisco wrote the FBI Director:

> **Original request for psychological profile of person authoring most recent Zodiac Letters has not been accomplished to date since Police chief Charles Gain, San Francisco, California Police Department has announced that Inspector David Toschi had actually written three letters himself to gain publicity for the Zodiac case. This police cooperation matter is considered closed by the Behavioral Science Unit, Training Division.**

In 1981, an article was shopped around by the son of a California police officer accusing David Toschi of *being* the Zodiac Killer. It was rejected by the *San Francisco Chronicle.* Law enforcement took notice and investigated it. In a memo dated June 4, 1981, the Special Agent in Charge of San Francisco informed the FBI Director that Toschi wasn't actually the Zodiac, just the cop who faked some letters:

> **Toschi is the original investigator of the Zodiac case; however, it is noted that Toschi is the author of letters to The Chronicle in 1979 purporting to be from the Zodiac. Toschi actually wrote the 1979 letters himself to get additional publicity for the case.**

The Special Agent in Charge made a slight error that has allowed Zodiac hucksters and true believers a bit of wiggle room to disregard this important memo—he incorrectly identified the famous Toschi hoax letter as being from 1979, when in fact it was from 1978.

A Zodiac letter was mailed to the *San Francisco Chronicle* on April 24, 1978. It was the first communication from the killer since 1974, when the Zodiac changed his writing style and seemed to fancy himself a film reviewer and a Gilbert and Sullivan enthusiast, offering his thoughts on *The Exorcist*:

> I saw + think "The Exorcist" was the best saterical comidy that I have ever seen.
>
> Signed, yours truley:
>
> He plunged him self into the billowy wave and an echo arose from the sucides grave tit willo tit willo tit willo
>
> Ps. If I do not see this note in your paper, I will do something nasty, which you know I'm capable of doing
>
> Me - 37
>
> SFPD - 0

The 1978 "I'm Back" letter represented a further stylistic departure for the Zodiac. It doesn't sound anything like the original just-the-facts 1969 letters. In it, Zodiac name-dropped the newspaper reporter Herb Caen and, strangely, complimented Toschi, writing, "This is the Zodiac speaking I am back with you. Tell herb caen I am here, I have always been here. That city pig toschi is good—but I am ~~bu~~ smarter and better."

In fact, the Zodiac seemed concerned primarily about fame when writing statements such as, "I am waiting for a good movie about me. who will play me."

Anyone who knew Inspector David Toschi personally or professionally knew that he was very concerned with who would be cast to play him in a movie about his life. It was a topic of conversation he was very fond of. He'd often ask others which Hollywood actor would do the best job playing him.

When the 1978 letter arrived, Toschi did something very odd for a seasoned detective who had been running the Zodiac case for nearly a decade. With a photocopy of the 1978 letter in his hand, he ran to get it authenticated by John Shimoda, the head of the Postal Service Crime Lab. However, Shimoda had never authenticated a Zodiac letter before the one from 1978. Without examining the original letter, which showed clear signs that the writer had copied from old Zodiac communications in an attempt to mimic the handwriting, Shimoda declared it authentic. Sherwood Morrill, the retired expert who examined over two dozen Zodiac communications and was responsible for all the verifications of all authentic Zodiac letters, also confirmed the 1978 letter was the real deal. Toschi knew better than to bring a photocopy for a letter authentication. The FBI was adamant in a number of communications with the local cops working Zodiac: Xerox copies or photocopies could not be authenticated. Toschi knew this better than anybody. So why did he take a weird short cut and bring the new guy Shimoda a photocopy of the letter instead of the actual letter?

Things got even weirder with Toschi. Shortly after the "I'm Back" Zodiac letter was published, the writer Armistead Maupin approached the police with some disturbing information. He believed he knew who had written the latest Zodiac letter. Maupin presented several fan letters, supposedly sent to him by college girls and young women, all expressing great affection for Inspector David Toschi.

Dear Editor
This is the Zodiac speaking I
am back with you. Tell herb caen
I am here, I have always been here.
That city pig toschi is good · but
I am ~~bu~~ smarter and better he
will get tired then leave me
alone. I am waiting for a good
movie about me. who will play
me. I am now in control of all
things.
Yours truly :
⊕ - guess
SFPD - 0

TOSCHI LETTER.
SAN FRANCISCO CHRONICLE,
MAY 4, 1981.

Maupin's serialized fiction column "Tales of the City" in the *San Francisco Chronicle* had featured a storyline about a San Francisco serial killer called the Tinkerbell Killer. To create a compelling story, Maupin needed a hotshot detective to go head-to-head with Tinkerbell—so he'd consulted with Toschi on the project. Inspector Henry Tandy, a character in the column, was entirely inspired by Toschi. Maupin even inserted the real Toschi into his fictional universe, where he served as a mentor to Tandy. As a result, Toschi made his debut in "Tales of the City," and the fan letters began pouring in to Maupin at the *San Francisco Chronicle*.

Maupin was surprised to see the college girls' letters asking for more Toschi. It was admittedly odd—why were young women so enamored with a forty-seven-year-old detective who was most famous for failing to crack the Zodiac Killer case after years of trying? Maupin not only recognized the handwriting in the fan letters as Toschi's, but he also believed that the tone and handwriting of the April 24, 1978, letter published in the *Chronicle* matched Toschi's as well. If Toschi was capable of writing one Zodiac letter, what's to say he didn't write them all?

Maupin didn't bite his tongue, either. In his column, the fictional Inspector Tandy, inspired by the real-life Inspector Toschi, began to send notes to himself from the Tinkerbell Killer. Inspector Tandy even had a revelation about Toschi that inspired him to write his own phony letters: "it hit me that here was a way I could make it as a super cop once and for all. Christ! Toschi and his goddamned Zodiac!" Inspector Tandy invented the Tinkerbell Killer to make himself famous. Tandy saw what the Zodiac had done for Toschi's career and created his own character in the press to further his own career, and the press just went along with it. Tandy was Tinkerbell as sure as Toschi was the Zodiac. The monster lives in the media. These were wild allegations.

The SFPD took Maupin's suspicions and evidence seriously. Jack O'Shea, the head of the SFPD's intelligence division, personally investigated the claims. The police enlisted three independent experts to re-authenticate the letter that

Toschi was accused of writing. The SFPD would never have brought in outside consultants if they hadn't believed the allegations had some merit. This time, John Shimoda examined the original letter, not Toschi's photocopy. He, plus Terrance Pascoe of the California Questioned Documents Bureau and a former LAPD chief, Ken Woodward, all agreed that the 1978 letter was a forgery. Suddenly, Toschi didn't trust the science of graphology. He told United Press International, "Handwriting analysis is like psychiatry. Ten different people can give you 10 different opinions."

Sherwood Morrill, the renowned expert on Zodiac communications, declined to re-examine the letter. When asked for his opinion, he said, "I've heard they're accusing Toschi of writing them. If Toschi wrote the last one, he's the Zodiac. He (Zodiac) wrote them all."

In 1978, Inspector Toschi was officially investigated by the SFPD for writing the "I'm Back" Zodiac letter as well as the 1974 "Exorcist" letter. Chief Charles Gain was visibly disgusted when he told the press, "The writing is manufactured by someone that knows a great deal about the background and the Zodiac's M.O. They knew every little detail of how he wrote."

The newspapers jumped all over the Toschi letter hoax story, but they weren't out to shine a light on the awful truth about Toschi as they would with any other crooked cop falsifying evidence in America's most famous unsolved serial killer case. Instead, they were zealously defending him. After all, he was the media's cop—their go-to source for information. He brought the stories to them and could always be relied on for a quote. It was a classic quid pro quo. One hand washed the other.

Nonetheless, the police investigation intensified. Toschi was questioned by SFPD Internal Affairs about his whereabouts during the Paul Stine murder. For the first time, they treated him as a genuine Zodiac suspect, not just a fame-hungry cop who wrote letters to the newspaper. Toschi's world began to fall apart. He, too, was falling apart. Toschi mentioned pills and booze in a rambling newspaper interview. He couldn't sleep for days at a time. The SFPD's deputy chief of investigations, Clement DeAmicis, ordered him to see the department physician. The police doctor told Toschi he shouldn't be working. He went on sick leave and filed a disability claim with the retirement board, saying he was "emotionally distressed because of inference made about the Zodiac letters and long hard work on the Zodiac case."[93] His claim was denied.

When Toschi was confronted by DeAmicis about the letter-writing, he copped to writing the letters to Maupin praising himself under fake names. However, he continued to deny any involvement with the Zodiac letters. He took responsibility for the small thing while continuing to proclaim innocence for the bigger, more serious thing.

Ultimately, he was cleared of writing fake Zodiac letters—by a team of his own buddies, bosses, and co-workers. Of course he was. Look, internal police investigations are largely self-serving. The investigators are hardly impartial. Inspector Toschi had facilitated over 100 murder convictions based on evidence he had gathered, confessions he had obtained, and testimony he had given in court. If the departmental charges were upheld and Toschi was found to be corrupt, his entire career would be tarnished. His reputation, along with that of the SFPD, would be irreparably damaged.

The city of San Francisco wasn't about to risk bankruptcy over some king shit cop who lost control of his ego. If Toschi went down for falsifying evidence with the Zodiac letters, it would be a nuclear scandal. If the departmental charges stuck, they would turn into criminal charges and Toschi would be branded as the type of cop who tampered with and fabricated evidence. Once that kind of misconduct was proven in one case, even the worst lawyer in the Bay Area could get it to apply to any other case where convictions depended on Toschi's investigations or testimony. Hundreds of cases he had closed could be overturned and the city could face millions of dollars in damages. The SFPD spared themselves the embarrassment of admitting that the guy they put in charge of the Zodiac investigation was actually pretending to be the Zodiac and sending letters to the paper.

"My recommendation," DeAmicis told the *San Francisco Chronicle,* "was that because of ego problems we thought it in the best interest of Dave Toschi and the department to reassign him to the pawnshop detail."

The fact that the SFPD demoted the once-celebrated Dave Toschi from lead Zodiac investigator to a lowly pawn-shop detail shows that they knew he had written the Zodiac letters but weren't willing to publicly admit it. A police chief is a political appointee. In a major city, the chief is less of a cop and more someone who works for the mayor, with the primary responsibility of averting lawsuits, shielding the police department from scandal, and protecting the mayor's image. Chief Gain did exactly what he was hired to do.

While publicly declaring that the 1978 Zodiac letter Toschi was accused of writing was a fake and that Toschi was a "disturbed personality," the SFPD found Toschi innocent of forging it or the 1974 "Exorcist" letter. Despite that interdepartmental ruling, Chief Gain quietly informed the FBI that Toschi had indeed written multiple Zodiac letters. Subsequently, the FBI removed Toschi's 1978 letter from their criminal profile of the Zodiac. About that profile: the only Zodiac letter writer ever named in hundreds of pages of FBI reports on the case is Inspector David Toschi. The Feds not only knew—they documented it in official reports and communications.

Toschi took others down with him. His boss, Jack Jordan, head of homicide, and Jack O'Shea, head of the SFPD's Intelligence Bureau, were both demoted and transferred due to their knowledge of Toschi's letter-writing scheme. That's not the kind of thing that happens to innocent, high-ranking police officials when a cop under their supervision is cleared of wrongdoing. Jordan and O'Shea obviously knew. O'Shea, the man who personally investigated Armistead Maupin's claims, told Maupin, on the record, "Frankly Toschi's a joke in the department. He can get things in the newspaper, but that's about it." Officially and publicly, Toschi was exonerated of being the Zodiac letter hoaxer. Behind the scenes, and between cops, Toschi's role in writing fake Zodiac letters was the second-worst-kept secret in California law enforcement.

Armistead Maupin revealed in a press conference that when researching Toschi for an article in *New West* magazine he had learned from Inspectors Deasy and Tedesco, who had taken over the Zodiac case after Toschi was booted off it, that Toschi was "sabotaging their investigation into his decade-long investigation of the Zodiac murders."[94] What was Toschi afraid Deasy and Tedesco would find? In 1989, Deasy told the documentary filmmakers producing *Crimes of the Century* that he "proved Toschi wrote the last letter."

Still, Toschi had powerful friends. Dianne Feinstein, who would become San Francisco's mayor, California's senator, and one of the most powerful people in the United States, was on the San Francisco Board of Supervisors in 1978. She visited Toschi at his home to support him, then defended the disgraced former homicide detective to the press, claiming that the department had "crucified" him with the public transfer to his new role.[95]

Why did this politician on the rise get involved in Toschi's mess? Well, they had history. Two years earlier, Feinstein had been working late at City Hall when she found a letter from the Zodiac in her mail:

Did you miss me? I was busy doing some nefarious, dastardly work, for which I am well suited.

Understandably, Feinstein was shaken—terrified that the Zodiac Killer had somehow gotten into City Hall and left her a letter. Inspector Toschi inserted himself into her world, coming to her rescue. He met with Feinstein and reassured her, telling her the letter was a fake. He even took time to teach her personal safety tips. They became friends.

Just so we're clear—the future mayor of San Francisco got a fake Zodiac letter, and the guy who comforted her and became her ally was a guy who wrote fake Zodiac letters.

What a grift.

Toschi spun a yarn in the press about the Feinstein caper. He told the reporter Guy Wright that a drunkard with mental-health issues had written the letter to Feinstein. Toschi called the guy Old Tom and claimed he was a chronic fake Zodiac letter writer Toschi had been acquainted with for years. According to Toschi, he kept two separate files for Zodiac letters: one for Old Tom's fake letters and one for the real Zodiac's.

The *San Francisco Examiner* printed a whole column about Old Tom.[96] In it, Toschi expressed frustration that Old Tom would likely get locked up in a psych ward and then be kicked loose by lenient judges. To give this tale some weight, Toschi named Judge Francis Mayer as the one who sprang Old Tom. The fact-checkers must have taken that day off. Mayer couldn't have been the one who kicked Old Tom loose, as he was a juvenile court judge.[97] He wouldn't rule on an adult criminal or mental-competency case. The whole thing was bullshit. Toschi fed a fantastical story to the newspaper, and they printed it the way he wanted it to read.

This kind of thing happened with alarming regularity. In his excellent book *Motor Spirit,* the Zodiac researcher Jarrett Kobek detailed a number of instances of Toschi planting fake stories in the *San Francisco Examiner*:

> **On 3 October 1975, *The Examiner* publishes a story about how Toschi helps the child of an overdosed woman. . . . On 24 October, the paper prints mail from a reader named Mrs. G. Richel from San Francisco. "I am pleased too by the questioning conducted by Inspector David Toschi. The gentleness he displayed shows we still have decent policemen in San Francisco."**

Kobek's research showed the letter-writer was not listed in a San Francisco city directory. Not only did they not live in San Francisco, there's no evidence that this person ever existed. Someone was writing phony letters praising Dave Toschi and sending them to the newspaper. That someone was Dave Toschi.

Kobek found an even more batshit-crazy Toschi letter in the *Examiner* on Christmas Eve of 1975. A seventeen-year-old girl named Angel Marks wrote to the paper, describing how Toschi and his partner had tracked down her and her mother in a downtown hotel "in October." He informed them that her sister, Danni Price, had been arrested in Kentucky with her "traveling companion," a man named Jim Stewart from Portland, Oregon, for the murder of an Iranian general's son. Angel wrote to the paper because she wanted to give Toschi a special Christmas thank-you and "a sense of pride and accomplishment" for helping her.[98]

However, Angel never specified how Toschi had helped her. The letter was vague, offering little more than multiple pats on the back. It's also somewhat odd that, with the explosion of violent crime and murder in mid-'70s San Francisco, two homicide detectives had nothing better to do than go to a hotel to notify someone that their sister got arrested in Kentucky. Small-town police departments don't dispatch cops to hotels to notify tourists that their relatives were arrested thousands of miles away, and the busy SFPD would never send their top homicide detective to do it. The entire premise of this convoluted story is ridiculous. The vibes were completely off on this whole thing.

Angel even gave Toschi (and everyone else in San Francisco) an update on the case: Danni was exonerated and Jim confessed to everything. Later in the letter, Angel reflected on how difficult the work of a homicide detective must be in a manner that sounded oddly world-weary and wise beyond her years: "I'm sure there's not many rewards for you guys in homicide—the things you must see and try to cope with." Toschi gave a quote to the reporter: "I told her (Angel) to be totally honest and I was sure that everything would be all right."[99]

The only problem? None of these people existed in real life. No Angel, Danni, or Jim. And there is no record of an Iranian general's son being killed in Kentucky or anywhere else in the United States. Someone made up a crime that never happened, sent that letter to the newspaper, and signed a fictitious name. In other words, it was another fake Toschi fan letter sent by him or someone close to him.

Kobek also discovered that Guy Wright, the reporter behind the "Old Tom" piece, had written an article on February 1, 1976, about a quick-thinking twenty-two-year-old Vietnamese immigrant named Truong Van Truong. In a feel-good story about a heroic young man new to the country, Truong detained a murder suspect at the hotel he worked at until police arrived. Toschi and his new partner Frank McCoy managed to secure some column-inches by expressing gratitude to Truong and nominating him—despite being a non-citizen—for the Citizen of the Year award.

Three weeks later, Guy Wright's column featured a reader letter praising Toschi for recognizing the fine, young Vietnamese immigrant for the award. Strangely, the letter focused almost entirely on Toschi's acknowledgment, while relegating Truong—the actual hero—to a secondary role in the story. The letter was from Mrs. J. Whipple. No such person existed in San Francisco. More bullshit. Another letter printed in the column (this time from a Mr. William Chalker) also praised Toschi and his partner McCoy for their great "public relations" but made no mention of brave, young Truong. Guess who else didn't exist? Mr. William Chalker.

Kobek discovered more fugazi letters praising Toschi in Wright's March 15, 1976, column. In *Motor Spirit,* Kobek writes:

> **The correspondents are Tom Dougherty, Mrs. Murial Sanchez, and Fred Woebber. Dougherty thinks that Toschi is the only person who knows how to do his job. Mrs. Sanchez can't believe that Toschi hasn't said to hell with it. After all, he faces the stupidity of the liberal establishment. Fred Woebber has the same thought, he has no idea how Toschi can deal with murderers, let alone lawyers and psychiatrists. Polk's directories for 1975 and 1976 reveal no trace of either Dougherty or Woebber. On the basis of her last name and marital status, Mrs. Sanchez cannot be traced in the directory. Genealogical searches reveal no one of that name living in San Francisco or the surrounding counties.**

The letters praising Toschi from people who didn't exist kept on coming, and the *Examiner* continued to print them. Toschi was doing remarkable work as his own press agent and the *Examiner* printed his press releases in the form of fake letters praising his heroics. In August 1977, all that perseverance paid off when the *Examiner* published an article about Toschi called "The City's Super Cop." Solving the big cases didn't get Toschi the article—he had a surprisingly low closure rate for his high-profile cases. It was his relentless letter-writing campaign that finally brought him the spotlight he believed he deserved.

With the *CSI*-ification of the world, the public often demands DNA evidence to back up any claim. If that sounds like you, this next bit might be of interest. Alan Keel, who worked at the SFPD crime lab from 1996 to 1999 before becoming a private-sector forensics expert at Forensic Science Associates, was approached by Lyndon Lafferty—a Zodiac researcher and former California Highway Patrol cop—about DNA evidence from the Zodiac letters as part of research for his 2012 book *The Zodiac Killer Cover-Up: The Silenced Badge*. Keel told Lafferty, "The 1974 and 1978 letters were written by Toschi, but he won't cooperate and give us any body fluids so we can test the DNA." Keel, who worked with Zodiac DNA, came right out and said Toschi did it. And since Keel had worked for the SFPD, this meant the department must have been aware of it. The SFPD knew it so well that they put a gag order on Inspectors Carroll and Maloney who were working the Zodiac as a cold case in the late '90s and early 2000s. Ultimately, the SFPD brass shut down the entire Zodiac investigation in 2004. Lt. John Hennessy, head of the homicide unit, confirmed the move, telling *SFGate*, "The case is being placed inactive."

Keel, now a civilian no longer employed by the SFPD, kept talking. "The '74 and '78 envelopes were full of DNA cells; but . . . the earlier letters, it's almost like they were sealed with tap water because there were virtually no cells at all," he said.

This information is surprising. It means that the original 1969 Zodiac letter-writer was more forensically aware than the top homicide inspector in San Francisco. Toschi licked the envelopes. The Zodiac didn't. Toschi left a palm print. The Zodiac didn't.

Lafferty asked Keel if the results from the DNA on the '74 and '78 letters matched. Keel said they did.

Keel conveyed the same information to the top Zodiac researcher Mike Rodelli, author of *Hunt for Zodiac: The Inconceivable Double Life of a Notorious Serial Killer*:

> **(Keel) revealed that there were two letters in possession of the department that, in contrast to the "true" Zodiac letters, had**

> **abundant saliva and DNA-containing oral epithelial cells on them, that DNA was easily extracted from these two letters, and that the DNA extracted from these two letters matched between them. These two letters were considered forgeries, since the "true" Zodiac verifiable letters had not been licked by the sender.**

Rodelli further explained the process of matching the letters:

> **In contrast [to earlier communications] Keel analyzes two other letters, one of which is the 1978 forgery, and finds that this letter and one of the 1974 letters are loaded with saliva and cells. He then easily extracts DNA from both of these letters using the more primitive DNA technology of that time and finds that the DNA matches between those two letters, thus proving that one person sent both.**

The only DNA match between letters or crime scenes in the entire Zodiac case is the '74 and '78 letters. Those letters were fakes, written by Dave Toschi, the guy in charge of catching the Zodiac. What a disaster for the SFPD, the Zodiac case, and the victims of the supposed Zodiac killer who'd never get justice because some cop liked seeing his picture in the paper.

Lafferty presented Keel with the opportunity to run a sample of Toschi's DNA, obtained by Lafferty's partner Jerry Johnson, against the 1978 Toschi letter. Keel couldn't say yes fast enough. He was totally on board—until he wasn't. He changed his mind. Did the gag order apply to the SFPD crime lab too?

Keel left a rambling and confusing voicemail message, asking Lafferty and Johnson not to bring their Toschi DNA sample to him. Abruptly, Keel had stopped talking about the Zodiac.

What we do know is damning enough. Toschi wrote fake letters to newspapers detailing crimes that never happened. Toschi, with the help of friendly reporters, planted stories in the newspaper. And, according to the FBI, Toschi wrote Zodiac letters.

Knowing all this about Toschi, how are we expected to give him the benefit of the doubt when it comes to the Zodiac case? After all, the entire Zodiac case is tied together not by physical evidence, matching eyewitness descriptions, or a similar modus operandi and victimology but by letters to the newspaper.

Without the letters, there's no Zodiac. The guy who authenticated every Zodiac letter and communication was Toschi's friend Sherwood Morrill. The same Sherwood Morrill who claimed "If Toschi wrote the last one, he's the Zodiac," about the 1978 letter that Toschi had written.

TL;DR: Toschi was assigned a routine taxicab robbery-turned-homicide in Presidio Heights and, through the magic of letter-writing and a torn piece of Paul Stine's bloody shirt, it became a high-profile Zodiac case. And once Zodiac finally struck in San Francisco, the Zodiac Killer became a compelling national Manson-era cat-and-mouse news story starring super-cop Inspector David Toschi. In the end, Toschi won. In 1971, he sat in the cinema and watched the Hollywood legend Clint Eastwood play him on the screen in the blockbuster film *Dirty Harry*.

CHAPTER 12: THE CELEBRITY LAWYER

EVERY GENERATION HAS ITS CELEBRITY LAWYERS. Americans have a love/hate relationship with litigators like Johnnie Cochran, Gloria Allred, Clarence Darrow, Robert Kardashian, and Robert Shapiro. Sure, their loophole-seeking hijinks might seem distasteful when you read about them in the newspaper, but if you're guilty of a high-profile crime they're the people you want representing you. If you're a celebrity with a reputation that needs protection, they're the first ones you call. And if you're a regular slob who suffered a civil wrong or needs a personal-injury lawyer, having one of them in your corner is practically a winning lotto ticket.

Melvin Belli was that guy in the 1960s. He was known as the "King of Torts" because of the big-money awards he won for his clients in personal-injury cases in the 1940s and 1950s. He was also known for his dramatic presentations in court: he was an early user of photos, movies, scale models, skeletons, prostheses, and other attention-getting methods of demonstrating evidence. He had a large hand in shaping our current litigious culture (and how we depict court cases in movies and on TV). He got really famous when he represented Jack Ruby pro bono after Ruby shot and killed John F. Kennedy's assassin Lee Harvey Oswald on live television. Belli was the lawyer for Mae West, Muhammad Ali, Chuck Berry, Tammy Faye Bakker, Lana Turner, and Errol Flynn when they faced public embarrassment and punishment.

A '60s San Francisco celebrity, it didn't take long for Melvin Belli, star of the *Examiner* and the *Chronicle,* to find himself sharing headlines with the Zodiac Killer.

On October 22, 1969, Oakland police received a call from a man claiming to be the Zodiac Killer. This Zodiac told the cops that he wanted a superstar tabloid attorney—F. Lee Bailey—to appear on a local call-in television talk show called *A.M. in San Francisco,* hosted by Jim Dunbar. If the cops could get the lawyer, the Zodiac would call in and have a chat with him on live television. Bailey was in Boston and couldn't make it to San Francisco in time for the taping, but the caller agreed to the next best thing: Melvin Belli.

The cops contacted Belli, and he leaped at the opportunity to join the Zodiac circus. He loved a legal challenge almost as much as he loved the publicity he would get for cleverly overcoming one of these challenges.

The cops woke Dunbar up at two in the morning and briefed him on what was happening. When Dunbar arrived at the television studio, Melvin Belli and every media outlet in San Francisco were already there.

Sure enough, the big, bad Zodiac Killer called in and apparently his name was "Sam":

DUNBAR: Talk to us. Just, tell us what's going on, inside you, right now. Please.
CALLER: I have headaches.
DUNBAR: Right.
BELLI: How long have you had those headaches, uh, Sam? Been a long time?
CALLER: Since I killed a kid.
BELLI: Well, was it before December that you had the headaches?
CALLER: (pause) Yes.
BELLI: If, did, were you in service, that you might have had an injury in service, did you ever fall out of a tree or down stairs? Were you ever unconscious?
CALLER: (pause) I don't know.
BELLI: You don't remember. Does aspirin do you any good?
CALLER: No.
BELLI: Doesn't do you any good?
CALLER: No.

JIM DUNBAR AND MELVIN BELLI, *ROCHESTER POST-BULLETIN*, OCTOBER 23, 1969.

DUNBAR: Sam—

BELLI: Damn stuff never did me any good either.

. . .

DUNBAR: Well, let's find out why he wanted to talk to—Why did you want to talk to Mr. Belli, Sam?

CALLER: I don't want to be hurt.

"Sam," who had headaches, mumbled a few words and hung up the phone. "Sam" repeated this fifty-four times over two hours. Everyone was watching. And I mean everyone. Don Sherwood, "the World's Greatest DJ," was working live on another network, and even he told his viewers to change the channel and watch the drama unfold on Jim Dunbar's show. At the time it must have been riveting live television. Watching clips in hindsight, it's completely cringeworthy and excruciating. It's a two-hour-long crank call divided into fifty-four parts. It's not interesting, informative, thrilling, or tense. The whole thing feels like a bad improv theater skit without a punchline.

Cops took the matter seriously. According to *SFGate*, "A surrender location was arranged for a spot in Daly City, and Dunbar recalls seeing sharpshooters on the rooftops along the drive out Mission Street. A cop staking out the meeting spot was disguised as a priest, with a gun under his robe. All that was lacking was the presumed Zodiac, who never showed up or called again."[100]

Three Zodiac ear witnesses—the police dispatchers Nancy Slover and Dave Slaight, who had taken the calls from the Zodiac boasting about his murders at Blue Rock Springs, Lake Herman Road, and Lake Berryessa, along with the surviving Lake Berryessa victim Bryan Hartnell—agreed that the person who called in to the Jim Dunbar show had a different voice from the person they spoke to.

It was a fraud. The caller was a hoaxer. The SFPD concluded that the caller was a mental patient named Eric Weil who called from Napa State Hospital. Once again, the Zodiac lived in the media, not in real life.

Belli pivoted from his role as Zodiac interviewer to helping the Rolling Stones organize a concert on December 6, 1969, at the Altamont Speedway. Belli can be seen negotiating the deal in the documentary *Gimme Shelter*.

Altamont was a cluster-fuck. Festival organizers had hired the Hells Angels to do security and plied them with all-you-can-drink beer. The bikers kicked the shit out of hippies as the Stones provided the live soundtrack. A twenty-year-old Hells Angels member named Alan Passaro stabbed and killed a concertgoer.

Altamont, along with the Manson Family and the Zodiac Killer, feature prominently in the pop-culture obituary of the peace-and-love '60s. Altamont was the closing ceremony of the flower-power era.

The Rolling Stones, the Hells Angels, and the owner of the Altamont Speedway were in deep shit with the law and the press. They brought in Belli to fix their legal and public-relations mess. Apparently, the dead concertgoer had been armed and had pointed a gun at Mick Jagger. This was caught on video by the *Gimme Shelter* documentary film crew.

Belli encouraged the Angels to locate the gun. The owner of Altamont delivered the gun to Belli's office. The D.A.'s office didn't go after Altamont or the Stones or the Angels. In 1971, the D.A. filed first-degree murder charges against Alan Passaro. The jury believed it was a clear case of self-defense and Passaro beat the rap.

His two-hour-long Zodiac shitshow on live television should have been the end of Belli's involvement with the Zodiac case, but it wasn't. Just when he thought he was not-so-gracefully getting out, they dragged him back in.

Belli went to Munich, Germany, on December 20, 1969, for a legal conference—it was the first anniversary of the Lake Herman Road murders. That same day, the Zodiac mailed a letter to Melvin Belli's home. The letter contained a piece of Paul Stine's bloody shirt to prove it was authentic. Belli's maid sent the letter to his office. His office staff opened the letter and called the cops. The letter read:

> Dear Melvin
>
> This is the Zodiac speaking. I wish you a happy Christmass. The one thing I ask of you is this, please help me. I cannot reach out for help because of this thing in me wont let me. I am finding it extreamly difficult to hold it in check. I am afraid I will loose control again and take my nineth + possibly tenth victom. Please help me. I am drownding. At the moment the children are safe from the bomb because it is so massive to dig in + the triger mech requires much work to get it adjusted just right. But if I hold back too long from no nine I will loose all controol of my self + set the bomb up. Please help me I can not remain in control for much longer.

This Zodiac had very nice penmanship. This letter looked nothing like the earlier Zodiac letters. It was neatly printed and formatted differently, and the tone was nothing like the earlier letters. The FBI lab was very non-committal about this letter coming from the same person who wrote the original Zodiac letters. The FBI report (part 5, page 57) states, "the hand printing on the Qc85 letter to the Qc100 letter [the Qc85-100 is every authenticated Zodiac communication from October 13, 1969, to April 24, 1978] shows a wide range of variation and various printing speeds. . . . For the above reason, the hand printing examination of these letters was inconclusive."

This is an often-overlooked fact in the Zodiac investigation. In a memo dated October 20, 1969, the FBI lab upheld the notion that the Zodiac letters following the murder of Darlene Ferrin at Blue Rock Springs were "probably prepared by one person." The FBI only says "probably" because they were not furnished with all original documents. Local cops made the error of sending the FBI lab Xerox copies of Zodiac letters and envelopes. They asked them to do the impossible—find latent fingerprints and perform handwriting analysis on photocopies. The FBI, being qualified professionals, wouldn't give a definitive statement without access to the original documents. How the hell were they supposed to discover print evidence and compare handwriting based on photocopies?

In a memo from the FBI lab to the San Francisco Field Office dated October 17, 1969, the lab laments, "The only original evidence received in this matter was Q1 to Q3 [Q1 to Q3 was a three-page letter sent to the *San Francisco Examiner* on August 4, 1969, beginning, "Dear Editor This is the Zodiac speaking"]. The other specimens have been photocopies, some of which were made after the evidence was treated for latent fingerprints. Such photocopies do not show sufficient detail to permit an adequate handwriting examination."

A copy of this memo was sent to Inspector David Toschi in 1969. He was told that photocopies weren't good enough to make a valid comparison. Despite knowing this, he still tried to get a photocopy of the letter he was accused of writing verified by a new document-examiner. Nine years later, the same FBI lab, when asked to analyze only the Zodiac communications following Dave Toschi's involvement in the case with the murder of Paul Stine until he was kicked off the case in 1978, found the identity of the author inconclusive because of "a wide range of variation and various printing speeds." This includes the letters with pieces of Paul Stine's bloody shirt and the handwritten notes associated with the murder of Cheri Jo Bates. That's wild. This is a fact that not enough people know. Sure, the FBI says that one person "may have prepared the letters," but "may" is a downgrade from "probably" and the FBI can't say conclusively one way or the other if the same person wrote the post-Stine letters or if they were the work of multiple writers.

The timing of this FBI info-dump is even wilder. The letter on FBI lab stationery was dated June 7, 1978. That's right in the middle of the Toschi–Zodiac letter fiasco. And the recipient of this information from the FBI was Toschi's boss, the SFPD chief Charles Gain. Gain wanted to know just how dirty his cop was, and he reached out to the FBI for confirmation. Had Toschi been writing letters since the Stine murder? To be clear: the FBI lab told Chief Gain that they couldn't determine if the same person was responsible for Zodiac letters, starting with the one sent two days after the Paul Stine murder—the letter that included a piece of Stine's bloody shirt, the only piece of evidence linking the crime scenes and letters in the case.

The first four Zodiac letters concerning the Blue Rock Springs and Lake Herman Road murders were "probably" from the same guy—the FBI was confident of that. But, according to the best forensic crime lab on Earth, the author of every other Zodiac communication after Toschi arrived on scene was up in the air. That was the message delivered to Chief Gain as Inspector

David Toschi, his lead investigator on the Zodiac case, was being investigated for faking Zodiac letters.

The FBI didn't offer this opinion because they were influenced by 1978 headlines—they were never fully on board with the Zodiac letters. In 1972, years before the "Exorcist" and Toschi letters, the FBI noted, "These are letters received in the Zodiac case. It has not definitely been established that all letters were written by the Zodiac" (part 4, p. 77 of the Zodiac FBI File).

The FBI could not and would not verify that any of the Zodiac letters sent after the SFPD got involved in the case were from the same letter-writer as the original Zodiac letters. Nor would they confirm that the letters from before or after the original four Zodiac letters were from the same person. The absence of a conclusive answer about this matter speaks volumes. The FBI wasn't backing up the SFPD, Gain, or Toschi—they were throwing their arms up. While the FBI didn't outright say that the letters were all bullshit once Toschi took charge of the case, they certainly didn't say the opposite.

People selling the urban-legend version of the Zodiac don't like to talk about this. They gloss right over this mess. They'll ban you from their online forums for screen-shotting the FBI report that mentions this inconvenient truth. It goes against the traditional Zodiac Killer narrative. That's bad for their little Zodiac cottage industries. If you have any doubts about what I'm saying, go check it out for yourself on vault.fbi.gov.

Unsurprisingly, the document expert Sherwood Morrill verified every single one of these supposed Zodiac letters as authentic Zodiac communications, including a poem etched on a desk at Riverside Community College and letters about the 1966 murder of Cheri Jo Bates, which neither the FBI nor the Riverside police believe to be the work of Zodiac.

Inspector Toschi was a bent copper to some degree, but how bent was he? Let's have a look at the letter containing a piece of Paul Stine's bloody shirt that was sent to the tabloid celebrity Melvin Belli and compare it to the Toschi forgery from 1978: Zodiac researcher Richard Grinell reported on the striking similarities between the letter sent to Belli and the letter Toschi was investigated for. Grinell writes on his excellent zodiacciphers.com website:

> **From August 4th, 1969, to March 13th, 1971, the Zodiac Killer mailed 12 authenticated letters (inc. Fairfield letters) that carried the introduction of "This is the Zodiac speaking" on the first line**

of the message. Of these 12 letters, only the Melvin Belli letter on December 20th, 1969, failed to keep the "This is the Zodiac speaking" introduction exclusively on the main first line . . . The author of the April 24th 1978 "I am back with you" letter (if a hoaxer) had every opportunity to just mimic any one of these common introductions, yet he chose to mimic the Melvin Belli letter on December 20th 1969, which broke with tradition. The Melvin Belli message began with "This is the Zodiac speaking I" but was grammatically incorrect in failing to place a comma or full-stop between "speaking" and "I." Therefore, the author of the 1978 letter (if a hoaxer) chose to imitate the message on the opening line of the Melvin Belli letter (including the punctuation error) rather than the standard introduction used by the Zodiac Killer.[101]

That isn't the only similarity. According to Grinell,

The Melvin Belli letter on December 20th, 1969, and the April 24th, 1978, letter both inserted an unnecessary word (just once) into the correspondence, spelled it correctly one alphabetical letter shy of completion, and then very neatly (almost ruler like) crossed out each word. Not only did the 1978 letter carry the identical introduction and punctuation error as the Melvin Belli letter, as well as being very deliberately and carefully written, but both inserted an unrequired word into the message before crossing it out, despite it being spelled correctly thus far. These are the only two communications up to April 24th, 1978, that carried both of these features."[102]

Only two Zodiac letters contained these quirks: the one sent to the celebrity lawyer Melvin Belli and the one written by the celebrity detective David Toschi. We know Toschi wrote fake Zodiac letters. So is it possible that Toschi wrote the letter to Belli? The handwriting and tone of the letter have nothing in common with the authenticated Zodiac correspondences. But the printing and formatting look a lot like the '78 Toschi letter that's a known hoax. Plus, the writing and formatting look similar to Toschi's fake fan letters to Armistead Maupin.

The FBI file says that Toschi wrote three Zodiac letters. Was the Belli letter, which shares quirks with the Toschi letter, one of them?

The Belli letter is considered real because a piece of Paul Stine's shirt accompanied it. If that bloody shirt swatch hadn't been included, there would be a lot of questions about the letter and it would probably be considered a fake.

But it should be noted that neither the police report nor the coroner's report mentions anything about a giant piece of Stine's shirt that was cut or torn out. The clothing the deceased wore is examined as a standard part of a postmortem. Nothing in the medical examiner's report indicates irregularities with Stine's shirt. How is it possible that nobody noticed this giant gaping hole? Do an image search for Paul Stine's shirt. The only published images of the shirt occurred after the Zodiac letter arrived with a piece of the shirt. It's obvious that the shirt was tampered with. There's no way all those people could have missed it.

The Paul Stine murder went from a routine cab robbery to a sensationalized Zodiac murder with a couple of snips from Paul's shirt. That was the proof that the Zodiac did it. The FBI concluded that "the hand printing examination of these letters was inconclusive" when compared to the earlier, conclusive Zodiac letters. The letter to the *Chronicle* containing a piece of Paul Stine's shirt two days after Paul's murder is the first "inconclusive" letter.

Two days after Toschi caught the case, the letters became inconclusive. The M.O. and victimology in the Stine attack were completely different from the previous Zodiac attacks. This Zodiac robbed solo men in the big city instead of attacking couples at lover's lanes. This Zodiac sent souvenirs to newspapers and lawyers. This Zodiac wrote "inconclusive" letters. This Zodiac sent a letter to Melvin Belli that had an awful lot of quirks in common with the fake 1978 Toschi letter.

Inspector Toschi, the guy in charge of the Paul Stine crime scene, was a known Zodiac letter-writer, described by his chief as a "disturbed personality" for his obsession with the media and publicity.

Florian Cafiero and Jean-Baptiste Camps, the computational-linguistics experts featured in the documentary series *The Myth of the Zodiac Killer,* came to a shocking conclusion about the letters. Their analysis showed that there were "visible shifts in style throughout the letters," particularly before and after the murder of Paul Stine." [103]

Thomas Henry Horan, M.F.A., an author, Zodiac researcher, and creative-writing professor, has a keen editorial eye. He's an experienced writer and teacher. He's uniquely attuned to recognizing a writer's voice. He noticed that the voice in the Zodiac letters dramatically changed after the murder of Paul Stine many years before the computational-linguistics algorithm noticed it.

If the letters sent after the Stine murder were hoaxes, the writer would almost certainly have had to be someone who was on the scene following Stine's murder. The letters contain detailed complaints about the police response—gripes that the Zodiac couldn't have known if he had been truly there and busy escaping. These remarks come from the perspective of an observer, not a fleeing criminal. The tone is strikingly similar to that of a disgruntled cop, pissed off over the SFPD's mishandling of the Stine murder. It reads more like a (snarky, badly spelled) critical after-action report from within the department than a letter from the killer:

> So as you can see the police don't have much to work on. If you wonder why I was wipeing the cab down I was leaving fake clews for the police to run all over town with, as one might say, I gave the cops som bussy work to do to keep them happy. I enjoy needling the blue pigs. Hey blue pig I was in the park—you were useing fire trucks to mask the sound of your cruzeing prowl cars. The dogs never came with in 2 blocks of me + they were to the west + there was only 2 groups of parking about 10 min apart then the motor cicles went by about 150 ft away going from south to north west.
>
> Must print in paperps. 2 cops pulled a goof abot 3 min after I left the cab. I was walking down the hill to the park when this cop car pulled up + one of them called me over + asked if I saw anyone acting suspicious or strange in the last 5 to 10 min + I said yes there was this man who was runnig by waveing a gun the cops peeled rubber + went around the corner as I directed them + I disappeared into the park a block + a half away never to be seen again.
>
> Hey pig doesnt it rile you up to have your noze rubed in your booboos?

Besides the two officers who may have seen or stopped and questioned the guy but never put it over the radio, how many people (besides the Zodiac) knew about Fouke and Zelms encountering a man who matched the description the Robbins kids gave? When Zodiac dropped the "2 cops pulled a goof" bombshell about Fouke and Zelms, he told the world he was keyed into SFPD gossip. Fouke (one of the goofs) didn't write his memo about his encounter with the white male subject until November 12, 1969, a month after Paul Stine was murdered, and a couple of days after the Zodiac made the information public. The Zodiac scooped Fouke and the SFPD.

The Zodiac indicated that the paper "must print" the bit about two cops pulling a goof. That's the part that was important to the Zodiac. The whole Fouke-and-Zelms-meet-Zodiac saga didn't even make it into Pelissetti's very detailed report about the murder of Paul Stine. The circle of people who would know about Fouke and Zelms potentially playing "catch and release" with the killer would likely be very small, limited to the man they encountered and the officers working the crime scene—a crime scene run by Inspector Dave Toschi.

One of the most bothersome aspects of the Presidio Heights fiasco is the impact it had on the reputation of Officer Donald Fouke. A distinguished member of the SFPD, Fouke's career was marked by exceptional bravery and service. In 1967, he was honored as one of the "10 Most Esteemed Police Officers" by the International Association of Police Chiefs and received the Gold Medal of Valor—SFPD's highest award—for his heroic actions in Golden Gate Park. When a gunman opened fire in a crowded area, Fouke showed remarkable restraint, choosing not to return fire despite being shot at five times, in order to avoid endangering civilians. Instead, he charged toward the assailant, disarmed him with a swift kick to the weapon, and subdued him without further harm.

Fouke's courage was recognized again in 1971 when he was awarded the Bronze Medal of Valor. On that occasion, he risked his own safety to rescue two helicopter pilots who had crashed into San Francisco Bay, as well as a good Samaritan who had attempted to assist them. His actions exemplify the highest standards of law enforcement, making the damage to his reputation in the aftermath of Presidio Heights all the more troubling.

Donald Fouke was an excellent police officer. He was never reprimanded for the incident that may or may not have happened at Presidio Heights. To the contrary, he was promoted a year later.

It should be noted that the Zodiac letter claiming "2 cops pulled a goof" didn't come two days after the murder but nearly a month after. If the Zodiac was so obsessed with mocking and outsmarting the police, why did he wait a month to put that information in his letter? Could it be that the Zodiac letter-writer was unaware of this bit of information when he sent the first letter immediately after the Stine murder? Dave Toschi told Robert Graysmith that he had learned days later that Fouke and Zelms may have encountered Zodiac and Toschi had reassured Fouke, telling him he "did the right thing" by coming forward.

Donald Fouke claimed to have never met or spoken with Dave Toschi in his life. On the other hand, Toschi readily supplied Robert Graysmith with tales of Fouke crying to him about letting the Zodiac escape and how the composite sketch was not as accurate as the original sketch. Was it Toschi who ruined Fouke's reputation with gossip? Did any of this actually happen or was it all a tall tale Toschi told Robert Graysmith?

The third Stine shirt letter was mailed to Melvin Belli on December 20, 1969. This letter also differed in tone from the North Bay letters, and this one had the added feature of completely different handwriting.

But the inclusion of the shirt must mean the letter is legit, right? Not necessarily. The piece of shirt was sent two months after Stine's murder, and the chain of custody for Paul Stine's shirt was a complete disaster. It wouldn't take a lawyer as good as Melvin Belli to get this lousy piece of evidence thrown out of court based on the number of people who laid hands on it. These shirt pieces had been touched by more people than the Shroud of Turin. Once it arrived at the *Chronicle,* it was passed around like a hot potato. Even the Belli household and office staff got in on the act.

Now let's talk Toschi. The Paul Stine crime scene looked like a standard taxi robbery/homicide until it got an infusion of big B-movie drama courtesy of the Zodiac letters sent with pieces of Paul Stine's bloody shirt. This sensational evidence came right on the heels of the Manson Family tabloid explosion in L.A. It propelled Dave Toschi from being just Baymous (famous in the Bay Area) to being capital-F Famous, the internationally renowned inspector who inspired Dirty Harry and was played by Clint Eastwood on the silver screen. Dave Toschi, a media-savvy ham, finally hit the big time. But surely a guy like Toschi wouldn't hoax a bunch of letters to gain publicity for himself, right? Chief Charles Gain called Toschi "a disturbed personality" because of his need for publicity. Such a craving might have impaired his work as an investigator, Gain told the *Oakland Tribune* for its July 18, 1978, issue.

This mess would be torn apart in court if the D.A. could even get a true bill of indictment with this compromised evidence (which would have been unlikely in San Francisco). The Zodiac case was poisoned by Toschi's hoaxing.

CHAPTER 13: PRETTY GIRLS MAKE GRAVES

THE MEDIA CARE A HELL OF A LOT MORE ABOUT murders when the victims are beautiful blonde women. The overrepresentation of media coverage for young, blonde, female murder victims in proportion to their percentage of the population and per-capita standing as a murder-victim demographic is absurd. It's a cliché, but it's only a cliché because it's so obviously true and noticeable. The media push these stories like dope-dealers and the public latches onto them like fiends. The combination of pretty, dead, and blonde keeps the lights on in the newsroom and at the true-crime factory. The hook is obvious. If the killers could get someone as valuable as Cheri Jo Bates, who was born beautiful and was destined to have every advantage available to a woman, imagine what they'd do to you—someone who probably doesn't look like a young Cybil Shepherd? Imagine what they'd do to your average-looking kids? The news media sell fear. Fear is their business . . . and business is good. This is a proven, effective sales tactic.

If all the beautiful California blondes mentioned in this book competed in a Ms. True Crime Victim beauty pageant, they'd all be competing for second place. Cheri Jo Bates could roll out of bed with no makeup, pajamas, and bedhead and she'd still have that beauty contest locked down. Cheri Jo was the blondest and most beautiful of them all. That's probably why the story of her murder had two separate lives in the media in just a five-year period. There were 11,040 murders in the United States in 1966 and none of the victims got more media coverage than Cheri Jo Bates.

Cheri Jo was born of pure Midwestern cornhusker stock in Omaha, Nebraska, in 1948. Her family moved to California when her father got a good paying job as a machinist for the military-industrial complex at the Corona Naval Ordnance Laboratory near Riverside. Cheri Jo was born to be a varsity cheerleader and fulfilled her birthright at Ramona High School. She dated a college football player, Dennis Highland, attended Riverside City College, made her own clothes, worked at the bank, played piano, participated in student government, drove a little green Volkswagen Beetle, and aspired to be a stewardess. The thing that stood out to classmates most about Cheri Jo was how nice she was. People as good-looking as Cheri Jo, who get chosen to be "junior princess" at homecoming, don't need to be nice to anyone, but she chose to be nice to everyone. She didn't hang out with the cool clique. She didn't have a clique at all. Cheri Jo was egalitarian in her friendships.

A woman named Cherie Curzon spoke to the Riverside City College newspaper *Viewpoints* about the time her friends bailed on her for the school talent show and Cheri Jo casually dressed up in a sailor suit and joined her on stage to sing "I'm Gonna Wash That Man Right out of My Hair" from the musical *South Pacific.*

"For me, the best part of our story was, I was an underclass person who she wanted to help out. The people who were going to do the talent contest with me backed out and she volunteered to be my partner. I will never forget her kindness . . . We had so much fun rehearsing and then performing, I loved her generosity and kindness toward me . . . She did it because of who she was; just a wonderful person."[104]

If that's not wholesome enough for you, on her last day on earth Cheri Jo went to Sunday mass with her father at St. Catherine of Alexandria Catholic Church. After receiving the body and blood of Jesus Christ in Holy Communion, the father and daughter ate breakfast together at Sandy's Restaurant as they always did. After breakfast, dad went full SoCal and invited Cheri Jo to hang out at the beach, something her family regularly did together. Cheri Jo had to pass on the invite. She needed to work on a research paper at the school library. When dad got home from the beach, he found a note from Cheri Jo taped to the refrigerator: "Dad—went to the RCC library."

According to true-crime lore, Cheri Jo worked on her paper at the library from around 6:00 p.m. until it closed at 9:00 p.m. But not a single eyewitness can confirm that she was ever inside the library that night. A student library worker said he may have seen her in the library that night, but he couldn't be sure. It might have been another night. Cheri Jo's friends who happened to be at the library did not see her. People who look like Cheri Jo never go unnoticed. If she was in the library, someone would have remembered. Someone described in the November 1968 issue of *Inside Detective* magazine as "a young Mexican-American student" claimed to have seen Cheri Jo at the library, "writing something with a blue ball point pen in her blue spiral notebook." [105] He told detectives he was "outside the library at 5:30 p.m. waiting for it to open at 6:00 p.m. and it was then he saw the girl." Seven people came forward and told cops they saw Cheri Jo between 3:45 and 6:15 p.m., but none of them saw her inside the library.

Cheri Jo didn't return home that night. That was out of character for her. Her father anxiously waited up for her. He called her friends. She wasn't with them. Mr. Bates filed a missing-persons report with Riverside police at 5:43 a.m. on October 31, 1966.

Less than an hour later, a maintenance worker found the body of Cheri Jo Bates in a gravel paved alley between two unoccupied houses on the campus of Riverside City College.

Crime scenes tell stories. This crime scene told the tale of how Cheri Jo bravely fought for her life. Her autopsy revealed skin fragments under her fingernails and a clump of brown hair in her bloody right hand. She scratched the hell out of her attacker and pulled some of his hair out. Her autopsy also revealed she was kicked in the head, stabbed in the chest twice, stabbed in the shoulder, slashed in the face, slashed on her chest, and stabbed in the neck. Her killer didn't rob or sexually assault her. The struggle between Cheri Jo and her killer was so intense that the ground where she was killed was described in her autopsy report as "looking like a freshly plowed field."

Cops examined the scene and found a men's Timex watch with paint splatters on it ten feet from Cheri Jo's body. The watch likely came off in the violent struggle between Cheri Jo and her attacker. The killer got away, but Cheri Jo made sure the killer didn't leave unscathed. Cops found footprints made by a military boot, eight to ten inches in length. That corresponds with a man's shoe between size five and size eight. The average American man wore a size 6½ in the 1960s (the average size is 10 today).[106] The guy who left the footprint was an average-sized man.

CHERI JO BATES.
GRAND RAPIDS PRESS,
NOVEMBER 1, 1966.

Cheri Jo's VW Beetle was parked about seventy-five yards east of where her body was found. Her key was in the ignition, library textbooks on the U.S. government lay on the front passenger seat, and the windows were rolled down. Investigators discovered her car was deliberately disabled by someone who pulled the ignition wiring and the distributor out. Cheri Jo's car had been tampered with. When she got in her car and tried to start it, it wouldn't turn over. Her killer likely disabled her car and pounced when she found herself stuck. Or he might have used the disabled car as a distraction and offered Cheri Jo his assistance, like a wolf in sheep's clothing.

Cops found a bunch of greasy, smeared palm prints and fingerprints on the exterior of the car. These prints didn't belong to Cheri Jo, her family members, or her friends.

Riverside police worked the case hard. They interviewed nearly 100 people, paying particular attention to RCC students and airmen stationed at March Air Force Base—just a twenty-minute drive from RCC. A female RCC student told cops she saw a guy creeping around in the dark across the street from Cheri Jo's car. She described him as being a white guy, nineteen or twenty years old, about five-foot-eleven with brown hair. That describes half the men who attended the college and half the airmen at the base.

This investigation was important to the Riverside police. Det. Sgt. David Bonine put out a casting call for a reproduction of the night of October 30, 1966, at the RCC library starring the people who were actually there. This was a smart way to get witnesses to come forward. Sixty-two students, two librarians, and the custodian who were in or around the library the night Cheri Jo was murdered returned to the library to participate in some live theater. Capt. Irv Cross directed the show. He had them wear the same clothes they wore that night and take their places exactly where they were on the night before

Halloween to do exactly what they did that night inside the library and in the parking lot. All interviews and interactions were tape-recorded by Riverside police. A fingerprint sample and a lock of hair were obtained from every male participant. Conspicuous by their absence were a heavyset man with a beard and a woman talking together in the library annex. Despite the unprecedented effort put into this exercise, not a single useful lead came from it.

A month after the murder, a typewritten confession letter was sent to the Riverside police headquarters and the *Riverside Press-Enterprise* newspaper. The letter reads:

> **THE CONFESSION BY__________________**
> **SHE WAS YOUNG AND BEAUTIFUL. BUT NOW SHE IS BATTERED AND DEAD. SHE IS NOT THE FIRST AND SHE WILL NOT BE THE LAST. I LAY AWAKE NIGHTS THINKING ABOUT MY NEXT VICTIM. MAYBE SHE WILL BE THE BEAUTIFUL BLOND THAT BABYSITS NEAR THE LITTLE STORE AND WALKS DOWN THE DARK ALLEY EACH EVENING ABOUT SEVEN. OR MAYBE SHE WILL BE THE SHAPELY BLUE EYED BROWNETT THAT SAID NO WHEN I ASKED HER FOR A DATE IN HIGH SCHOOL. BUT MAYBE IT WILL NOT BE EITHER. BUT I SHALL CUT OFF HER FEMALE PARTS AND DEPOSIT THEM FOR THE WHOLE CITY TO SEE. SO DON'T MAKE IT TO EASY FOR ME. KEEP YOUR SISTERS, DAUGHTERS, AND WIVES OFF THE STREETS AND ALLEYS. MISS BATES WAS STUPID. SHE WENT TO THE SLAUGHTER LIKE A LAMB. SHE DID NOT PUT UP A STRUGGLE. BUT I DID. IT WAS A BALL. I FIRST PULLED THE MIDDLE WIRE FROM THE DISTRIBUTOR. THEN I WAITED FOR HER IN THE LIBRARY AND FOLLOWED HER OUT AFTER ABOUT TWO MINUTS. THE BATTERY MUST HAVE BEEN ABOUT DEAD BY THEN. I THEN OFFERED TO HELP. SHE WAS THEN VERY WILLING TO TALK TO ME. I TOLD HER THAT MY CAR WAS DOWN THE STREET AND THAT I WOULD GIVE HER A LIFT HOME. WHEN WE WERE AWAY FROM THE LIBRARY WALKING, I SAID IT WAS ABOUT TIME.**

SHE ASKED ME, "ABOUT TIME FOR WHAT". I SAID IT WAS ABOUT TIME FOR HER TO DIE. I GRABBED HER AROUND THE NECK WITH MY HAND OVER HER MOUTH AND MY OTHER HAND WITH A SMALL KNIFE AT HER THROAT. SHE WENT VERY WILLINGLY. HER BREAST FELT WARM AND VERY FIRM UNDER MY HANDS, BUT ONLY ONE THING WAS ON MY MIND. MAKING HER PAY FOR THE BRUSH OFFS THAT SHE HAD GIVEN ME DURING THE YEARS PRIOR. SHE DIED HARD. SHE SQUIRMED AND SHOOK AS I CHOAKED HER, AND HER LIPS TWICHED. SHE LET OUT A SCREAM ONCE AND I KICKED HER IN THE HEAD TO SHUT HER UP. I PLUNGED THE KNIFE INTO HER AND IT BROKE. I THEN FINISHED THE JOB BY CUTTING HER THROAT. I AM NOT SICK. I AM INSANE. BUT THAT WILL NOT STOP THE GAME. THIS LETTER SHOULD BE PUBLISHED FOR ALL TO READ IT. IT JUST MIGHT SAVE THAT GIRL IN THE ALLEY. BUT THAT'S UP TO YOU. IT WILL BE ON YOUR CONSCIENCE. NOT MINE. YES, I DID MAKE THAT CALL TO YOU ALSO. IT WAS JUST A WARNING. BEWARE . . . I AM STALKING YOUR GIRLS NOW.

CC. CHIEF OF POLICE

ENTERPRISE

This letter sounds like a proto-Zodiac. This letter sounds like Jack the Ripper fan fiction written by an incel. The letter writer claimed, "SHE DID NOT PUT UP A STRUGGLE." The writer was very wrong about that. Cheri Jo put up a hellacious fight. The writer was also wrong when he bragged that he "FINISHED THE JOB BY CUTTING HER THROAT." Her throat was not slashed in real life, only in local gossip. Some true-crime writers went as far as to say Cheri Jo was "nearly decapitated" by her killer's furious slashing. That's simply not true and the autopsy report proves it. She was stabbed in the neck by a very small knife. Riverside police believed that despite the fact that the letter-writer offered zero unique information about the crime that wasn't printed in the newspaper or the subject of local gossip, he was the killer. They believed he knew Cheri Jo and was involved in some type of romantic relationship with her.

A month later, in December of 1966, a custodian found this sadboy emo poem carved into a desktop in the RCC library:

Sick of living/unwilling to die
cut.
clean.
if red,
clean.
blood spurting,
dripping,
spilling;
all over her new
dress.
Oh well,
it was red
anyway
life draining into an
uncertain death.
she won't die.
this time
someone ll find her.
just wait till
next time.
rh

On April 30, 1967, Cheri Jo's father, Joseph Bates, the *Press Enterprise,* and the Riverside police each received a handwritten note that said, "Bates had to die. There will be more."

Despite everyone's best efforts, the Bates case went cold.

Nearly three years later, after Bryan Hartnell and Cecelia Shepard had been attacked at Lake Berryessa, Chief Kincaid of the Riverside police contacted the Napa County sheriff, Earl Randol, on October 20, 1969, to let him know that he had a case with "a similar M.O. of your 'Zodiac.' . . . There are numerous similarities in your homicide and our [Bates homicide]. I thought you should be aware that we are working a similar-type homicide investigation."

This law-enforcement cooperation didn't yield any results for the Bates or Zodiac cases.

On November 16, 1970, Cheri Jo and the Zodiac made the front page of the *Los Angeles Times* together.

Paul Avery, a reporter for the *San Francisco Chronicle* who wrote extensively about the Zodiac, got a tip about Cheri Jo Bates being a Zodiac murder. Avery went down to Riverside to investigate and report the story. Shortly after, SFPD detectives met with investigators in Riverside. Everyone's favorite questioned-document expert Sherwood Morrill got involved and, to the surprise of absolutely no one who has been reading this book, he certified that the envelopes from the confession letter to the newspaper and police were from the Zodiac. Morrill also certified a match between the handwritten "Bates had to die" notes. According to him, they were written by the Zodiac. Incredibly, Sherwood Morrill was even able to match the Zodiac's handwriting with the poem scratched into the desk with a blue ballpoint pen at the library. Under the best of circumstances, handwriting analysis is a pseudoscience. Comparing felt tip pen writing from the Zodiac letters to characters scratched on a desk and coming up with a match is completely out of pocket and ridiculous. This was charlatanism. It was a parlor trick passing itself off as forensic science. Sherwood Morrill was the worst thing to ever happen to the Zodiac case.

Not only is handwriting analysis junk science, but Morrill was also a nepo-baby. He had no accredited professional training in document examination or the pseudoscience of handwriting analysis. According to an article in the May 14, 1974, issue of the *San Francisco Chronicle,* Morrill got his job at the State Bureau of Criminal Identification and Investigation because his father, Clarence Morrill, the man who started the State Bureau of Criminal Identification and Investigation, trained him. Sherwood Morrill's father invented a state job. When Sherwood didn't make it to the major leagues as a baseball player, his father passed the job he created on to his son. It's pure nepotism. And that son was perfectly content to be a self-taught expert, refusing to keep up with advancements in a field that was making an attempt to be somewhat scientific.

Zodiac investigators led by David Toschi considered Cheri Jo Bates a Zodiac murder victim. Of course they did. The Zodiac–Bates connection got Toschi back in the newspaper. The Zodiac case was forgotten in the press until the Cheri Jo connection. Toschi was back in the limelight with this new/old Zodiac murder. The Zodiac and, more importantly, Dave Toschi were front-page news again. Investigators from Riverside didn't agree with their colleagues from Northern California. Riverside investigators did not believe Cheri Jo had

SHERWOOD MORRILL.
SOLANO-NAPA NEWS CHRONICLE,
MAY 23, 1973.

been killed by the Zodiac. They believed Cheri Jo had been killed by a local guy whom she knew, possibly an ex-boyfriend she had dumped for Johnny Football Hero. The overwhelming majority of female murder victims (76%) are killed by someone known to them.[107] Only 12% of female murder victims are killed by strangers.[108] Riverside cops had a suspect they believed committed the Bates murder. They weren't on board for the Toschi Morrill Zodiac media circus. They offered information to Zodiac investigators about a similar murder that predated Zodiac by two years, and the Zodiac investigators took the opportunity to add the Riverside case to their tally once the story resurfaced in the papers. When Riverside police reached out directly in 1969, the Zodiac investigators blew their chief off. When the story made the front page of the biggest newspaper on the West Coast, suddenly Toschi and the boys made waves about the Bates case and had to take a field trip to Riverside.

The Zodiac exists in the media, not in real life. The *San Francisco Chronicle* and the *Los Angeles Times* turned the Cheri Jo Bates murder into a Zodiac murder. The police had already investigated the similarities and links and dismissed the notion a year earlier. The monster lives in the media. The cops were being led around by the nose by newspaper reporters. Avery investigated and the cops reacted, instead of the cops investigating and Avery reporting on it.

The absurdity continued. This Zodiac wrote to the *L.A. Times* on March 13, 1971, and took responsibility for Cheri Jo's murder, claiming, "I do have to give [the police] credit for stumbling across my Riverside activity, but they are only finding the easy ones. There are a hell of a lot more down there." This feels like an old band doing a half-hearted reunion tour. Zodiac was back-ish. This Zodiac thinks the cops did a good job. This Zodiac gives cops credit despite the fact that it was a reporter via a tipster, and not the police, who made the connection. This Zodiac sounds like a phony letter-writer we know who wrote Zodiac letters to the *Chronicle* and planted fake stories and letters praising himself in the *San*

Francisco Examiner. This Zodiac writes to L.A. papers, not Bay Area ones. Like the other Zodiacs, this Zodiac took credit for a crime he didn't commit.

In 2021, the Riverside police's cold-case unit published a Cheri Jo Bates update on their website:

> **In April 2016, investigators received a letter postmarked from San Bernadino, California. This letter was typed and appeared to have been generated from a computer. The author of the anonymous letter admitted to writing the handwritten letters [the "Bates had to die" letters to her father, the cops, and the newspaper]. The author apologized for sending the letters and said it was a sick joke. The author admitted that he was not the Zodiac Killer or the killer of Cheri Jo Bates and was just looking for attention.**
>
> **In 2020, the Homicide Cold Case Unit and the FBI Los Angeles Investigative Genealogy Team submitted the stamp from the letter for additional DNA analysis and subsequent interviews were conducted. The individual linked to the DNA evidence on the stamp admitted to writing the letter and sending it to the Riverside Police Department.**
>
> **Investigators confirmed the person was not involved in the murder of Cheri Jo Bates or involved in the murders associated with the "Zodiac Killer." Additional information was developed regarding a separate set of letters sent to Northern California police agencies. The author claimed to be the "Zodiac Killer," but the author ultimately admitted to sending the letters to keep the investigation going.**
>
> **Early in the investigation, a potential suspect was identified in the killing of Cheri Jo Bates. Based on the evidence, the person of interest remained the primary suspect over the years and continues to be the focus of the investigation.**[109]

Riverside wanted nothing to do with the Zodiac mess. They made that clear. They even took a shot at Toschi's Zodiac letter hoaxing in their update. The Riverside police has had a suspect since the 1960s. It's a case of Riverside police believing they know who killed Cheri Jo but never having had enough evidence to prove it in court. The police believe that people who know the suspect had additional information that could lead to charges or a conviction, but as of yet those people have not shared it with them. They want to distance their investigation from Zodiac.

Cheri Jo was a Zodiac victim only in the media. The cops who investigated her case did not consider her a Zodiac victim. Paul Avery, a *Chronicle* reporter who found out about a desk in storage for years with a goofy poem scratched on it, was the main proponent of Cheri Jo as a Zodiac victim. All he had to do was get the publicity hound Toschi and his good buddy Sherwood Morrill to sign off on this nonsense. It got them all a lot of publicity and probably sold a lot of papers. Mission accomplished.

In 1971, the "top suspect" Arthur Leigh Allen attempted to insert himself into the investigation by telling cops he had been in Riverside around the time of the Bates murder. I can't believe for an instant that a sharp investigator like David Toschi legitimately thought that a middle-aged, balding, 250-pound Arthur Leigh Allen was able to go undetected while he was scratching a poem into a desktop in a college library full of eighteen- and nineteen-year-olds.

The Zodiac didn't kill Cheri Jo Bates. The Zodiac is bullshit.

CHAPTER 14: OFFICER ZODIAC: WAS THE ZODIAC A COP?

HAVE YOU EVER SEEN A PLAINCLOTHES COP WORKING in the field and completely made them? Maybe they were a little too clean-cut for the role they were supposed to be playing or spoke and acted like a cop instead of who they were pretending to be. Whether consciously or not, you noticed that something was off and saw through the disguise. You were able to notice someone trying to conceal the fact they're a police officer while looking more like a cop than they would have if they had been in uniform. Despite the many tells that just scream "cop" to everyone around them, the plainclothes officer doesn't know you know. They think they're blending in.

I feel this way when I read the Zodiac letters. I feel like I'm looking at something very obviously written by a cop pretending not to be a cop. These letters couldn't give more cop vibes if they had a high and tight haircut, a professional sports jersey (untucked to conceal the gun on their hip or waistband), a pair of 1990s Oakley sunglasses, camouflage cargo shorts, and a pair of suburban-dad Nikes.

I was a police officer for seven years. Maybe that's why I'm attuned to these vibes. I was an average-at-best patrol cop. Oftentimes I felt more like a mall cop than a real cop. I was a 9/11 first responder and worked rescue and recovery at the World Trade Center crime scene for nine months following the attack. I retired on a line-of-duty disability pension. I have post-traumatic stress disorder, panic disorder, and a mild case of agoraphobia. That means I've got a lot of time on my hands to sit in my apartment and read old police reports, newspaper accounts, and interviews with the people involved with this case. When I exhausted the available Zodiac information, I set out to get more. I set up an Ancestry.com account and a Classmates.com account, and searched for people adjacent to these cases, as well as other criminals in the Zodiac era who haven't been interviewed and might want to chat. I focused on similar crimes in the area and paid extra attention to people the original investigators had been interested in. I believe that the cops working the cases in 1968 and 1969 had a pretty good idea of what they were dealing with before these crimes became mythological Zodiac murders. I wanted to talk to the people they talked to. I wanted to talk to the people (looking at the case in hindsight) they wish they'd spoken to back then. Sometimes I'd cold-call them. Sometimes I'd email them. A lot of people wanted to talk about their former lives. A few wanted nothing to do with it. Everyone I communicated with had their own theories about the Zodiac Killer and almost everyone had their own suspect. Quite a few people have been waiting over fifty years to tell their stories. I was never an investigator and can offer no professional insights from that point of view. But what I can offer is an anthropological insight into law-enforcement officers and police culture. I can spot a cop a mile away. And I spotted a cop in the Zodiac letters.

The first three letters are obvious. The Zodiac plagiarized police reports and copied mistakes right out of those reports. His tell was delivering facts without narrative. He listed how many rounds were fired and the type of ammo recovered and that Darlene was wearing a "slack dress" as though he were the reporting officer preparing an incident report about the crime instead of a crazed killer boasting about his kills. He followed the conventions of police-report writing. Habits are hard to break.

The fourth letter, the one where Chief Stiltz asked for more information, is where the Zodiac proved he was a liar when he bragged about affixing pencil lights and spraying bullets. That was pure fantasy. In reality, David Faraday was shot once in the head at point-blank range, execution-style.

The letters following the Paul Stine murder in San Francisco have cop written all over them too. The specific details the Zodiac harps on sound as though they were written by someone who was on scene. The letters read as if the Zodiac is offering a scathing critique of police tactics in the aftermath of the Paul Stine murder. It's an audit of what went wrong, written from the point of view of someone who was giving a play-by-play of the ineffectiveness of police procedures deployed, not someone who had just murdered a cabbie and was frantically making his escape from the police.

How could the Zodiac have witnessed all of this if he was truly escaping? The area was flooded with cops and K-9 units. A killer who had just shot a man at close range in a taxicab would likely be covered in blood. That man wasn't hanging around the Presidio taking notes on the failure of police standard operating procedures in the aftermath of the Stine murder. If he had been, SFPD officers would have caught him. The Zodiac could not have witnessed these things unless he had been right there, on scene, hiding in plain sight. The Zodiac does a bitter assessment of the uselessness of special units on scene: motor patrol, K-9, and a fire-department searchlight. The focus is on failed police tactics, not that of a killer offering details of a murder. The Zodiac, who had supposedly stolen Paul Stine's wallet, doesn't use his name. He refers to him as the cab driver. Zodiac writes, "The S.F. Police could have caught me last night if they had searched the park properly instead of holding road races with their motorcicles seeing who could make the most noise. The car drivers should have just parked their cars and sat there quietly waiting for me to come out of cover." This is certainly a departure from earlier Zodiac communications, when he didn't write like an expert witness on police tactics.

There's a great deal of very specific complaining about the police response to Stine's murder. The gripes in the letters come from an observer's point of view, not a fleeing criminal's. He sounds a lot like a disgruntled cop, furious over SFPD's poor handling of the Stine murder. It sounds like a critical after-action report from a police officer. The letter-writer isn't interested in the murder or the victim; he's laser-focused on the cops and their mistakes:

> So as you can see the police don't have much to work on. If you wonder why I was wipeing the cab down I was leaving fake clews for the police to run all over town with, as one might say, I gave the cops som bussy work to do to keep them happy. I enjoy needling the blue pigs. Hey blue pig I was in the park—you were useing fire trucks to mask the sound of your cruzeing prowl cars. The dogs never came with in 2 blocks of me + they were to the west + there was only 2 groups of parking about 10 min apart then the motor cicles went by about 150 ft away going from south to north west.

> Must print in paperps. 2 cops pulled a goof abot 3 min after I left the cab. I was walking down the hill to the park when this cop car pulled up + one of them called me over + asked if I saw anyone acting suspicious or strange in the last 5 to 10 min + I said yes there was this man who was runnig by waveing a gun + the cops peeled rubber + went around the corner as I directed them + I disappeared into the park a block + a half away never to be seen again.
>
> Hey pig doesnt it rile you up to have your noze rubed in your booboos?

This Zodiac doesn't care about the murder of Paul Stine. He offers no insight into this supposed crime he committed. His hyper-focus on the police response is a little too aware, too inside baseball, when he mentions the encounter with the police.

Apart from the two officers who may have seen, or stopped and questioned, a white man near the scene of the crime but never put it over the radio, how many people (besides the Zodiac) knew about Fouke and Zelms encountering a man who more or less matched the description the Robbins kids gave? When the Zodiac drops the "2 cops pulled a goof" bombshell about Fouke and Zelms, he tells the world he's keyed into SFPD gossip. Officer Fouke (one of the goofs) doesn't write his memo about his encounter with the male white subject until November 12, 1969, a month after Paul Stine was murdered and a couple of days after the Zodiac made the information public with his letter.

The Zodiac scooped Fouke and the SFPD. The Zodiac demanded that the paper "must print" the bit about two cops pulling a goof. That's the part that was important to the Zodiac. The whole Fouke-and-Zelms-meet-Zodiac saga never made it into Armond Pelissetti's very detailed SPFD incident report about the murder of Paul Stine. The circle of people who'd know about Fouke and Zelms playing catch-and-release with a possible killer would likely be very small and confined to the man they encountered and the cops working the scene—a scene run by Inspector Dave Toschi.

The Zodiac letter-writer seemed to be knowledgeable about police investigations long before his letters following the Paul Stine murder. The first three Zodiac letters and three-part cipher code arrived at the *San Francisco Examiner, San Francisco Chronicle,* and *Vallejo Times-Herald* on July 31, 1969. The FBI was unable to get directly involved or open its own investigation because the murders were local crimes and didn't fall under federal jurisdiction. But extortion through the mail is a federal crime. The FBI reasoned that the Zodiac's letters to the newspapers constituted extortion through the mail. The FBI approached all three newspapers about pressing charges as victims of extortion. If they filed, it would allow the top law-enforcement agency in the United States to conduct its own Zodiac investigation. The *Chronicle* and the *Examiner* flat out said no. They weren't interested in pressing charges against the Zodiac. The *Vallejo Times-Herald* agreed to press charges with the Feds. The FBI prepared an extortion case.

Strangely, the Zodiac never wrote to the Vallejo paper again.

The fact that the Zodiac deemed the *Vallejo Times-Herald* important enough to send a copy of his first letter and one-third of his cipher to, and actually got the front page he demanded (as opposed to the San Francisco papers), then never sent that newspaper another letter once they agreed to cooperate with the FBI indicates he might have had knowledge and understanding about the Zodiac investigation. If he had continued sending the *Vallejo Times-Herald* letters, he would have had to deal with the FBI opening a case against him and acting as lead investigator in an extortion case. If the FBI had had this case in August of 1969, it might have been solved quickly. How many civilians would have been aware of these investigatory machinations? Whoever wrote the letters seemed to understand the media as well as police investigations. The letter-writer may have pretended to be crazy, but he wasn't stupid. He wanted local cops investigating him, not G-men.

The sheer lack of forensic evidence present on the real Zodiac letters is remarkable. The letter-writer likely used gloves to avoid leaving a fingerprint. The letter-writer likely used water to seal the envelopes and affix the stamps instead of the more common practice of licking them. This was in 1969. DNA wasn't used in criminal cases until 1986, but this criminal didn't take any chances with leaving clues about himself behind. In 1969 it would have been possible to detect blood type from saliva. The Zodiac knew there was evidentiary value to saliva and opted to use water to seal the letters and stamp them. Not many people would possess this level of working forensic knowledge in 1969. If they had been a cop, they would be an incredibly smart and careful cop. The Zodiac letters that Inspector Toschi wrote contained saliva samples and a big, fat palm print. The Zodiac understood forensics better than super-cop Toschi.

CHAPTER 15: MEDIA MONSTER

ON APRIL 19, 1970, A FORTY-YEAR-OLD SAN FRANCISCO lamp-designer named Robert Salem was found murdered in his apartment. His ear was cut off and taken as a trophy by the killer. Salem was stabbed in the back and the chest, and his throat was slashed ear to ear in an attempt to decapitate him. Someone wrote, "SATAN SAVES ZODIAC," using Salem's blood on the wall of the apartment. The message was accompanied by the Egyptian ankh symbol. An ankh appears somewhat similar to the Zodiac symbol, but it's something entirely different. Paul Avery wrote an article about it called "The Bloody Satan Murder." The Zodiac Killer didn't commit this murder, but someone inspired by Manson wanted the world to think it was Zodiac. It was a messy copycat killing.

On November 2, 1970, the assistant district attorney for Livingston, Montana, called the SFPD to let them know that an inmate at Warm Springs State Hospital had told doctors about his involvement with the Robert Salem murder. This was no ordinary inmate. It was Stanley Dean Baker, the "Hippie Satanist Cannibal Killer." On July 13, 1970, a simple motor vehicle accident near Big Sur had turned into something out of a horror movie when two longhaired occupants of a van fled the scene on foot. The driver of the other car called the cops about the accident and Highway Patrol picked up the two men who fled, Stanley Dean Baker, age twenty-two, and Harry Allen Stroup, age twenty. Baker turned his pockets out and revealed a recipe for LSD, a copy of Anton LaVey's *Satanic Bible,* and a human finger bone that had been gnawed on. He then confessed to the highway patrolman, "I have a problem. I'm a cannibal."[110] It turns out he wasn't lying. The finger belonged to a twenty-two-year-old social worker named James Michael Schlosser who had picked up Baker and Stroup when they were hitchhiking near Yellowstone. Baker confessed to killing Schlosser, then cutting out and eating his heart. Fingerprints found in Robert Salem's San Francisco apartment belonged to Stanley Dean Baker (which explains the missing ear).[111] Despite Baker confessing to Salem's murder and the SFPD discovering his fingerprints in Salem's apartment, the San Francisco district attorney chose not to prosecute him for Salem's murder because Baker had already been given a life sentence in Montana. Did that have anything to do with the fact that Salem was an out and proud flamboyant gay man? Maybe. Or maybe it was pure pragmatism, like Solano County failing to prosecute Magris and Holmberg for the murders of David Faraday, Betty Lou Jensen, and Matthew Burrell because they were already on death row for another murder. Strangely, Baker's cannibal murder of Salem is hardly spoken about in the true-crime world outside of the fact that it was, for a short period of time, Zodiac-adjacent, which strengthened the legend of the Zodiac while leaving Salem largely forgotten to history.

On September 6, 1970, a Lake Tahoe resident named Donna Lass went missing after leaving the casino where she worked. In 1971 the *San Francisco Chronicle* got a Lake Tahoe postcard supposedly from the Zodiac. It arrived with the words "sought victim number 12," possibly referring to Lass. That was enough for the media to include Donna Lass in their Zodiac narrative. Her skull was found in 1986 and identified in 2023. According to NBC news, "South Lake Tahoe police Sgt. Nick Carlquist said that there has been speculation about Lass being connected to the Zodiac cases, 'but there has not been a definitive, evidence-based connection to support that.'" There is no evidence the Zodiac killed Donna Lass, but her murder fueled the Zodiac legend. When Zodiac fan websites run out of things to say about the five canonical Zodiac murders, they trot out Donna Lass and Cheri Jo Bates.

On October 12, 1970, the *San Francisco Examiner* put out an article linking the Zodiac to light opera and Gilbert and Sullivan. The unnamed investigator who tipped the newspaper with this blind item thought the Zodiac may have played a role in a production of the opera *The Mikado* due to the similarities between the Zodiac's letters and the lyrics in the opera. As it turns out, the lead investigator, Dave Toschi, was a keen fan of musicals and light opera and was known as a guy who was "always singing." This nonsense has nothing to do with the Zodiac case, but someone from the SFPD with a close relationship to the press and an interest in opera (I wonder who?) gave a reporter a tip. Anything to get the Zodiac back in the paper. That's where he's most powerful.

On June 28, 1972, the *Examiner* printed an article titled "Zodiac Pet Killer at Large." Thirty pets had been killed by poisoning in the Eureka Valley over a dozen years. The writer, Almena Lomax, really tried to make the Zodiac Pet Killer thing happen. It didn't catch on. Awesome headline, though.[112]

On March 22, 1970, Kathleen Johns, a seven-months-pregnant mother of a one-year-old told police she had encountered the Zodiac after leaving her mother's house in Petaluma, California. She told the police that, while driving with her one-year-old, a car had come up behind her and started flashing its lights, indicating that the driver was trying to get her attention. She pulled over. He warned her about a loose tire. She checked and the tire really was loose. He offered to drive her to a gas station. She accepted his ride but left the keys in her car and her headlights on. He turned her headlights off and pocketed the keys. They drove around for two hours. He never made an advance on her or bothered her, but he talked and rambled a lot, which made her nervous. She jumped out of his car at a stop sign, holding her young daughter like a football. He drove away. A couple of farmers took her and her kid to the police station. Once in the station, she saw the composite drawing of the Zodiac from Presidio Heights. She started screaming and crying, saying, "That's that man. My God, that's the man that picked us up." Cops found Johns's car torched on Highway 132.[113] The news media had a new Zodiac victim. The monster needs to be fed. The articles need to be pumped out. Her story didn't check out. Cops doubted that anything even happened. They wrote her off as a person experiencing an episode of mental illness who might have burned her own car and made up a Zodiac story. Kathleen Johns is not considered a Zodiac victim by professional investigators. Some of the more desperate and content-starved Zodiac fans and amateur sleuths still want to believe, and the Kathleen Johns joyride-from-hell story makes the rounds on the Zodiac entertainment websites.

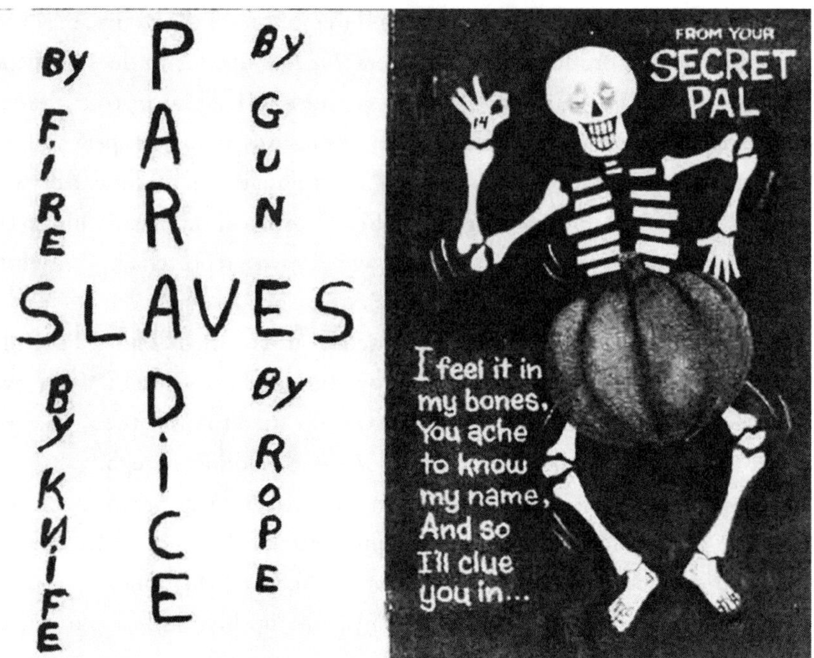

HALLOWEEN CARD. *MIAMI HERALD*, NOVEMBER 1, 1969. AP WIREPHOTO.

On October 31, 1970, Paul Avery got a Halloween card from the Zodiac.

On Easter 1971, an eighteen-year-old high-school honor student named Kathy Bilek was found dead in Saratoga, California. The *San Francisco Examiner* reported that the Zodiac Killer may have murdered her because her body was found in a park. Cops immediately said the Zodiac didn't do it, but the paper got a few salacious articles out of the connection.

Even Sherwood Morrill got in on the act with his tale of several Zodiac sightings at his own home. While Sherwood was out, a man and a woman rang the bell to his house and spoke to his wife. Mrs. Morrill was certain the Zodiac was standing in front of her in the doorway. The beefy man said, "Tell your husband he was correct about the letter"—meaning the fake 1978 Toschi letter that Morrill had declared was real. The guy came back another time and had a long conversation with Sherwood. According to the handwriting expert the guy had "an uncanny knowledge of the case. He knew things only the police knew. He even told me the make of the sewing machine the hood was stitched on." The guy came back again, and he and Sherwood hung out and chatted. This time the guy revealed to Morrill that he had just moved from

Petaluma—coincidentally, the same town Kathleen Johns, who was believed to be a Zodiac victim, had visited before encountering a man (not the Zodiac) who warned her about a loose tire. Sherwood asked him to write his address and phone number down, but that old sly fox Zodiac was too smart to write something for the handwriting expert. "I'm not going to write anything down for you," Totally-Not-the-Zodiac said. Sherwood Morrill checked the guy out (though he doesn't mention going to authorities with his Zodiac suspicions), but amazingly the guy never wrote anything by hand, ever, not even job applications. The guy typed everything.[114]

Graysmith's book came out right as America was in the grips of a full-scale Satanic Panic. The hippies sold out and had turned into yuppies by the mid-'80s. They were about as threatening as sitcom parents. If the media really wanted to scare people, they had to go old-school and bring back one of the classics: Satan. Satanic conspiracy theorists began popping up all over television in the 1980s. Maury Terry wrote a book called *The Ultimate Evil* about how New York's "Son of Sam" killer was assisted in carrying out his murders by a massive underground network of satanists. Naturally, this book became a bestseller, and its author became a go-to expert on occult and satanic crimes. Apparently, according to Terry, devil-worshippers were everywhere, committing ritual Satanic abuse against the innocent children of America via sexual molestation and even human sacrifices. The public really believed this nonsense. Teachers, babysitters, and daycare workers were accused of the most vile crimes carried out in the name of the devil. The McMartin family, who ran a daycare, were accused of 321 counts of ritual abuse that included sacrifices, blood-drinking, shit-eating, rape, and sodomy against forty-eight kids. None of this happened. It was pure unhinged bullshit from the sick imaginations of the parents and quack therapists who coached the kids into making these accusations and the reporters who turned this mess into a terrifying story that drew eyeballs. It took the family the better part of a decade and multiple court cases to finally beat the charges and clear their name as much as it could be cleared after allegations like those. These totally normal people were railroaded in a modern-day witch hunt and the news media gleefully covered the story. Disgusting.

In West Memphis, Arkansas, three teenage metalhead dirtbags—Damien Echols, Jesse Misskelley, and Jason Baldwin—got death sentences for the supposed Satanic ritual murders of three young boys. There wasn't a single shred of evidence that tied the West Memphis Three to those murders other than the fact that they wore black, acted creepy, had unironic mullets, and listened to Metallica, but an occult expert with a correspondence doctorate from a degree mill was able to convince a jury that they were Satanic murderers. Echols was sentenced to death and the others were given life sentences. In 2011, with the Satanic Panic far in the rear-view, and after nearly twenty years in prison, the West Memphis Three were allowed to cop an Alford plea, a legal compromise that allowed the three men to be released from prison while the state of Arkansas was able to keep their guilty verdict.

The British heavy-metal band Judas Priest were taken to trial in Reno, Nevada, in 1990 because of a drunken 1985 suicide pact between two metal fans, Raymond Belknap and James Vance. Belknap and Vance smoked some weed, drank some beers, listened to some Priest, then took a twelve-gauge shotgun to a church playground and shot themselves. Belknap died at the scene; Vance survived but was badly injured. He died from drug use three years later. Vance's parents sued Judas Priest and CBS Records for millions of dollars, claiming that their musical recordings contained hidden subliminal satanic messages that one could only hear when the records were played backwards or slowed down, and those messages encouraged the boys to commit suicide. This trial went on for five weeks before the judge ruled that it was a nonsensical case and the band wasn't liable for the deaths of the two young men.

During the Satanic Panic years of the 1980s and 1990s, the Zodiac case was viewed under a different, Satanic-cult-focused lens, and talk-show hosts such as Geraldo Rivera and Sally Jessy Raphael exploited that for ratings. Serial killers and Satan were big business during those years. The narrative around the Zodiac murders, especially concerning Darlene Ferrin, became occult-tinged. Darlene was accused of being a Satanic witch involved in a cult who attended a Black Mass at the Church of Satan in San Francisco, and "experts" hinted that she may have been killed by Satanists.

In 1991, an interview clip with Det. Ed Rust on the program *Now It Can Be Told* seemed to show him endorsing the theory that Darlene had been killed by Satanic conspirators who might have even been connected to Vallejo-area cops. Another original Zodiac investigator, Sgt. John Lynch, told the camera that he was informed that Darlene was involved with a witch and a cult. Dave Peterson, a journalist who covered the Zodiac for the *Vallejo Times-Herald,* endorsed the Darlene-was-in-a-Satanic-cult bullshit. Peterson was tied in with Howard Davis, an author who believed that the Zodiac murders were committed by the Manson Family and that the Los Angeles district attorney covered up the connection, including the infamous Zodiac hood supposedly being found at Manson's ranch during a search after Charlie's arrest. This is all ridiculous. What each of these people fails to realize is that the Satanism for sale at Anton LeVey's Church of Satan was not devil worship. Quite the opposite, it was non-theistic self-worship. The concept of gods and devils were a joke to LaVey and his pals who hung around the Black House in San Francisco. LaVey was selling hedonistic libertarian atheism and a touch of pop psychology and self-help wrapped up in a spooky showman's razzle-dazzle. It served as an even more underground alternative to San Francisco's flower-power counterculture, but it certainly wasn't devil worship. There are no supernatural entities in LaVeyan Satanism. The fictional character of Satan and imagery associated with Satan represent pride, carnality, survival of the fittest, and self-centeredness. The church rejects the supernatural. LaVey was into using curvy naked women, embodying the Earth Mother, as an adornment for his altar, not murder cults and a literal Satan. His Satan was symbolic, just part of his schtick and sales pitch. LaVey himself described satanism as "just Ayn Rand's philosophy with ceremony and ritual added."

On May 31, 1990, 78-year-old Joseph Proce was shot in the back by a man with a mustache and an improvised zip gun as he entered his Brooklyn brownstone. He died in the hospital three weeks later. Cops found a strange note at the crime scene: "This is the Zodiac the twelve sign will die when the belts in the heaven are seen." It was signed with the familiar Zodiac symbol from the 1969 Bay Area murders and the astrological signs Scorpio, Gemini, and Taurus. Unlike the letter writer from the '60s, this 1990s New York Zodiac was actually into astrology and knew about the signs of the Zodiac.

Like any good Zodiac copycat, the killer sent letters to the newspaper. The *New York Post* was the recipient, and this Zodiac was claiming three victims in three months, "the first sign is dead on march 8 1990. The second sign is dead on march 29 1990. The third sign is dead on may 31 1990."

Cops discovered that Mario Orozco, a Pisces, had been shot in the back with a zip gun on March 8, 1990. He survived with a bullet lodged near his spine. Jermaine Montenesdro, an Aries, was shot with a zip gun and the bullet went through his liver. He also survived. This copycat Zodiac shot nine people, killing three. He also left a series of taunting letters and cipher codes based on maritime flags at the crime scenes and sent them to the *New York Post*. This

Zodiac picked his victims based on their star signs. This Zodiac was more of a Zodiac Killer than the "real" Zodiac Killer. The NYPD called in a professional astronomer to predict when the killer would strike based on the stars. The father-in-law of a *Post* reporter and World War II naval-intelligence officer was able to crack the code based on maritime signal flags. The fifty NYPD detectives working the case considered Robert Graysmith's book *Zodiac* to be their "bible" for understanding the killer and finding clues.[115] Graysmith was back on the promotional hustle. He traveled to New York to have a look at the crime scenes. He came to the conclusion that the killer must be a census-taker, which would explain why he knew accurate star-sign information on the victims. Graysmith called the New York Zodiac's letters "an imitation of the San Francisco Zodiac's, but not a very good one." Graysmith lamented, "I wrote a book to catch a killer, not to inspire another one."[116] Sales of his paperback *Zodiac,* now in its tenth printing, doubled with the emergence of the New York Zodiac. At least somebody made good from this mess.

Four years went by, and the New York Zodiac hadn't been caught. In March of 1994, the NYPD stopped, questioned, and frisked a guy named Heriberto Seda when they noticed a gun-shaped bulge in his jacket pocket. That bulge turned out to be a zip gun. The twenty-six-year-old unemployed high-school dropout who lived with his mother was arrested. Seda, who made money by stealing coins from payphones and vending machines, experienced what he thought was a miracle that proved he was beyond consequences when his public defender got the weapons charges against him thrown out. On June 11, 1996, Seda got into an argument with his sister and her boyfriend. This led to a standoff with police, a hostage situation, and Seda shooting his sister in the ass. Seda surrendered more than a dozen homemade zip guns to the cops and cops found two pipe bombs during a search of his mother's apartment. Seda was not suspected in the Zodiac murders, but he signed a statement with the Zodiac symbol and cops put two and two together. Seda, an unkissed, friendless virgin who slept his days away, claimed to have been inspired by a PBS television program about the Zodiac Killer. He thought he'd follow the Zodiac's example and get "famous."[117] He was tried twice, getting an eighty-three-year sentence, followed by a 152-year sentence. He wasn't the only one to use the legend of the Zodiac Killer to achieve a measure of fame.

The Zodiac was a myth, no more real than Slenderman and other Internet-era boogeymen decades later. When staring into the abyss of the harsh, uncaring reality of life, it is tempting to fill that abyss with myths and legends. David Faraday, Betty Lou Jensen, Darlene Ferrin, and Paul Stine were all brutally murdered and the cops never caught their killers. The world makes sense if they were victims of a criminal mastermind who evaded capture for five and a half decades. That explanation requires one sentence and zero thought. It's a lot harder to process how the justice system denied the Faraday and Jensen (and Burrell) families and everyone who loved David and Betty Lou justice by failing to bring the thrillkiller David Magris to trial for their murders. It's easier to believe that a mysterious Zodiac Killer existed and murdered the kids because he wanted their souls as "slaves in Paradise" than it is to believe that Solano County authorities "knew" who committed the murders, as well as the murder of Matthew Burrell, and just sat on their hands instead of pursuing justice. The horror-tinged story sells better than the bleak story of the former ballet dancer and his buddy hopped up on a psychosis-inducing cocktail of methedrine and LSD driving around Vallejo killing people for fun. The real horrors are too much to handle. The Code Killer is easier to digest.

Statistically speaking, Darlene Ferrin was probably murdered by a man she knew, likely someone who was once an intimate partner. There's a chance that man might have even worn a police uniform. Her murder was banal evil. It was likely motivated by sexual jealousy. That's terrifying because it could happen to anyone and be carried out by anyone. Her killer wasn't a monster or a mastermind, or a frothing-at-the-mouth maniac. He was an ordinary man. He probably had a job and a family and people who loved him. The cops didn't catch him. Maybe they weren't trying too hard. It's unsettling to look back at all the women murdered in the Vallejo area in the Zodiac era and see how the police shitcanned the investigations and made them go away because they didn't care enough to make the effort if the murdered woman slept around, dated cops, or managed a strip club. Just rule it a suicide. Tell the reporters she tried killing herself in the past. Shrug your shoulders and say, "Maybe it was a maniac." Don't look too hard or you might find an answer. Answers are messy. Nobody wants the truth. They want to believe that Dave Toschi spent a decade in pursuit of the Zodiac. They don't want to hear that he faked Zodiac evidence and used the murders to get media attention for himself.

No one would be talking about the Zodiac today if it weren't for a former *San Francisco Chronicle* political cartoonist named Robert Graysmith. When the rest of the world stopped caring about the Zodiac Killer, Graysmith registered a copyright for a book he hoped to write about the case. Graysmith had worked as a political cartoonist at the *Chronicle* when the Zodiac letters were coming in. He developed a friendship with Dave Toschi and used him as a source for a lot of his material. He had access to the investigators and some of the police reports when nobody else did. He was obsessed. Graysmith spent nearly a decade writing and researching his book, and in the late 1970s he began to shop it around to publishers.

After Toschi's great Zodiac letter-writing scandal of 1978, interest in the case was practically non-existent. The hippie-era boogeyman seemed, in the disco era, like a mass delusion based on a silly hoax. But Graysmith was undeterred. Robert Graysmith either believed he had cracked the Zodiac's "340 cipher" or thought having a go at it would be a great way to publicize the book he was hawking. The 340 cipher was a then-unsolved 340-character cryptogram included with the Zodiac's November 8, 1969, letter to the *San Francisco Chronicle.* Graysmith contacted the FBI and presented them with his code solution. It was as follows:

Herb Caen: I give them hell too
to dead hell is a clue.
there some see a name below
a killer's game is pills parole
me. Cops met to talk to me.
Such time. These fools helpd me.
Mad killer places a mask.
Bull S.
Alone pleasured I'd like to kill.
Scared I eat a pilll.
Asshole I plan to harm phone ask.
CB sells slaves because all
collection either please to lie in hell.
He's me. Toschi the pig leads me.
Collects eighth some mail KT

If this solution seems incredibly odd to you, you're not the only one. Why would the Zodiac have cared about Dave Toschi way back in November of 1969? Toschi had just caught the case a couple of weeks earlier. The Zodiac

ROBERT GRAYSMITH. *TIMES COLONIST*, MARCH 4, 2007.

had never mentioned a police investigator by name before. And why Toschi? Sergeant Lundblad, Sergeant Lynch, Detective Rust, and Detective Narlow had all been on the case longer. And more troublingly, why does Graysmith's solution sound so similar to Toschi's fake 1978 letter? Here's a refresher on the letter Toschi had written:

> Dear Editor
> This is the Zodiac speaking I am back with you. Tell herb caen I am here, I have always been here. That city pig toschi is good - but I am ~~bu~~ smarter and better he will get tired then leave me alone. I am waiting for a good movie about me. who will play me. I am now in control of all things.
> Yours truly:
> ⊕ - guess
> SFPD – 0

This whole thing stinks, but it got Graysmith some much needed press in the local newspapers for the Zodiac manuscript he was trying to sell to a publisher in 1979. Graysmith included a version of this cipher solution in his 1986 book *Zodiac* in the form of a poem. I'm not making that up. It really happened. He really did that. The FBI thought the whole thing was garbage. Here's what they had to say about Graysmith's attempt at code breaking:

> **Based upon the information available, it is the opinion of respondent that the solution is not a valid decryption. . . . The total feeling generated toward the decrypted solution is that the solution has been forced. First the random-like transposition system permitted the various vowels and consonants to be forced into words, then the words were forced into being poetry in an effort to give them meaning. Just about any random selection of words could be arranged to be as "logical" as those in the supposed poetic solution. (It is noted that the initial ZODIAC decrypted message was particularly clear as to the meaning ZODIAC desired to communicate.) When a cryptogram has been decrypted properly there is an unmistakable sense of rightness about the solution. This sense of rightness is completely absent in the proposed solution.**

For some reason, the FBI failed to notice or mention how similar his solution was to his buddy's fake Zodiac letter. The Zodiac had been off the radar for at least four years if you believe the "Exorcist" letter is legit (and you shouldn't). Then, after years of radio silence, Toschi fakes a letter. Right after that, Graysmith publicly pretends he cracked the 340 code, and it sounds just like Toschi's letter. Nobody involved in profiting from the Zodiac-industrial complex calls bullshit on this absolute nonsensical chain of events. They treat it as a simple code-breaking error on Graysmith's part due to exuberance. Graysmith, the person who most benefited from the Zodiac case, made Toschi the hero of his bestselling book (and we know how much Toschi loved being a hero), yet nobody suspects that they colluded to get a new Zodiac letter and a solution to a Zodiac cipher in the press to promote Graysmith's book. Fascinating.

In 2020, three actual experts—the American computer programmer David Oranchak, the Belgian computer programmer Jarl Van Eycke, and the Australian applied mathematician Sam Blake—cracked the Zodiac's 340 code. Here's the Zodiac message that was hidden in the cipher for over a half-century:

I HOPE YOU ARE HAVING LOTS OF FUN IN TRYING TO CATCH ME
THAT WASNT ME ON THE TV SHOW
WHICH BRINGS UP A POINT ABOUT ME

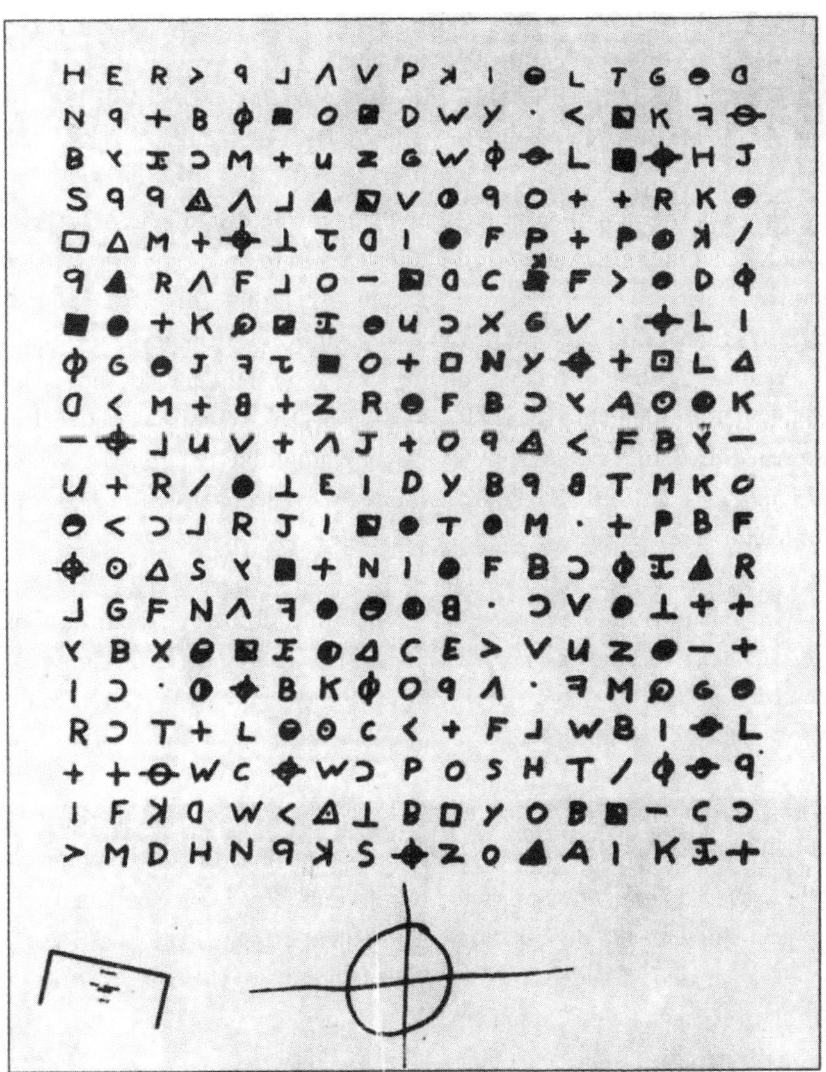

340-CIPHER. *BILLINGS GAZETTE*, MARCH 4, 2007.

I AM NOT AFRAID OF THE GAS CHAMBER
BECAUSE IT WILL SEND ME TO PARADICE ALL THE SOONER
BECAUSE I NOW HAVE ENOUGH SLAVES TO WORK FOR ME
WHERE EVERYONE ELSE HAS NOTHING WHEN THEY REACH PARADICE
SO THEY ARE AFRAID OF DEATH
I AM NOT AFRAID BECAUSE I KNOW THAT MY NEW LIFE IS
LIFE WILL BE AN EASY ONE IN PARADICE DEATH

This was the most significant movement in the case in the nearly two decades since the SFPD had made the 2004 decision to declare the investigation inactive. Civilian Zodiac researchers accomplished this. This Zodiac sounds like the original Zodiac from the three-part cipher. He's talking about "slaves in Paradice" again. He's talking about the fiasco on Jim Dunbar's show. This Zodiac doesn't sound like the Zodiac who wrote Dave Toschi's fake letter. This isn't a televised stunt where DNA is for some reason collected from the outside of a stamp that any cop, secretary, or postal employee could have touched. This is something real in a case littered with bullshit.

On January 1, 1986, St. Martin's Press published Robert Graysmith's book titled *Zodiac: The Full Story of the Infamous Unsolved Murders in California*. Four months later, someone purporting to be the Zodiac wrote a letter to the *San Francisco Chronicle*:

This is the Zodiac speaking I am still out here and crack proof. I want you to know about my latest slaves that I have collected about two weeks ago up by Sacramento California. I will give you clue to help you with the mystery. They were killed by a freeway. The Blue Meanies almost caught me. The Body count is growing nearly 100+ all over the state of Ca and Na.
SFPD - 0
Zodiac - 100+

Despite rumors of the band being back together, this wasn't the real deal. This letter is as close to the real Zodiac as an Elvis impersonator in Laughlin, Nevada, is to the King of Rock 'n' Roll. It's good, but it's another crank letter in the long tradition of crank Zodiac letters. Maybe the writer was inspired by Graysmith's book. Maybe the letter was a not-so-clever ham-fisted way to garner publicity for Graysmith's book. Maybe something else. Whatever the case, it's bullshit. The cops wanted nothing to do with it and the papers didn't run with it despite the claim that the Zodiac had over 100 victims.

A letter postmarked October 27, 1987, was sent to the *Vallejo Times-Herald*:

> This is the Zodiac speaking I am crack proof. Tell Herb Caen that I am still here. I have always been here. Tell the blue pigs if want me I will be driving around on Halloween in my death machine looking for some kiddies to run over. Cars make nice weapons. The pigs can catch me if they can find me out there just like in the movie The Car. Tell the kiddies watch before they cross the street on Halloween night. Tell Tochi my new plans. Yours Truly:
>
> Zodiac - quess
>
> VPD - 0

Artificial-intelligence programs like ChatGPT didn't exist in 1987, but this letter sounds like a Zodiac parody generated by a computer using the earlier letters as reference. It's the greatest-hits medley. Toschi's name is back again, but the spelling is wrong. Herb Caen's back too. The Zodiac's still talking about Blue Meanies like a sixties hepcat in 1987. The letter is bullshit. The cops and the papers don't even pretend this time. After the embarrassment caused by the 1978 letter fiasco, nobody takes the bait. It's not taken seriously. Not even the most ardent Zodiac true believers and hucksters are trying to pass this letter or the 1986 one off as legit. Nobody's buying it this time. That joke isn't funny anymore. Even Graysmith thinks it's bullshit. He tells the *San Francisco Examiner,* "There's nothing original about it. . . . And he misspelled Toschi. I can't imagine him doing that. Zodiac has a lot of respect for Toschi."[118] The Zodiac has a lot of respect for Toschi? What? Why would Graysmith say that? That might be the most unhinged statement in this completely unhinged story. How would Graysmith know how the Zodiac felt about Toschi? Graysmith presents an extremely odd reason for discounting the letter. Even more unbelievable is Toschi telling the *Examiner* he hadn't seen the letter, then adding, "I know there are a lot of copycats out there."[119] Toschi would never miss a chance to see his name in the paper. The *Examiner* wrote about Toschi on July 11, 1978: "he is a man done in by his own admiration for newspaper stories that mentioned his name."

The letter-writer is a competent copycat artist. It kind of looks like the real thing, and it sounds like the real thing. He hits all the right notes and takes extraordinary measures to appear authentic, but that copycat band isn't Led Zeppelin no matter how well they mimic the look and sound. If you close your eyes and force yourself to believe, then maybe for a second you might, but as soon as you open your eyes and the fog machine subsides it's clear that they're Kingdom Come or Bonham and not the genuine article.

Why would the Zodiac care about Dave Toschi in 1987? Toschi had been removed as an investigator in the Zodiac case in 1978. Jim Deasy had overseen investigating Zodiac for nearly a decade. The case was frozen cold. The SFPD had shipped their Zodiac files to Sacramento and weren't interested. Toschi had retired from the SFPD on July 3, 1985, and become the director of security at St. Luke's Hospital in the Mission district. Toschi wasn't out there conducting an independent investigation, determined to catch the Zodiac at all costs, like some kind of madman movie cop. Toschi was basking in his return to prominence following Graysmith's book. He had Hollywood in mind when he told the *Examiner,* "I'd like to be technical director" if the bestselling Zodiac book in its third printing was ever made into a movie.[120] No one on earth was invested in getting Dave Toschi's name in the newspaper as much as Dave Toschi was invested in getting his name in the newspaper. The guy couldn't help himself. The letter comes from someone who knew the Zodiac letters well enough to copy even the smallest details on the envelope and get them right. Toschi was so knowledgeable about the letters, he fooled the experts until Armistead Maupin sounded the alarm and people started to look at Toschi and the Zodiac evidence sideways. The Zodiac wasn't writing letters about a retired cop. A retired cop and wannabe technical director was still writing letters to the paper pretending to be the Zodiac.

Toschi once told reporters about a particularly distressing time in his life at an SFPD press conference—when a reporter asked police senior officers, "Could Toschi be Zodiac?"[121]

That's a fair question. Was he the serial killer calling himself the Zodiac who terrorized the Bay Area in 1968 and 1969? No, he absolutely wasn't. He was a lot of things, but he wasn't a killer. Still, Toschi was the Zodiac as much as anyone else was the Zodiac. The Zodiac didn't exist in real life—he only existed on the pages of the newspapers and in the imagination of a titillated public. Toschi played a significant part in creating and expanding the Zodiac legend not only with his position as the media-friendly lead detective trying to catch the Zodiac but with the letters he wrote claiming to be from the Zodiac. Toschi's friend Sherwood Morrill used the pseudoscience of handwriting analysis to authenticate these letters. Without Morrill's credulity stretching authentications, the Zodiac wouldn't exist. Sherwood Morrill was the Zodiac too. Toschi's other pal Robert Graysmith popularized the Zodiac legend to millions of people with a mass-market paperback. Graysmith was the Zodiac's greatest promoter. He turned a myth into a legend. Graysmith was the Zodiac too. Without Toschi's grandstanding and Graysmith's trade paperback, Zodiac would have been a long-forgotten relic of the 1960s. They kept him alive and allowed him to reach greater heights than he had in his sixties heyday. Paul Avery's articles allowed the Zodiac to live on in the newspaper years after the alleged crime spree ended. He turned the Cheri Jo Bates murder into a canonical Zodiac crime for decades in the public's imagination until the cops put the kibosh on that. Avery was the Zodiac too.

David Magris confessed to being involved in the two Zodiac murders at Lake Herman Road, but David Magris wasn't the Zodiac. David Magris was the anti-Zodiac; he was the real killer, not the guy pretending to be him in silly letters to the newspaper. The guy with access to police reports who wrote the letters following the murder of Darlene Ferrin, taking credit for Magris's murder while Magris was in jail, was the creator of the Zodiac character. The letter-writer was Stan Lee and Zodiac was his Spider-Man. The Solano County district attorney's office could have killed the Zodiac myth before it started by taking Magris and his partner to trial for the murders of Betty Lou Jensen and David Faraday. After securing a murder conviction and the death penalty for Magris, the county wasn't keen on another long and expensive Magris circus trial. Their pragmatic inaction created the vacuum that allowed the Zodiac to exist. Eric Weil, who spoke to Melvin Belli on Jim Dunbar's show from a phone in a mental hospital, didn't commit any of the murders, but he was the Zodiac for two hours. Every single crank-letter-writer pretending to be the Zodiac was the Zodiac.

David Fincher made a massive Hollywood movie about Graysmith's obsession with the case. It was supposed to be about the Zodiac murders based on Graysmith's book, but when Fincher and his team of researchers investigated the case and found discrepancies between reality and Graysmith's book, they pivoted and made a movie about a reporter and a cop obsessed with an unsolvable case. That movie was brilliant and brought renewed interest to the Zodiac case in the age of the podcast and YouTube video. Fincher was the Zodiac too. So were the podcasters, streamers, webmasters, true-crime authors, and forum posters. They're all the Zodiac. All of these Zodiacs kept the legend alive decades past its expiration date. Without these people, the Zodiac story wouldn't have the oxygen needed to survive past 1969.

Everyone was the Zodiac.

No one was the Zodiac.

⌖

ACKNOWLEDGEMENTS

I want to thank my wife, Meirav Devash, for supporting me during this project. I can't believe you put up with my nonstop Zodiac info dumping and pretended to be cool with me tracking down some truly terrifying people.

None of this would have been possible without the interest and support of Christina Ward and Jessica Parfrey of the mighty Feral House. Thank you to Chris Roth for your attention to detail and helpful edits. Thank you to Ron Kretsch for the killer design.

A special thank you goes to Mike Lewi for coming up with the title *Zodiactually*, and inviting me to bounce my theories off the unsuspecting public at House of Know. Thanks to Daniel McGowan for taking an early interest in my project and welcoming me to speak at Tiny Raccoon Books. Additionally, I want to thank Nick Braccia, Ilise S. Carter, Christine Colby, James Fitzsimmons, and Mike Monello for listening to me hash out, in excruciating detail, my many discoveries along the way.

I'd like to extend a huge thank you to the former kids of Vallejo, now in their seventies, for taking the time to talk and message with me and set the record straight about what was really going on there in the late '60s. Thanks to the former criminals of the Bay Area who took an uncomfortable trip back to the bad old days with me. I'd also like to thank Dale Bromell, the Doyel family, Brendan Riley, Dian Stevens, and George Waters for answering my questions. I'd like to further thank the California Department of Corrections and Rehabilitation, Solano County Courts, Solano County Historical Society, Vallejo Public Library, and all the retired and active members of law enforcement who helped or heard me out.

Finally, I owe a debt of gratitude to the many Zodiac experts and obsessives for all the investigative work they've done over the years, including Mike Bassham, Sandy Betts, Michael Butterfield, Michael Cole, Max Daly, Ned DeHan, Bernie Doherty, Ray Grant, Robert Graysmith, Richard Grinell, Thomas Horan, Jarrett Kobek, Mike Morford, Mike Rodelli, Joseph Shores, and Tom Voigt. I have learned so much from all of you.

NOTES

1 "100 Women: The Truth behind the 'Bra-Burning' Feminists," *BBC News*, September 18, 2018, https://www.bbc.com/news/world-45303069.

2 Lindsy Van Gelder, "There Was Grit and Talent Galore," *JSTOR Daily*, June 18, 2020, https://daily.jstor.org/there-was-grit-and-talent-galore/.

3 Greg Marx, "Fact-Checking Bra-Burning, and Related Thoughts," *Columbia Journalism Review*, November 15, 2009, https://www.cjr.org/the_kicker/factchecking_braburning_and_re.php.

4 Carrie A. Rentschler, "The Physiognomic Turn," *Journal of Communication* 4 (2010): 231-365; Robert D. McFadden, "Winston Moseley, 81, Killer of Kitty Genovese, Dies in Prison," *New York Times*, April 4, 2016.

5 "Winston Moseley, 81, Killer of Kitty Genovese, Dies in Prison," *New York Times*, April 4, 2016.

6 Sam Roberts, "Sophia Farrar, Witness in Kitty Genovese Case, Dies at 90," *New York Times*, September 2, 2020.

7 Vincent Bugliosi, *Helter Skelter: Part Eight of the Shocking Manson Murders* (ebook), Cornerstone Digital, 2015, https://www.penguin.co.uk/books/431733/helter-skelter-part-eight-of-the-shocking-manson-murders-by-vincent-bugliosi-and-curt-gentry/9781473519055.

8 A. L. Bardach, "Jailhouse Interview: Bobby Beausoleil," *Bardach Reports*, https://www.bardachreports.com/death-trips-new-yorks-unwanted-dead-1.

9 Donna Beth Weilenman, "Citizens Police Academy: Signs of the Zodiac," *Benicia* [Calif.] *Herald*, June 2, 2013.

10 "Large Quantity of Marijuana" (article), https://attachment.tapatalk-cdn.com/11510/202309/10762221_cf423e55230eb639a1807de82933e756.jpeg.

11 "Search Evidence Asked Suppressed," *Vallejo* [Calif.] *Times-Herald*, March 1, 1969, p. 7

12 "This Is the Zodiac Speaking," YouTube, uploaded by Pedrosbox, January 27, 2013, https://www.youtube.com/watch?t=3m5s&v=HI0jnsbZwys&feature=youtu.be.

13 "Benicians Not Keeping off the Grass," *Solano-Napa* [Calif.] *News Chronicle*, August 8, 1967, p. 7.

14 "Benicia," *Vallejo Times-Herald*, May 7, 1967, p. 2.

15 "Lake Herman Road Police Report," p. 52, ZodiacKiller.com, https://www.zodiackiller.com/LHRPR52.html.

16 "Lake Herman Road Police Report," p. 34, ZodiacKiller.com, https://www.zodiackiller.com/LHRPR34.html.

17 "Lake Herman Road Police Report," p. 53, ZodiacKiller.com, https://www.zodiackiller.com/LHRPR53.html.

18 "Lake Herman Road Police Report," p. 48, ZodiacKiller.com, https://www.zodiackiller.com/LHRPR48.html.

19 "19 SCSO Police Report, Case No. V22564," p. 34.

20 "Lake Herman Road Police Report," p. 48, ZodiacKiller.com, https://www.zodiackiller.com/LHRPR48.html.

21 Tom Voigt, *Zodiac Killer: Just the Facts*, Brainjar Media, p. 66.

22 "Reward Fund Grows in Vallejo Murders," *Vallejo Times-Herald*, February 13, 1969, p. 13.

23 "Lake Herman Road Police Report," p. 34.

24 "Hunt Maniac in Murders of Teenagers," *Vallejo Times-Herald*, December 23, 1968, p. 1.

25 Richard Grinell, "The White Chevrolet Impala," *Zodiac Ciphers*, March 16, 2015, https://www.zodiacciphers.com/zodiac-news/the-white-chevrolet-impala.

26 "Hunt Maniac in Murders of Teenagers", *Vallejo Times-Herald*, December 23, 1968, p. 1.

27 "Gunman Slays Vallejoan," *Napa Valley Register*, January 4, 1969, p. 2.

28 "Local Youth Dances with Soviet Troupe," *Solano-Napa News Chronicle*, December 4, 1964, p. 7.

29 D. Patrick Miller, "A Brutal Sadness," *Sun Magazine*, August 1993.

30 "Police Arrest 8 Persons," *Solano-Napa News Chronicle*, August, 9, 1968, page 2.

31 "Parents of 6 Neglected Tots Hunted," *San Francisco Examiner*, June 19, 1956, p. 3.

32 "Hells Angels, Girl Friends Battle Cops," *Concord* [Calif.] *Transcript*, May 29, 1967, p. 3.

33 "Murder Defendant's Kin at Drug Charge Hearing." *Vallejo Times-Herald*, July 31, 1969, p. 6.

34 "Warrants Issued for Four," *Reno* [Nev.] *Gazette-Journal*, July 8, 1967, p. 2.

35 "Girl Questioned about Conflicts," *Vallejo Times-Herald*, June 21, 1969, p. 4.

36 David M. Fergusson, Joseph M. Boden, and L. John Horwood, "Psychosocial Sequelae of Abortion: A Long-Term Study," *British Journal of Psychiatry* 208(3) (2016): 273-80.

37 "Witnesses Tell Court Magris Has Killed and Robbed Before," *Daily Republic* (Fairfield, Calif.), November 16, 1969, p. 2.

38 "Trial," *Vallejo Times-Herald*, November 15, 1969, p. 2.

39 "Trial," p. 7.

40 Miller, "A Brutal Sadness."

41 "David Luis Magris, June 2, 1948–August 17, 2023," Scobee-Combs-Bowden Funeral Home, August 17, 2023, https://www.scobeecombsbowdenfuneralhome.com/obituaries/David-Magris/#!/Obituary.
42 "Frank Zona Obituary," Legacy.com (from *Whittier* [Calif.] *Daily News*, February 3-4, 2015), https://www.legacy.com/us/obituaries/whittierdailynews/name/frank-zona-obituary?id=6897327.
43 "Agents Testify about Drug Raid," *Vallejo Times-Herald*, September 30, 1971, p. 17.
44 "Vallejo Man, Wife Are Sentenced on Nine Drug Charges,", *Vallejo Times-Herald*, October 23, 1971, p. 7.
45 "Convicted Slayer Linked to Another Murder in Vallejo," *Vallejo Times-Herald*, November 15, 1969, pp. 1-2.
46 "Partners in Crime Went Free," *Sacramento Bee*, November 13, 1995, p. 8.
47 "Suspect Linked to Defendant Jailed on Burglary Count," *Solano-Napa News Chronicle*, June 26, 1969, p. 3.
48 "Judge," *Vallejo Times-Herald*, September 3, 1969, p. 2.
49 John Johnson, "Zodiac Case: New Evidence Emerges," *Los Angeles Times*, July 28, 1996.
50 "Young Attendant Shot in Attempted Murder," *Vallejo Times-Herald*, September 21, 1969, p. 1.
51 "Youth Unshaken on Telling Story," *Vallejo Times-Herald*, November 1, 1969, p. 2.
52 "Vallejo Okays Protection for Two Shooting Victims," *Sacramento Bee*, August 23, 1969, p. 5.
53 "Jury Life-Death Decision Nearing," *Vallejo Times-Herald*, November 19, 1969, p. 2.
54 "Convicted Slayer Linked to Another Murder in Vallejo," *Vallejo Times-Herald*, November 15, 1969, p. 1.
55 "Gun Link to Earlier Slaying," *Solano-Napa News Chronicle*, November 14, 1969, p. 1.
56 "Girlfriend Gives Trial Testimony." *Vallejo Times-Herald*, October 22, 1969, p. 12.
57 "Former Partners in Crime Go Straight, Grow Apart," *Tribune*, November 23, 1995, p. 45.
58 "Solano Jurors Will Decide Life or Death for Killers," *Vallejo Times-Herald*, November 20, 1969, p, 10.
59 "Zodiac Killer: COTC47," ZodiacKiller.com, https://www.zodiackiller.com/COTC47.html.
60 "Zodiac Killer: COTC48," ZodiacKiller.com, https://www.zodiackiller.com/COTC48.html.
61 "Police Disagree about …," https://imgur.com/a/RzfHIJn.
62 "Appeals Court Upholds Decision," *Vallejo Times-Herald*, May 3, 1973, p. 4.
63 "Zodiac Killer: COTC1," ZodiacKiller.com, https://www.zodiackiller.com/COTC1.html.
64 "Two Counties Show 23 Murders in Year," *Vallejo Times-Herald*, October 26, 1969, p. 6.
65 "Cunningham for Sheriff," advertisement, *Vallejo Times-Herald*, May 25, 1970, p. 4.
66 "Gun Traced in Shooting," *Vallejo Times-Herald*, November 20, 1972, p. 10.
67 "County Jail Sentence in Shooting Case Here," *Daily Republic*, June 11, 1971, p. 3
68 "Vallejo Police, Firemen Strike," *San Mateo* [Calif.] *Times*, July 18, 1969, p. 41.
69 "The Great Danger of False Alarms," *Vallejo Times-Herald*, July 20, 1969, p. 1.
70 "Search Evidence Asked Suppressed," *Vallejo Times-Herald*, March 1, 1969, p. 7.
71 Anna E. Jaffe *et al.*, "Is the Risk for Sexual Revictimization Cumulative? A Prospective Examination," *Women's Health Issues* 33, no. 2 (March–April 2023): 208–214, https://www.ncbi.nlm.nih.gov/pmc/articles/PMC10023376/.
72 Sandy Betts, Zodiac Killer FR Forum, Tapatalk, October 5, 2018, https://www.tapatalk.com/groups/zodiackillerfr/viewtopic.php?p=133637#p133637.
73 "Morf13," Zodiac Killer FR Forum, Tapatalk, January 15, 2022, https://www.tapatalk.com/groups/zodiackillerfr/viewtopic.php?p=194064#p194064.
74 Betts, Zodiac Killer FR Forum, Tapatalk, October 15, 2018, https://www.tapatalk.com/groups/zodiackillerfr/viewtopic.php?p=133637#p133637.
75 "Lake Herman Drug Bust," Zodiac Killer Forum, Forumotion, July 28, 2015, https://zodiackiller.forumotion.com/t89-lake-herman-drug-bust.
76 "Lake Herman Road Crime Scene Photograph," ZodiacKillerFacts.com, https://zodiackillerfacts.com/gallery/displayimage.php?album=48&pid=515#top_display_media.
77 "Benicia Mother Takes Own Life," *Vallejo Times-Herald*, January 26, 1972, p. 4.
78 Jennifer L. Hughes *et al.*, "Suicide and the Criminal Justice System: Understanding the Role of Arrest and Incarceration," *Health & Justice* 10(1) (2022).
79 Interview with Bryan Hartnell, *Shadow of the Zodiac*, October 30, 2019, https://www.shadowofthezodiac.com/bryan-hartnell/.
80 "Lake Berryessa: A Survivor's Story," ZodiacKillerFacts.com.
81 Richard Grinell, "Through the Mask," ZodiacCiphers.com.
82 Grinell, "Lake Berryessa: Killer and Caller the Same?", ZodiacCiphers.com, https://www.zodiacciphers.com/zodiac-news/lake-berryessa-killer-and-caller-the-same.
83 Brendan Riley, "Brendan Riley's Solano Chronicles: Mafia Soldier Once Lived in Vallejo," *Vallejo Times-Herald*, September 30, 2018.

84 "#5—Allen: Another Investigation," ZodiacKillerFacts.com, https://zodiackillerfacts.com/zodiac-theories/the-accused-the-accusers/allen-primed-suspect/allen-part-5/.

85 "#5—Allen: Another Investigation," ZodiacKillerFacts.com.

86 "Vallejo Police Have Sent Zodiac Killer DNA to a Lab," *Sacramento Bee*, April 30, 2018.

87 "New Info on Zodiac Killer Bloody Fingerprints," YouTube video, uploaded by Zodiac Killer Official, May 7, 2023, https://www.youtube.com/watch?v=TsD2zxRG04w.

88 "This Is the Zodiac Speaking," YouTube video, uploaded by Zodiac Killer Documentaries, June 2, 2016, https://www.youtube.com/watch?v=1t7qpDNU4RM.

89 "New Zodiac Outburst Possible in Shooting of S.F. Cab Driver," *Los Angeles Times*, January 26, 1970, p. 1.

90 "The Day the Police Blew the Lid off a Pot-Smoking Bus Boy," *San Francisco Examiner*, May 20, 1970, p. 64.

91 Grinell, "The Fingerprint of a Killer," ZodiacCiphers.com, https://www.zodiacciphers.com/zodiac-news/the-fingerprint-of-a-killer.

92 Jon Blistein, "Zodiac Killer Letters Were Analyzed by an AI—and the Results Are Terrifying," Yahoo Entertainment, October 2, 2023, https://www.yahoo.com/entertainment/zodiac-killer-letters-were-analyzed-201601857.html.

93 "Zodiac Cop Files a Claim for Disability," *San Francisco Examiner*, September 1, 1978, p. 6.

94 "Maupin Tells His Version of the 'Zodiac' Fan Letters to Toschi," *San Francisco Examiner*, July 15, 1978, p. 12.

95 "Dianne Feinstein Backs Toschi," *Napa Valley Register*, July 15, 1978, p. 5.

96 "In S.F. Sanity is a Relative Thing," *San Francisco Examiner*, August 27, 1976, p. 35.

97 "Tom Dumb-Dumb Becomes Tom the Avid Biologist," *San Francisco Examiner*, November 18, 1974, p. 4.

98 "Just a Note to Let Cops Know," *San Francisco Examiner*, December 24, 1975, p. 5.

99 "Just a Note to Let Cops Know."

100 "Last Call: Innovator Jim Dunbar Retiring after 50 Years on Bay Area Radio," *SFGate*, May 30, 2005, https://www.sfgate.com/bayarea/article/last-call-innovator-jim-dunbar-retiring-after-3240279.php.

101 Grinell, "The 1978 Letter May Be Genuine after All," ZodiacCiphers.com, https://www.zodiacciphers.com/zodiac-news/the-1978-letter-may-be-genuine-after-all.

102 Grinell, "The Greatest Copycat in Town," ZodiacCiphers.com, https://www.zodiacciphers.com/zodiac-news/the-greatest-copycat-in-town.

103 Cydney Contreras, "The Zodiac Letters Were Analyzed by AI—Here are the Results," *Oxygen*, July 11, 2023, https://www.oxygen.com/crime-news/what-does-ai-say-about-the-zodiac-killer-letters.

104 "It's Time to Remember Cheri Jo," Viewpoints Online, November 2013, https://viewpointsonline.org/2013/11/its-time-to-remember-cheri-jo/.

105 "Inside Detective: Zodiac—A New Look at the Infamous Case" (originally published in *Inside Detective*, July 1971), ZodiacKiller.com, https://www.zodiackiller.com/InsideDetective5.html.

106 Peter Verry, "What Is the Average Shoe Size for Men? Experts Weigh In," *Footwear News*, August 17, 2023, https://footwearnews.com/shoes/mens-footwear/average-shoe-size-men-1202752232/.

107 Bureau of Justice Statistics, *Female Murder Victims and Victim–Offender Relationship*, 2021, U.S. Department of Justice, Office of Justice Programs, https://bjs.ojp.gov/female-murder-victims-and-victim-offender-relationship-2021.

108 Bureau of Justice Statistics, *Female Murder Victims and Victim–Offender Relationship*, 2021.

109 Riverside Police Department, "Cold Case Unit," City of Riverside, https://www.riversideca.gov/rpd/about-contact/operations/investigations-division/cold-case-unit.

110 "Yesterday's Crimes: The Hippie-Cannibal Satanist," *SF Weekly*, March 21, 2018.

111 "Cannibal's Clue," *San Francisco Examiner*, November 21, 1970, p. 3.

112 "Zodiac Pet Killer at Large," *San Francisco Examiner*, June 28, 1972, p. 19.

113 "Rode with Zodiac, Woman Claims," *San Francisco Examiner*, March 23, 1970, p. 4.

114 "Zodiac Complex," *San Francisco Examiner*, December 21, 1986, p. 148.

115 "NYPD Combs 'Zodiac' Thriller for Clues," *San Francisco Examiner*, July 19, 1990, p. 22.

116 "NYPD Combs 'Zodiac' Thriller for Clues."

117 Esther Haynes, "Kiss of the Scorpion Woman," *New York Magazine*, March 14, 2004.

118 "A Letter of Threats by 'Zodiac,'" *San Francisco Examiner*, October 29, 1987, p. 2.

119 "A Letter of Threats by 'Zodiac.'"

120 "Zodiac Breath," *San Francisco Examiner*, March 27, 1986, p. 39.

121 Rae Alexandra, "How the Zodiac Killer Investigation Fell Apart in 1978 . . . Because of Armistead Maupin," KQED, October 2, 2023, https://www.kqed.org/arts/13966297/zodiac-killer-forged-letter-david-toschi-armistead-maupin-tales-of-the-city.

V+■UZQPFHME⊕ꟼ⅃HMᗡJUO●Z◩◪
ᑭRWΦƎꟼS⊡⊡ᗡᗡΛ◬KTΦ+V⊙◩ꓘ⊙ↃN
FSꟻꞮƎL\ꓘΛ+TJ⅃O□KꞮЯ●T⊥6F⊡
YꝖꟼKƎZЯHUIYꟻZꞮΦWFIᗡ⊼KIMΔ
O/ΔDRSVᗡYLLM⅃H6F⊼⊙ƎIꞮQNC
UFIEDƎZ●⊖NꝖᗡЯZƎ+⊥LꓘLY⊕NX
DZSK⊡YꝖ+KLMꟼ■+⊡K●⊖⊙⊥ZPF■
ZJI●ꞮHMPD/SVXYL◬O⊕⅃⊼ZЯKᗡ
O⊡Y⊥NꞮQWↃE\□LMUΛRAᗡY◪ꟻOW
Ↄ⊙Я⊖6ↃN⅃Φ□O++⊕IX●⊖ᑭΛ/SVX
YL6D□HMΔORЯ◬A

⊕